CAMBRIDGE
UNIVERSITY PRESS

Chemistry

for the IB Diploma

WORKBOOK

Jacqueline Paris

Shaftesbury Road, Cambridge CB2 8EA, United Kingdom

One Liberty Plaza, 20th Floor, New York, NY 10006, USA

477 Williamstown Road, Port Melbourne, vic 3207, Australia

314–321, 3rd Floor, Plot 3, Splendor Forum, Jasola District Centre, New Delhi – 110025, India

103 Penang Road, #05–06/07, Visioncrest Commercial, Singapore 238467

Cambridge University Press is a department of the University of Cambridge.

It furthers the University's mission by disseminating knowledge in the pursuit of education, learning and research at the highest international levels of excellence.

www.cambridge.org
Information on this title: www.cambridge.org/9781009052672

First published 2017
Second edition 2023
20 19 18 17 16 15 14 13 12 11 10 9 8 7 6 5 4 3

Printed in Malaysia by Vivar Printing

A catalogue record for this publication is available from the British Library

ISBN 978-1-009-05267-2 Workbook with Digital Access (2 Years)

Additional resources for this publication at www.cambridge.org/go

CAMBRIDGE DEDICATED TEACHER AWARDS — 2022

Teachers play an important part in shaping futures. Our Dedicated Teacher Awards recognise the hard work that teachers put in every day.

Thank you to everyone who nominated this year; we have been inspired and moved by all of your stories. Well done to all of our nominees for your dedication to learning and for inspiring the next generation of thinkers, leaders and innovators.

Congratulations to our incredible winners!

WINNER

Regional Winner
Australia, New Zealand & South-East Asia

Mohd Al Khalifa Bin Mohd Affnan
Keningau Vocational College, Malaysia

Regional Winner
Europe

Dr. Mary Shiny Ponparambil Paul
Little Flower English School, Italy

Regional Winner
North & South America

Noemi Falcon
Zora Neale Hurston Elementary School, United States

Regional Winner
Central & Southern Africa

Temitope Adewuyi
Fountain Heights Secondary School, Nigeria

Regional Winner
Middle East & North Africa

Uroosa Imran
Beaconhouse School System KG-1 branch, Pakistan

Regional Winner
East & South Asia

Jeenath Akther
Chittagong Grammar School, Bangladesh

For more information about our dedicated teachers and their stories, go to
dedicatedteacher.cambridge.org

CAMBRIDGE UNIVERSITY PRESS

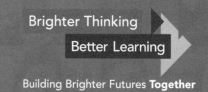

Brighter Thinking
Better Learning
Building Brighter Futures **Together**

> Contents

> How to use this series

This suite of resources supports students and teachers of the IB Chemistry Diploma course. All of the books in the series work together to help students develop the necessary knowledge and scientific skills required for this subject.

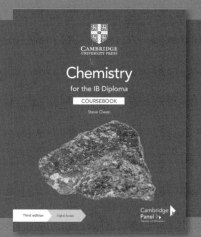

The coursebook with digital access provides full coverage of the latest IB Chemistry Diploma course.

It clearly explains facts, concepts and practical techniques, and uses real world examples of scientific principles. A wealth of formative questions within each chapter help students develop their understanding, and own their learning. A dedicated chapter in the digital coursebook helps teachers and students unpack the new assessment, while exam-style questions provide essential practice and self-assessment. Answers are provided on Cambridge GO, to support self-study and home-schooling.

The workbook with digital access builds upon the coursebook with digital access with further exercises and exam-style questions, carefully constructed to help students develop the skills that they need as they progress through their IB Chemistry Diploma course. The exercises also help students develop understanding of the meaning of various command words used in questions, and provide practice in responding appropriately to these.

The teacher's resource supports and enhances the coursebook with digital access and the workbook with digital access. This resource includes teaching plans, overviews of required background knowledge, learning objectives and success criteria, common misconceptions, and a wealth of ideas to support lesson planning and delivery, assessment and differentiation. It also includes editable worksheets for vocabulary support and exam practice (with answers) and exemplar PowerPoint presentations, to help plan and deliver the best teaching.

> How to use this book

A chapter outline appears at the start of every chapter to introduce the learning aims and help you navigate the content.

CHAPTER OUTLINE

In this chapter you will:

- describe the structure of the atom and the relative charges and masses of protons, neutrons and electrons

- describe how protons, neutrons and electrons behave in electric fields

- deduce the number of protons, neutrons and electrons in atoms and ions.

KEY TERMS

Definitions of key vocabulary are given at the beginning of each chapter.

You will also find definitions of these words in the glossary.

Exercises

Exercises help you to practise skills that are important for studying Standard Level and Higher Level Chemistry.

TIP

Tip boxes will help you complete the exercises, and give you support in areas that you might find difficult.

EXAM-STYLE QUESTIONS

Questions at the end of each chapter are more demanding exam-style questions, some of which may require use of knowledge from previous chapters. Answers to these questions can be found in digital form on Cambridge GO.

Visit Cambridge GO and register to access these resources at www.cambridge.org/GO

KEY EQUATIONS

In these boxes you will find chemical equations in the form of symbols and formula.

> Unit 1

The nature of matter

> Chapter 1

The particulate nature of matter

CHAPTER OUTLINE

In this chapter you will:

- understand the terms *element, compound* and *mixture*

- understand the differences between heterogeneous and homogeneous mixtures

- understand how to separate the components of a mixture

- use kinetic molecular theory to understand the properties of solids, liquids and gases

- understand that temperature in K is proportional to the average kinetic energy of particles

- understand how to convert temperatures between K and °C

- use state symbols in chemical equations

- use kinetic molecular theory to explain changes of state.

KEY TERMS

Make sure you understand the following key terms before you do the exercises.

atom: the smallest part of an element that can still be recognised as that element; in the simplest picture of the atom, the electrons orbit around the central nucleus; the nucleus is made up of protons and neutrons (except for a hydrogen atom, which has no neutrons)

element: a chemical substance that cannot be broken down into a simpler substance by chemical means. Each atom has the same number of protons in the nucleus

compound: a pure substance formed when two or more elements combine chemically in a fixed ratio

mixture: two or more substances mixed together. The components of a mixture can be mixed together in any proportion (although there are limits for solutions). The components of a mixture are not chemically bonded together, and so, retain their individual properties. The components of a mixture can be separated from each other by physical processes

CONTINUED

molecule: an electrically neutral particle consisting of two or more atoms chemically bonded together

heterogeneous mixture: a mixture of two or more substances, that does not have uniform composition and consists of separate phases. A heterogeneous mixture can be separated by mechanical means. An example is a mixture of two solids

chemical properties: how a substance behaves in chemical reactions

chromatography: a technique used to separate the components of a mixture due to their different affinities for another substance and/or solubility in a solvent

deposition: the change of state from a gas to a solid

filtration: a separation technique used to separate insoluble solids from a liquid or solution

physical properties: properties such as melting point, solubility and electrical conductivity, relating to the physical state of a substance and the physical changes it can undergo

solvation: a process used to separate a mixture of two or more substances, due to differences in solubility

states of matter: solid, liquid and gas

state symbols: used to indicate the physical state of an element or compound; these may be either written as subscripts after the chemical formula or in normal type: (aq) = aqueous (dissolved in water); (g) = gas; (l) = liquid; (s) = solid

boiling: change of state from a liquid to a gas at the boiling point of the substance

boiling point: the temperature at which a liquid boils under a specific set of conditions - usually we will be considering the boiling point at atmospheric pressure

distillation: a separation technique used to separate the solvent from a solution or separate liquid components of a mixture that have different boiling points

sublimation: the change of state from a solid to a gas

melting: the change of state from a solid to a liquid

freezing: the change of state from a liquid to a solid

melting point: the temperature at which melting occurs

homogeneous mixture: a mixture of two or more substances with the same (uniform) composition throughout the mixture – it consists of only one phase. Examples are solutions or a mixture of gases

CONTINUED

solution: that which is formed when a solute dissolves in a solvent

evaporation: the change of state from a liquid to a gas that can occur at any temperature above the melting point

solute: a substance that is dissolved in another substance (the solvent) to form a solution

solvent: a substance that dissolves another substance (the solute); the solvent should be present in excess of the solute

temperature: a measure of the average kinetic energy of particles

Exercise 1.1 Elements, compounds and mixtures

This exercise will check you understand the key terms **element**, **compound**, **mixture**, **atom** and **molecule**, which are important fundamental ideas in chemistry.

1   Approximately how many different elements are there?

2   Some elements exist as individual atoms, some as a small group of atoms bonded together into a molecule and others are bonded together into a giant structure.

    a   Name two elements that exist as giant structures at 25 °C.

    b   Name an element that exists as a single atom.

    c   Name an element that exists as a molecule made of two atoms joined together (a diatomic molecule).

3   Identify which of the following formulas represent atoms and which represent molecules:

    a   He

    b O_2

    c H_2O

    d   C

4   Identify which of the following formulas represent elements and which represent compounds:

    a   He

    b O_2

    c H_2O

    d   C

TIP

An atom is a single particle.

A molecule is made up of more than one atom.

The atoms in a molecule can be of the same element.

---

5   This statement is incorrect, explain why:

Elements are made of atoms and compounds are made of molecules.

6   An alloy is a mixture of a metal and other elements. Give one way in which the composition of an alloy differs from that of a compound.

7   Compounds have both different **chemical properties** and **physical properties** from the elements from which they are formed.

   a   What is meant by the term *physical properties*?

   b   What is meant by the term *chemical properties*?

8   Most everyday substances are mixtures although they are often labelled as pure. Pure orange juice is a common example. The manufacturers simply mean that nothing has been added to the orange juice. In chemistry, the term *pure* is not used in the same way.

   In chemistry, what is meant by the term *pure*?

9   Why do the components of a mixture retain their individual properties?

10   Group the following substances into elements, mixtures and compounds:

   air, water, sodium chloride solution, sodium chloride crystals, iron, chlorine gas, carbon dioxide gas.

11   What name is given to a mixture that has a uniform composition and only consists of one phase?

12   What name is given to a mixture that does not have a uniform composition and consists of separate phases?

13   Why is a mixture of the solids sodium chloride and sand not a **homogeneous mixture**?

14   When a small amount of salt and water is mixed together, it forms a homogeneous mixture, but this is not true when flour is mixed with water, why?

15   Are chemical or physical processes typically used to separate the components of a mixture?

TIP

Question 5 is linked to ideas in Chapter 6.

TIP

Solid, liquid, gas and solution are all examples of phases.

16 Match the name of the separation technique with the type of mixture it can be used to separate.

Technique		Types of mixture	
A	filtration	1	substances with very different solubilities in a **solvent**
B	distillation	2	an insoluble solid from a liquid
C	evaporation	3	a **solute** with very different solubilities in two different solvents
D	solvation	4	the solute from a **solution**
E	solvent extraction	5	a mixture of substances with small differences in their solubilities in a solvent
F	paper **chromatography**	6	liquids with a large difference in their boiling points
G	recrystallisation	7	a mixture containing a solute with different solubilities in a solvent at different temperatures

Exercise 1.2 Kinetic molecular theory

Kinetic molecular theory is used to explain the observed properties of solids, liquids and gases.

1 Complete Table **1.1**, which describes the arrangement and movement of particles in solids, liquids and gases.

Description	Solids	Liquids	Gases
diagram showing the arrangement of the particles			
relative distance of the particles from one another			
relative energy of the particles			
movement of particles			
relative force of attraction between the particles			

Table 1.1: Arrangement and movement of particles.

2 Which of the descriptions of particles in Table **1.1** can explain the fixed shape of solids and the lack of a fixed shape in liquids and gases?

3   Which of the descriptions in Table **1.1** explain why, at a given **temperature**, the volume of a gas is not fixed but the volume of solids and liquids are?

4   Younger students are often confused by the observed properties of a powder. A powder can flow like a liquid and take up the shape of its container but does not completely spread out into a puddle like a liquid.

    a   How would you explain that a powder is a solid?

    b   How would you explain the ability of a powder to flow like a liquid?

5   Which scale is the SI scale for temperature?

6   On the kelvin scale, what does zero K (or absolute zero) represent?

7   Complete Table **1.2** to show equivalent temperatures on the kelvin and Celsius scales.

Celsius scale	Kelvin scale
0	
	373
40	
	74
946	
	3
	500

Table 1.2: Equivalent temperatures on the kelvin and Celsius scales.

> **TIP**
>
> Absolute zero equals −273.15 °C, but you can use −273 °C for your chemical calculations.

8   Temperature is used in some chemical calculations. When it is, the kelvin scale is always used, unless the calculation involves a temperature change.

Explain why either Celsius or kelvin can be used to measure temperature change.

Exercise 1.3 Temperature and kinetic energy

Not all of the particles in a sample have the same amount of energy, and so, they do not all move with the same speed. In this exercise, you will explore the distribution of kinetic energies at different temperatures.

1   Consider a sample of oxygen at a constant temperature.

    a   Do all the oxygen particles have the same kinetic energy? Explain your answer.

    b   Do all the particles of the gas move at the same speed? Explain your answer.

2 Consider a mixture of the gases nitrogen and helium at a constant temperature.

    a The average kinetic energy of the particles will be higher for which gas?

    b The average speed of the particles will be higher for which gas?

3 Describe how the following change when the temperature of a gas is increased:

    a the average kinetic energy of the particles

    b the average speed of the particles

    c the most probable kinetic energy of the particles

    d the fraction of particles with the most probable kinetic energy.

> **TIP**
>
> The most probable kinetic energy is the energy at the peak of a Maxwell–Boltzmann distribution curve.

Exercise 1.4 Changes of state

Heating or cooling a substance can cause it to change state, as these processes involve the breaking or formation of forces of attraction between the particles. In this exercise, you will check that you understand these processes and can work out the state of a substance at a given temperature from its **melting point** and **boiling point**.

Figure **1.1** summarises the changes of state.

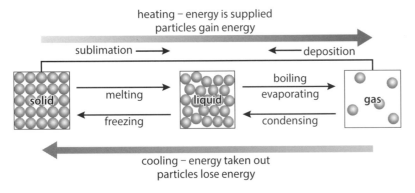

Figure 1.1: The changes of state.

1 Which change of state does not take place only at a fixed temperature for a given pressure?

2 Identify which changes of state are exothermic and which are endothermic.

3 What name is given to the temperature at which a substance changes from a liquid to a solid?

4 What name is given to the temperature at which a substance changes between gas and liquid?

5 Carbon dioxide and iodine are two examples of substances that undergo **sublimation**.

    a What is meant by the term *sublimation*?

    b What term is used to describe the reverse of sublimation?

> **TIP**
>
> The same name for the temperature at which the change in question 3 happens is used, no matter in which direction the change happens.

6   Complete the table to show whether a substance is a solid, liquid or gas at the
     temperature stated in the column header.

Substance	Melting point / °C	Boiling point / °C	State at −50 °C	State at 115 °C	State at 245 K
A	15	125			
B	253	578			
C	−83	78			
D	−169	−87			

7   Figure **1.2** shows the cooling curve for a substance.

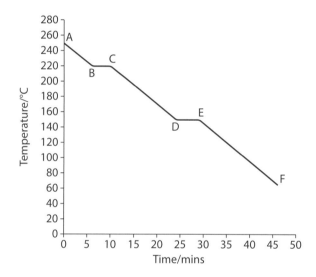

Figure 1.2: The cooling curve for a substance.

a   Label the diagram to show the following:

   i   the region where the substance is a solid

   ii   the region where the substance is a liquid

   iii   the region where the substance is a gas

   iv   the region where the substance is freezing

   v   the region where the substance is condensing

   vi   the melting point of the substance

   vii   the boiling point of the substance.

b   Explain, in terms of the movement and arrangement of the particles, why the
     temperature of the substance remains the same during a change of state.

EXAM-STYLE QUESTIONS

1 Which of the following lists substances that are all made up of molecules?

A C, O_2, CO_2

B Na, Cl_2, $NaCl$

C H_2, He, Li

D P_4, S_8, O_3

2 Which of the following statements is **true** of heterogeneous mixtures?

A Their components cannot be separated by physical means.

B They have the same composition throughout the mixture.

C The components are in a fixed ratio.

D The components are in separate phases.

3 Which of the following is **not** a heterogeneous mixture?

A cola

B tea with milk

C tea with sugar

D milk

4 Which of the following shows the correct sequence of the changes of state involved in distillation?

A boiling, condensing

B condensing, boiling

C evaporation, cooling

D boiling, cooling

5 What is the name given to the separation technique that is used to separate the components of a mixture that have different solubilities in a solvent at different temperatures?

A distillation

B recrystallisation

C evaporation

D paper chromatography

6 Mercury is a liquid at 25 °C, which of the following could be its melting and boiling points?

	Melting point	Boiling point
A	−38.9 °C	83.7 K
B	−38.9 K	629.7 °C
C	−38.9 K	356.7 K
D	−38.9 °C	356.7 °C

CONTINUED

7 Which is the correct equation for sublimation?

   A $CO_2(s) \rightarrow CO_2(g)$

   B $CO_2(g) \rightarrow CO_2(s)$

   C $H_2O(s) \rightarrow H_2O(l)$

   D $CO_2(g) \rightarrow CO_2(aq)$

8 Which statement is correct about melting?

   A The average kinetic energy of the particles increases, but the temperature stays the same.

   B The average kinetic energy of the particles increases, and the temperature increases.

   C The average kinetic energy of the particles stays the same, but the temperature increases.

   D The average kinetic energy of the particles stays the same, and the temperature stays the same.

9 Ammonia liquid boils at −33 °C and freezes at −78 °C at atmospheric pressure.

   a Predict the state of ammonia at

      i −50 °C

      ii −80 °C

      iii 200 K. [3]

   b Sketch a graph of temperature against time as a sample of ammonia is cooled from 0 °C to −50 °C. [4]

10 Some seaweeds accumulate iodide ions in their leaves, and so, are a good source of iodine. The seaweed must first be dried and then heated to burn off the organic matter. The remaining ash is then boiled in water and allowed to cool. The iodide ions dissolve in the water.

   a Suggest a suitable technique that could be used to separate the iodide solution from any insoluble impurities. [1]

   b State the type of mixture that remains after the insoluble impurities have been removed. [1]

   c When dilute sulfuric acid and hydrogen peroxide are added to the mixture, an aqueous solution of iodine is produced:

      $2H^+ + H_2O_2 + 2I^- \rightarrow I_2 + 2H_2O$

      Give the state symbols for I_2 and H_2O in the equation above. [2]

   d Iodine is not particularly soluble in water. It is much more soluble in organic solvents such as cyclohexane. Outline a method that could be used to separate the iodine from the solution. [3]

11 The statements below describe the analysis of a mixture of amino acids by paper chromatography.

   a Place the statements in the correct order:

      i spray the plate with a locating agent

      ii mark the position of the solvent front

      iii place a small sample of the unknown sample on the bottom of a piece of chromatography paper

      iv place the paper into a tank containing a suitable solvent

      v allow the solvent to rise up the paper [3]

CONTINUED

b Figure **1.3** shows the results of the experiment.

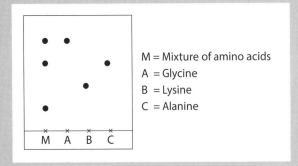

Figure 1.3: Chromatogram of an amino acid mixture.

Which amino acids did the mixture contain? [1]

c Why do substances A, B and C each only produce one spot on the chromatogram? [1]

> Chapter 2
The nuclear atom

CHAPTER OUTLINE

In this chapter you will:

- describe the structure of an atom

- understand the terms *atomic number* (Z) and *mass number* (A)

- calculate the numbers of protons, neutrons and electrons in atoms and ions

- understand the term *isotope*

- understand that isotopes of an element have the same chemical properties but different physical properties

- calculate the *relative atomic mass* (A$_r$) from the relative abundances of isotopes

- calculate the relative abundance of an isotope from the relative atomic mass.

> understand that the abundance of isotopes in a sample can be determined from a mass spectrum

> understand how to calculate relative atomic mass from a mass spectrum.

KEY TERMS

Make sure you understand the following key terms before you do the exercises.

ion: a charged particle that is formed when an atom loses or gains electron(s); a positive ion is formed when an atom loses an electron(s) and a negative ion is formed when an atom gains an electron(s)

atomic number (Z): the number of protons in the nucleus of an atom

isotopes: different atoms of the same element with different mass numbers, i.e. different numbers of neutrons in the nucleus. Isotopes have the same chemical properties but different physical properties

nuclear symbol: a symbol showing the atomic number and mass number of an element, $^{A}_{Z}X$

mass number (A): the total number of protons plus neutrons in the nucleus of an atom

CONTINUED

mass spectrometry: an analytical technique used to determine the relative abundance and mass (strictly mass to charge ratio) of gaseous particles. It can be used to determine the isotopic composition of an element

relative atomic mass (A_r): the weighted average of the masses of the atoms of the isotopes

Exercise 2.1 The structure of atoms

This exercise will check your understanding of the basic structure of an atom and how to calculate the number of protons, neutrons and electrons in atoms and **ions**.

1   Complete Table **2.1** to show the relative mass and charge of protons, neutrons and electrons and where in an atom these are found.

Sub-atomic particle	Relative mass	Relative charge	Location of the particle in the atom
proton			
neutron			
electron			

Table 2.1: Sub-atomic particles.

> **TIP**
>
> Question 1 asks for the *relative mass* and *charge* of each particle not the actual mass or charge. The actual masses are given in the IB data book.

2   Complete Table **2.2**.

Element	Atomic number (Z)	Mass number (A)	Number of protons	Number of neutrons	Number of electrons
phosphorus	15	31			
strontium	38	88			
		207	82		
bromine	35			44	
				109	74

Table 2.2: Structures of various atoms.

> **TIP**
>
> Question 2 is about *neutral atoms*, so the number of both the protons and electrons are the same as the **atomic number**: number of neutrons = mass number (A) – atomic number (Z)

3   Complete Table **2.3**.

Formula	Atomic number (Z)	Mass number (A)	Number of protons	Number of neutrons	Number of electrons
Na^+	11	23			
O^{2-}	8	16			
	29	64			28
Fe^{2+}		56		30	
			22	24	20

Table 2.3: Structures of various ions.

TIP

Ions have a negative charge if they *gain* an electron. A positive charge means that an electron has been *lost*. Remember that an ion should not be defined as a charged particle because protons and electrons are charged particles, but they are not ions.

Exercise 2.2 Isotopes

In this exercise, you will begin by considering the definition of an **isotope** and calculate the number of protons, neutrons and electrons in different isotopes. You will then explore relative atomic mass and how this is calculated from isotopic abundances. The last question uses data from **mass spectrometry**, which is for Higher Level students only.

1   In terms of the particles in an atom, describe what is meant by the term *isotope*.

2   In terms of the atomic number and **mass number** of an atom, describe what is meant by the term *isotope*.

3   Complete Table **2.4** to show the number of protons, neutrons and electrons in the following isotopes.

Nuclear symbol	Number of protons	Number of neutrons	Number of electrons
$^{79}_{35}Br$			
	35	46	35
$^{81}_{35}Br^-$			
$^{64}_{29}Cu^{2+}$			
	11	12	10
$^{19}_{9}F^-$			
	8	8	10

Table 2.4: Structures of various isotopes.

TIP

Questions 1 and 2 are asked in two different ways. Read the questions carefully.

TIP

Question 3 includes both atoms and ions.

4 Which atomic particles determine the chemical properties of atoms?

5 Look at the definition of **relative atomic mass, A_r**. What does the term *weighted* mean in this definition?

6 Calculate the relative atomic masses of the following elements, giving your answer to two decimal places.

    a carbon: % abundance: ^{12}C = 98.93, ^{13}C = 1.07

    b argon: % abundance: ^{36}Ar = 0.3365, ^{38}Ar = 0.0632, ^{40}Ar = 99.6003

7 Calculate the percentage of ^{35}Cl and ^{37}Cl in a sample given that the relative atomic mass is 35.45.

> **TIP**
>
> This calculation can be done by assuming that, in a sample of 100 atoms, x are ^{35}Cl and $100 - x$ are ^{37}Cl. The coursebook gives a worked example of how to do this. It also gives a shorter method using the formula
>
> $$\% \text{ of heavier isotope} = \frac{\text{relative atomic mass} - \text{mass number of lighter isotope}}{\text{difference in the mass numbers of two isotopes}} \times 100$$

8 **a** On the mass spectrum of copper in Figure **2.1** suggest the particle responsible for each peak.

    b Calculate the relative atomic mass of the element.

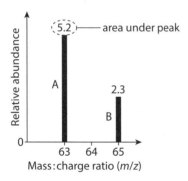

Figure 2.1: Mass spectrum of copper.

> **TIP**
>
> Note that abundance data are not given as a percentage. These do *not* need to be converted into a percentage.

EXAM-STYLE QUESTIONS

1 Which statement is correct?

    A Protons and electrons have the same relative mass.

    B Protons and neutrons have the same relative mass.

    C Electrons have zero mass.

    D The mass of a neutron is about 100 times more than the mass of an electron.

CONTINUED

2 Which statement is incorrect?

A The relative charge of an electron is zero.

B The relative charge of a proton is +1.

C The charge on a proton is 1.6×10^{-19} C.

D The charge of a neutron is zero.

3 Which of the following atoms contains the most neutrons?

A ^{40}Ca

B ^{40}Ar

C ^{39}K

D ^{37}Cl

4 How many protons are there in an atom of $^{208}Pb^{2+}$?

A 208

B 126

C 124

D 82

5 What is the charge on an ion that has an atomic number of 19, a mass number of 39 and 20 electrons?

A −1

B 0

C +1

D +2

6 Which statement is **not** true about $^{138}_{56}Ba^{2+}$?

A It has 56 protons, 82 neutrons and 58 electrons.

B The atomic number is 56 and the mass number is 138.

C It has more neutrons than protons.

D It has more protons than electrons.

7 Bromine (atomic number 35) has two naturally occurring isotopes and a relative atomic mass of 79.9. Which of the following statements can be deduced from this information?

A The two isotopes are ^{79}Br and ^{81}Br.

B The two isotopes are ^{78}Br and ^{81}Br.

C One isotope has more than 45 neutrons and the other has fewer than 45 neutrons.

D The two isotopes are found in approximately equal proportions.

8 A sample of boron is found to contain a mixture of 20% ^{10}B and 80% ^{11}B.
What is the relative atomic mass of boron in this sample?

A 10.8

B 10.6

C 10.4

D 10.2

CONTINUED

9 **a** Explain the terms *mass number* and *relative atomic mass*. [3]

 b **i** Compare the structure of ^{16}O, ^{17}O and ^{18}O in terms of the particles of which they are made. [2]

  ii What name is given to particles that differ in this way? [1]

 c A sample of oxygen was found to contain 99.76% ^{16}O, 0.04% ^{17}O and 0.20% ^{18}O.
Calculate the relative atomic mass of oxygen to two decimal places. [2]

10 What is the relative atomic mass of an element with the mass spectrum shown in Figure **2.2**?

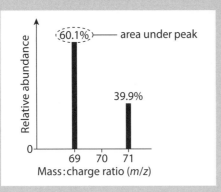

Figure 2.2: Mass spectrum of an element.

 A 70.0

 B 70.2

 C 69.5

 D 69.8

> Chapter 3
Electron configurations

CHAPTER OUTLINE

In this chapter you will:

- describe the emission spectrum of hydrogen

- understand how the lines in the emission spectrum of hydrogen arise

- describe the relationship between wavelength, frequency, energy and colour in the electromagnetic spectrum

- write full and condensed electron configurations for atoms and ions up to $Z = 36$

- understand what orbitals are and draw diagrams of s and p orbitals

- draw orbital diagrams for atoms and ions up to $Z = 36$.

> understand that the ionisation energy for hydrogen can be deduced from the emission spectrum

> calculate the first ionisation energy from the wavelength or frequency of the convergence limit

> understand what information about the electronic structure of atoms can be deduced from successive ionisation energy data

KEY TERMS

Make sure you understand the following key terms before you do the exercises.

continuous spectrum: a spectrum consisting of all frequencies/wavelengths of light

energy level: the energetic 'distance' of an electron from the nucleus of an atom

line spectrum: the emission spectrum of an atom consists of a series of lines that get closer together at higher frequency; only certain frequencies/ wavelengths of light are present

degenerate: a set of orbitals with the same energy

electromagnetic spectrum: the range of frequencies of radiation

CONTINUED

emission spectrum: electromagnetic radiation given out when an electron in an atom falls from a higher energy level to a lower one. Only certain frequencies of electromagnetic radiation are emitted – a line spectrum. Each atom has a different emission spectrum. For hydrogen, the emission spectrum in the visible region consists of a series of coloured lines that get closer together at higher frequency

principal quantum number: the number used to describe the main energy level or shell of an atom. The first shell has the principal quantum number one, the second two, and so on. The symbol n is sometimes used. The maximum number of electrons in a given shell can be calculated using the formula $2n^2$

electron configuration: the arrangement of the electrons in an atom or ion

Aufbau principle: the process of putting electrons into atoms to generate the electron configuration

condensed electron configuration: an abbreviated form of an electron configuration where the previous noble gas atom is written in square brackets followed by the remainder of the full electron configuration

energy sub-levels: the main energy levels, or shells, in an atom are divided into sub-levels. There are different types of sub-level, known as s, p, d and f sub-levels

convergence limit: the point in a line emission spectrum where the lines merge to form a continuum. The frequency of the convergence limit in the series of lines where the electron falls down to $n = 1$, may be used to determine the ionisation energy of hydrogen

convergence: when the lines in an emission spectrum get closer together at higher energy/frequency

ionisation energy: see first ionisation energy

first ionisation energy: the minimum amount of energy required to remove an electron from a gaseous atom/the energy required to remove one electron from each atom in one mole of gaseous atoms under standard conditions. The energy for the following process:

$$M(g) \rightarrow M^+(g) + e^-$$

second ionisation energy: the minimum energy required to remove the outermost electron from each ion in a mole of gaseous ions with a 1+ charge to form a mole of gaseous ions each with a 2+ charge under standard conditions:

$$M^+(g) \rightarrow M^{2+}(g) + e^-$$

orbital diagrams: diagrams that show the full electron configuration of atoms/ions using arrows (electrons) in boxes (orbitals)

orbital: a region of space in which there is a high probability of finding an electron; it represents a discrete energy level. There are s, p, d and f orbitals. One orbital can contain a maximum of two electrons

CONTINUED

Pauli exclusion principle: two electrons in the same orbital must have opposite spins

Hund's rule: electrons fill orbitals of the same energy (degenerate orbitals) to give the maximum number of electrons with the same spin

Exercise 3.1 The electromagnetic spectrum

In this exercise, you will consider the **electromagnetic spectrum**.

1   Describe the qualitative relationship between wavelength and frequency in the electromagnetic spectrum.

2   Describe the qualitative relationship between wavelength and energy in the electromagnetic spectrum.

3   Which has a higher frequency, red light or violet light?

Exercise 3.2 The hydrogen atom spectrum

Emission spectra are produced by all elements. The hydrogen **emission spectrum** is particularly useful, as hydrogen only has one electron, so its spectrum is easier to interpret. This exercise looks at how the hydrogen emission spectrum is formed and how it is interpreted.

1   What is meant by a **continuous spectrum**?

2   What is meant by a **line spectrum**?

3   Why is it possible to identify an element from its emission spectrum?

4   Passing an electric discharge or high voltage through a sample of gas causes the electrons in an atom to be excited. Suggest another method of exciting the electrons in an atom that can be used to identify the presence of some elements in a simple laboratory experiment.

5   How does the arrangement of electrons into **energy levels** provide an explanation for the production of a line spectrum rather than a continuous spectrum?

6   What do the different series of lines in the hydrogen emission spectrum represent?

7   Figure **3.1** shows part of the hydrogen emission spectrum that appears in the visible part of the electromagnetic spectrum that relates to transitions to the $n = 2$ energy level. Show what transitions cause the lines at each of the wavelengths shown.

TIP

Questions 1 and 2 ask for the qualitative relationship not the quantitative (mathematical) relationship.

TIP

The entire distribution of frequencies of radiation are given in the IB data book.

Spectrogram of the visible lines in the Balmer series of hydrogen

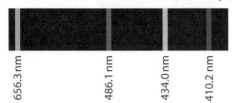

656.3 nm 486.1 nm 434.0 nm 410.2 nm

Figure 3.1: Part of the hydrogen emission spectrum.

TIP

The wavelength of the line is related to its energy. The longer the wavelength, the lower the energy. All of these lines relate to transitions from energy levels higher than 2 to $n = 2$.

8 Why do the lines in an emission spectrum series get closer together at shorter wavelengths?

9 The lines in the hydrogen emission spectrum representing transitions to the $n = 1$ level occur in the ultraviolet region of the electromagnetic spectrum.

    a What name is given to the point at which they merge?

    b What does this point represent?

Exercise 3.3 Electron configurations

Electron configuration is the term used to describe the arrangement of electrons in an atom or ion. The position of an electron is described in terms of its energy level rather than its distance from the nucleus. The position of an electron is described by its **principal quantum number**. The energy levels are divided into sub-levels and each sub-level is divided into a number of **orbitals**.

1 What formula can be used to calculate the maximum number of electrons in a main energy level?

2 Calculate the maximum number of electrons that can occupy each of the first four main energy levels.

3 Which letters are used to name the sub-levels?

4 Each sub-level is made up of a number of orbitals. What is meant by the term *orbital*?

5 Complete Table **3.1** to show how many orbitals there are in each sub-level and the maximum number of electrons these orbitals and sub-levels can hold.

Sub-level	Number of orbitals	Maximum number of electrons in each orbital	Maximum number of electrons in the sub-level
s			
p			
d			
f			

Table 3.1: Atomic orbitals and their occupancy.

6 Using the **Aufbau principle**, write the **sub-energy levels** up to the third energy level in order, starting with the sub-level of lowest energy.

7 A chlorine atom has 17 electrons.

  a Write the full electron configuration of chlorine.

  b Write the **condensed electron configuration** of chlorine.

8 Why is the condensed electron configuration of potassium [Ar] $4s^1$ and not [Ar] $3d^1$?

9 Give the full electron configuration of the following elements:

  a carbon

  b calcium

  c arsenic

  d chromium.

10 Which other element in the same period as chromium has an electron configuration that does not follow the Aufbau principle?

11 The periodic table can be used to work out the order in which the sub-levels are filled, although using this does not work for the elements that are exceptions to the Aufbau rules. Describe the relationship between the period number of an element and its electron configuration.

12 Describe the relationship between the group number of an element and its electron configuration.

13 Figure **3.2** shows an outline of the modern form of the periodic table.

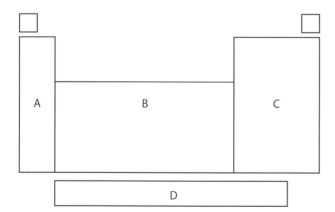

Figure 3.2: Outline of the modern form of the periodic table.

  a Identify the names of the blocks A–D.

  b What does the block in which an element is found tell you about that element's electron configuration?

14 Give the full electron configuration of the element that is found in Period 4 and Group 14.

15 Give the full electron configuration of the element with atomic number 35.

> **TIP**
>
> The condensed electron configuration is an abbreviated form of the full electron configuration and uses square brackets around the symbol for the preceding noble gas.

> **TIP**
>
> The electron configuration of chromium does not follow the Aufbau principle.

> **TIP**
>
> The relationship is slightly different in different parts of the periodic table. It would be a good idea to refer to the different blocks in your answer.

Exercise 3.4 Putting electrons into orbitals: Aufbau principle

In this exercise, you will look at the way that the electrons are arranged in orbitals, the idea of electron spin, the **Pauli exclusion principle** and **Hund's rule**.

1   How many different types of orbitals are there?

2   Sketch a diagram to show the shape of an s orbital.

3   Sketch a diagram to show the shape of a p orbital.

4   The p sub-level is made up of a number of different orbitals. In what way do they differ from each other?

5   How many different d orbitals make up a d sub-level?

6   The f sub-level can hold a maximum of 14 electrons. How many f orbitals is it made of?

7   The orbitals that make up a sub-level are said to be **degenerate**. What does this term mean?

8   How are the spins of an electron in an orbital represented in an **orbital diagram**?

9   Using your understanding of Hund's rule, draw an orbital diagram to show how three electrons would occupy a p sub-level.

10   Draw orbital diagrams for the following atoms:

a   nitrogen

b   sulfur

c   titanium.

11   Complete the orbital diagrams for phosphorus and copper in Figure **3.3**.

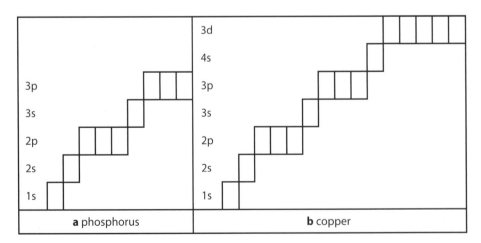

Figure 3.3: Orbital diagrams for phosphorus and copper.

12 Atoms form negative ions when one, or more, electron is gained. Draw the orbital diagram for each of the following negative ions:

a F^-

b O^{2-}

c N^{3-}

13 Atoms form positive ions by losing electrons. Draw the orbital diagram for each of the following positive ions:

a Li^+

b Na^+

c Al^{3+}

14 Which electrons are usually the first electrons removed from a transition element?

15 Give the full electron configurations of the following atoms and ions:

a V and V^{2+}

b Fe and Fe^{2+}

c Cr and Cr^{3+}

d Cu and Cu^{2+}

Exercise 3.5 Ionisation energy

At the end of exercise 3.2 you met the idea that the convergence limit of the lines in the hydrogen emission spectrum represent the point beyond which its electron is free from any attraction to the nucleus. The energy corresponding to this convergence limit is known as the ionisation energy. This exercise explores the definitions of ionisation energies and the information given by the trends in the successive ionisation energies of an element.

1 Define the term **first ionisation energy**.

2 Give an equation for the first ionisation energy of chlorine.

3 Give an equation for the **second ionisation energy** of potassium.

4 Give an equation for the sixth ionisation energy of sulfur.

5 Why is the amount of energy required to remove a second electron from an atom always greater than the amount of energy required to remove the first?

6 **a** How can the emission spectrum of an element be used to find the ionisation energy of its outermost electron?

   b A line in the emission spectrum of sodium has a wavelength of 598 nm. Calculate the energy of the photon emitted.

   c The convergence limit of helium is 50.4 nm. Calculate the ionisation energy of helium.

7 Successive **ionisation energy** data for an element can be used to deduce in which group of the periodic table it belongs.

Table **3.2** shows the successive ionisation energies for magnesium.

Ionisation energy number	Energy / kJ mol^{-1}
first	738
second	1451
third	7733
fourth	10 543
fifth	13 630
sixth	18 020
seventh	21 711

Table 3.2: Successive ionisation energies for magnesium.

> **TIP**
>
> When you sketch a graph, remember to include labels for the axes.

Explain why there is a large increase in the amount of energy required to remove the third electron compared to the second.

8 Sketch a graph of the successive ionisation energies for silicon.

9 Sketch a graph of the first 10 successive ionisation energies for an element in Group 17 of the periodic table.

10 Why are data on successive ionisation energies of a transition metal often not useful in assigning its group number?

EXAM-STYLE QUESTIONS

1 Which statements are **true** of the hydrogen emission spectrum?

I The lines in the spectrum are due to electron excitation.

II The line of highest frequency represents the energy gap between the innermost and outermost energy levels.

III The lines in each series get closer together because the energy gaps between the levels get smaller.

A I only

B II only

C I and II only

D II and III only

2 What is the maximum number of electrons in the $n = 3$ energy level?

A 3

B 6

C 10

D 18

3 What is the total number of p electrons in an atom of arsenic, atomic number 33?

A 3

B 7

C 15

D 33

4 What is the correct full electron configuration of titanium, atomic number 22?

A $1s^2\ 2s^2\ 2p^6\ 3s^2\ 3p^6\ 4s^2\ 3d^2$

B $1s^2\ 2s^2\ 2p^6\ 3s^2\ 3p^6\ 3d^4$

C $1s^2\ 2s^2\ 2p^6\ 3s^2\ 3p^6\ 4s^1\ 3d^3$

D $1s^2\ 2s^2\ 2p^6\ 3s^2\ 3p^6\ 4s^4$

5 What is the correct condensed electron configuration of potassium?

A $[Ne]\ 3s^2\ 3p^6\ 4s^1$

B $1s^2\ 2s^2\ 2p^6\ 3s^2\ 3p^6\ 4s^1$

C $[Ar]\ 4s^1$

D $4s^1$

6 What is the correct electron configuration of Ni^{2+}?

A $1s^2\ 2s^2\ 2p^6\ 3s^2\ 3p^6\ 4s^2\ 4p^6\ 3d^2$

B $1s^2\ 2s^2\ 2p^6\ 3s^2\ 3p^6\ 4s^2\ 3d^6$

C $1s^2\ 2s^2\ 2p^6\ 3s^2\ 3p^6\ 3d^{10}$

D $1s^2\ 2s^2\ 2p^6\ 3s^2\ 3p^6\ 3d^8$

CONTINUED

7   Which of the following orbital diagrams is correct for chromium?

A   [Ar] ⟨1↓⟩⟨1⟩⟨1⟩⟨1⟩⟨1⟩

B   [Ar] ⟨1⟩⟨1⟩⟨1⟩⟨1⟩⟨1⟩⟨1⟩

C   [Ar] ⟨1↓⟩⟨1↓⟩⟨1↓⟩⟨ ⟩⟨ ⟩

D   [Ar] ⟨ ⟩⟨1↓⟩⟨1⟩⟨1⟩⟨1⟩⟨1⟩

8   The first ten successive ionisation energies of an element are shown in Figure **3.4**.

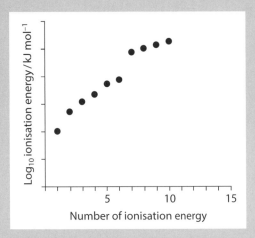

Figure 3.4: Successive ionisation energies of an element.

Which group of the periodic table could this element belong to?

A   Group 4

B   Group 6

C   Group 14

D   Group 16

9   Given that Planck's constant has a value of 6.63×10^{-34} Js, what is the energy of a photon of light with a frequency of 2.00×10^{14} Hz?

A 1.326×10^{-19} J

B 3.315×10^{-48} J

C 3.017×10^{47} J

D 1.326×10^{-20} J

10   Which of the following statements is **true** about the emission spectrum of an element?

A   The first ionisation energy is deduced from the convergence limit of the series with the longest wavelength.

B   The first ionisation energy is deduced from the convergence limit of the series with the shortest wavelength.

C   The lines of the spectrum represent the movement of electrons between energy sub-levels.

D   The number of lines on the spectrum indicates the number of electrons in an atom of the element.

CONTINUED

11   Neon gas glows orange–red when placed in an electric field and gives its name to coloured lights that can be used in advertising signs. The colour observed is due to the relative intensity of the different lines in its emission spectrum; the orange–red lines are more intense than the lines of the other colours that are produced.

    a   Describe what changes in an atom give rise to its emission spectrum.　[1]

    b   Explain why an emission spectrum, such as that of hydrogen, consists of a number of different series of lines.　[1]

    c   Sketch an energy level diagram showing the transitions that lead to the lines in the series of the hydrogen emission spectrum with the shortest wavelength.　[4]

    d   With reference to emission spectra, describe what is meant by the term *convergence*.　[1]

    e   What data can be calculated from the convergence limit of an emission spectrum?　[1]

12   Figure 3.5 shows the $\log_{10}$ of the successive ionisation energies of an element. Identify the element giving a reason for your answer.　[3]

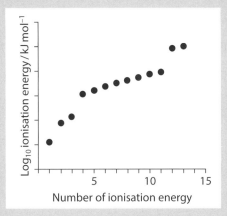

Figure 3.5: The $\log_{10}$ of the successive ionisation energies of an element.

> Chapter 4

Counting particles by mass: The mole

CHAPTER OUTLINE

In this chapter you will:

- understand the terms *relative atomic mass* and *relative formula mass*

- understand what a mole is

- calculate molar masses

- calculate amounts of a substance in mol from masses and vice versa

- carry out calculations involving amounts of a substance in mol, masses and number of particles

- understand what empirical and molecular formulas are

- deduce empirical and molecular formulas from experimental data

- understand what is meant by the concentration of a solution

- carry out calculations involving concentrations in mol dm^{-3} and g dm^{-3}

- understand Avogadro's law

- solve problems involving gases using Avogadro's law.

KEY TERMS

Make sure you understand the following key terms before you do the exercises.

relative formula mass: if a compound contains ions, the relative formula mass is the average mass of the formula unit relative to the mass of $\frac{1}{12}$ of an atom of carbon-12

mole: the unit of the amount of substance. The amount of substance that contains the Avogadro number (6.02×10^{23}) of particles (atoms, ions, molecules, etc.)

molar mass (*M*): the mass that contains 1 mol of particles (atoms, molecules, ions) and is its A_r or M_r in grams. The units of molar mass are g mol^{-1}

Avogadro constant: has the same numerical value as the Avogadro number but units of mol^{-1}, i.e. 6.02×10^{23} mol^{-1}. The symbol L or N_A is used for the Avogadro constant

CONTINUED

molecular formula: the total number of atoms of each element present in a molecule of the compound; the molecular formula is a multiple of the empirical formula

empirical formula: the simplest whole number ratio of the elements present in a compound

relative molecular mass (M_r): the average mass of a molecule of a compound relative to the mass of $\frac{1}{12}$ of an atom of carbon-12; M_r is the sum of the relative atomic masses for the individual atoms making up a molecule

concentration: quantity of solute dissolved in a unit volume of solution; the volume that is usually taken is 1 dm^3 (one litre); the quantity of solute may be expressed in g or mol, so the units of concentration are $g\,dm^{-3}$ or $mol\,dm^{-3}$

standard solution: a solution of known concentration

Avogadro's law: equal volumes of ideal gases measured at the same temperature and pressure contain the same number of molecules

KEY EQUATIONS

$n = \dfrac{m}{M}$

where

   n = number of moles, mol

   m = mass, g

   M = molar mass, $g\,mol^{-1}$

$N = n \times N_A$

where

   N = number of particles

   n = number of moles, mol

   N_A = Avogadro's constant = $6.02 \times 10^{23}\ mol^{-1}$

$n = CV$

(or $C = \dfrac{m}{V}$ to give the concentration in $g\,dm^{-3}$)

where

   C = concentration, $mol\,dm^{-3}$

   n = number of moles, mol

   m = mass, g

   V = volume, dm^3

$$\text{\% by mass of an element} = \frac{\text{number of atoms of the element} \times \text{atomic mass of the element}}{\text{relative formula mass}}$$

Exercise 4.1 Relative masses

The mass of an atom is so small that the actual masses of atoms and molecules are not used and *relative* atomic masses are more usual. In this exercise, you will explore this idea and practise calculating the relative mass of different substances.

1   In the terms **relative atomic mass, relative formula mass** and **relative molecular mass**, to what does the term *relative* apply?

2   Calculate the relative formula mass or relative molecular mass of the following substances:

    a CO_2

    b H_2O_2

    c $NaNO_3$

    d $(NH_4)_2SO_4$

    e C_2H_5OH

    f $(CH_3CH_2COO)_2Mg$

    g $H_3C_6H_5O_7$

> **TIP**
>
> Always use the values from the IB data book and be consistent with decimal places. The data book gives relative atomic masses to two decimal places. So, answers should be given to two decimal places.

Exercise 4.2 Moles

The **mole** is the fundamental SI unit of amount. Put simply, it is the unit we use to count things. It is used to count very large amounts.

1   In this exercise, you will use the formula $n = \dfrac{m}{M}$

    a   What do the symbols n, m and M represent?

    b   Give the units for n, m and M.

2   Using the formula $n = \dfrac{m}{M}$, calculate the amount in mol of the following:

    a   10.0 g of sodium

    b   0.5 kg of NaCl

    c   0.25 g of $KMnO_4$

    d   3.0 kg of CO_2

    e   15.0 g of Br_2

    f   1 g of H_2O

> **TIP**
>
> Take care to always note the number of significant figures used in the question.

3 Using the formula $n = \dfrac{m}{M}$, calculate the number of moles of hydrogen atoms in 1.00 g of each of the following substances:

a H_2O

b CH_4

c $C_6H_{12}O_6$

d $(NH_4)_2SO_4$

e C_2H_5OH

> **TIP**
>
> Each H_2O molecule contains two hydrogen atoms, so, however many moles of water there are, there must be twice that number of moles of hydrogen atoms.

4 Rearranging the formula $n = \dfrac{m}{M}$, calculate the mass of the following:

a 0.10 mol of NO_2

b 2.25 mol of $CuSO_4$

c 3.00 mol of $Cu(NO_3)_2$

d 0.050 mol of $Mg(HCO_3)_2$

e 0.23 mol of nitrogen gas.

5 Rearranging the formula $n = \dfrac{m}{M}$, calculate the following:

a The molar mass of a substance if 0.250 mol of the substance has a mass of 54.0 g.

b The molar mass of a substance if 1.5 mol of the substance has a mass of 180 g.

> **TIP**
>
> To calculate either the mass or the number of moles, the correct **molar mass** must be used, which means that the correct formula is essential. The formula for nitrogen gas is N_2.

Exercise 4.3 The mass of a molecule

This exercise uses **Avogadro's constant** to find the mass of a single particle of a substance and the number of particles in a given mass of substance.

1 What is the significance of Avogadro's constant?

2 In this exercise, you will use the formula $N = n \times N_A$

a What do the symbols N, N_A and n represent?

b Give the units for N, N_A and n.

3 Using the formula $n = \dfrac{m}{M}$ and number of particles, $N = n \times N_A$, calculate the following:

a The number of water molecules in 2.50 mol of water.

b The number of oxygen molecules in 64 g of oxygen.

c The number of oxygen atoms in 64 g of oxygen.

d The total number of atoms in 1 g of SiO_2.

> **TIP**
>
> Note that values should not be rounded until the very last step of a calculation.

e   The mass of one molecule of CO_2.

f   The mass of hydrogen atoms in 0.040 mol of C_2H_6.

Exercise 4.4 Empirical and molecular formulas

Not all substances are made of molecules, and so, the term **molecular formula** is not always appropriate. In the case of substances that have a giant structure (see Chapters 6, 7, and 8), an **empirical formula** is used. In this exercise, you will practise calculating the empirical and molecular formulas of different substances, so it is important that you know the meaning of these terms. You will start by first calculating the percentage composition of a compound from its formula using the following expression:

$$\% \text{ by mass of an element} = \frac{\text{number of atoms of the element} \times \text{atomic mass of the element}}{\text{relative formula mass}}$$

1   Calculate the percentage of iron in Fe_2O_3.

2   Calculate the mass of iron in 500 kg of Fe_2O_3.

3   Calculate the % composition by mass of each of the elements in $Mg_3(PO_4)_2$.

4   Calculate the mass of magnesium in 1 g of $Mg_3(PO_4)_2$.

5   For each of the following compounds, calculate the mass of substance that will contain 10.0 g of carbon:

a CH_4

b C_6H_6

c C_4H_{10}

6   All substances have an empirical formula but not all substances have a molecular formula. Explain this statement.

7   Deduce the empirical formula from the following molecular formulas:

a C_2H_2

b H_2O_2

c C_4H_{10}

d $(COOH)_2$

e NH_4NO_3

f $CH_3CH_2CH_2COOH$

8 The molecular formula of a substance is always a whole number multiple of its empirical formula. Complete Table **4.1**. The first row has been filled in as an example.

	Molecular formula	Empirical formula	Ratio, $\dfrac{\text{molecular formula}}{\text{empirical formula}}$
	H_2O_2	HO	2
a		NH_2	2
b	$C_6H_{12}O_6$		
c		CH_2	5
d		CH_2O	3

Table 4.1: Molecular and empirical formulas.

9 As the ratio of the molecular formula to the empirical formula is always a whole number, the molecular formula can also be calculated from the empirical formula if the molar mass is known. Deduce the molecular formula of the following substances:

   a Empirical formula P_2O_5 and a molar mass of 283.88 g mol^{-1}

   b Empirical formula CH_2 and a molar mass of 70.15 g mol^{-1}

   c Empirical formula CH_2O and a molar mass of 60.06 g mol^{-1}

10 Find the empirical formulas of the following compounds using the data given:

   a Ca 20.05%, Br 79.95%

   b Na 29.1%, S 40.5%, O 30.4%

   c C 53.3%, H 15.5%, N 31.1%

11 An oxide of phosphorus contains 56.4% phosphorus and 43.6% oxygen. Its relative molecular mass is 219.9. Find both the empirical and the molecular formula of the oxide.

12 In an experiment, 0.36 g magnesium was reacted in an excess of oxygen and the oxide formed was found to have a mass of 0.60 g.

   a Calculate the mass of oxygen in the compound.

   b Deduce the empirical formula of the compound.

13 1.50 g of an organic compound containing only the elements carbon, hydrogen and oxygen with a relative molecular mass of 90.04 was combusted in excess oxygen. 1.47 g of CO_2 and 0.30 g of water were formed.

   a Calculate the empirical formula of the compound.

   b Deduce its molecular formula.

Exercise 4.5 Solutions

A solution is formed when a solute is dissolved in a solvent. The **concentration** of a solution is normally given in mol dm^{-3}. In this exercise, you will practise calculating concentration in mol dm^{-3}, using $C = \frac{n}{V}$, and in g dm^{-3}, using $C = \frac{m}{V}$, and calculating the concentration when a solution is diluted. Finally, you will use a graphical method to find the concentration of a coloured solution.

1   Convert the following volumes:

   a   25 cm^3 into dm^3

   b   100 cm^3 into dm^3

   c   1 cm^3 into dm^3

   d   0.05 dm^3 into cm^3

   e 1.5×10^{-2} dm^3 into cm^3

   f 2.5×10^{-3} dm^3 into cm^3

2   Calculate the concentrations of the following solutions in both g dm^{-3} and mol dm^{-3}:

   a   200 cm^3 of solution containing 1 g of KOH

   b   25 cm^3 of solution containing 0.025 g of $CuCl_2$

   c 3.5×10^{-2} dm^3 of solution containing 14 mg of $KMnO_4$

3   Calculate the concentrations of the following solutions:

   a   10.2 g dm^{-3} $Pb(NO_3)_2$ in mol dm^{-3}

   b   4.6 g dm^{-3} $MgCl_2$ in mol dm^{-3}

   c   0.01 mol dm^{-3} NaOH in g dm^{-3}

4   Calculate the number of moles of solute present in each of the following solutions:

   a   25 cm^3 of HCl with a concentration of 0.010 mol dm^{-3}

   b 5.2×10^{-2} dm^3 of $CuSO_4$ with a concentration of 0.010 mol dm^{-3}

   c   100 cm^3 of $FeBr_2$ with a concentration of 2.5×10^{-5} mol dm^{-3}

5   Calculate the mass of solute present in each of the following solutions:

   a   10 cm^3 of $MnCl_2$ with a concentration of 1.5 mol dm^{-3}

   b   25 cm^3 of KI with a concentration of 0.020 mol dm^{-3}

   c   2.000 dm^3 of CH_3COONa, where $[CH_3COONa] = 0.010$ mol dm^{-3}

TIP

To convert concentration in g dm^{-3} into mol dm^{-3}, simply divide by the molar mass.

TIP

Make sure you use the correct units when calculating concentrations. Concentration can be measured in g dm^{-3} or in mol dm^{-3}, but a common mistake is to use cm^3. Convert volumes when necessary.

TIP

Note that the volume of the solution is given and not the volume of solvent that the solute is dissolved into. This is because the volume can change when a solute is added due to the forces of attraction between the solute and solvent particles.

6 Calculate the concentration of nitrate, NO_3^-, ions present in the following solutions:

   a $[NaNO_3] = 0.10$ mol dm³

   b $[Cu(NO_3)_2] = 0.50$ mol dm³

   c $[Al(NO_3)_3] = 1.5 \times 10^{-3}$ mol dm³

7 Calculate the total number of moles of ions present in 1 dm³ of each of the solutions in question 6.

8 Calculate the concentration in mol dm³ of the following **standard solutions**. The substances are all hydrated, so they contain water of crystallisation.

   a   100 cm³ of solution containing 1.00 g of $MgSO_4 \bullet 7H_2O$

   b   250 cm³ of solution containing 1.00g of $CuSO_4 \bullet 5H_2O$

> **TIP**
>
> Water of crystallisation is only found in solids. It can be thought of as water molecules trapped within the crystal structure. As crystal structures are regular, the amount of water trapped tends to be the same for a given substance. This is represented in a formula by a mid dot/bullet.

9 Calculate the concentration of a solution of HCl made by adding sufficient water to 25.0 cm³ of a solution with a concentration of 1.00 mol dm³ to a give a new volume of 100.0 cm³.

10 Calculate the volume of a $CuSO_4$ solution of concentration 0.250 mol dm⁻³ that will be required to make 200 cm³ of solution with a concentration of 0.150 mol dm⁻³.

Exercise 4.6 Avogadro's law

Knowing **Avogadro's law** makes some calculations more straightforward because, under the same conditions of temperature and pressure, the volume of a gas is equivalent to the number of moles of gas. Chapter 5 explores this idea about so-called *ideal* gases in more detail.

Assume that all the substances mentioned are ideal gases, and that both temperature and pressure remain constant, for all the questions in this exercise.

1 For the following reactions, calculate the final volume of the mixture if the quantities stated were reacted with each other.

   a $H_2(g) + F_2(g) \rightarrow 2HF(g)$
      100 cm³ 100 cm³

   b $2H_2(g) + O_2(g) \rightarrow 2H_2O(g)$
      200 cm³ 100 cm³

   c $C_6H_6(g) + 3H_2(g) \rightarrow C_6H_{12}(g)$
      100 cm³   300 cm³

> **TIP**
>
> The use of square brackets around the formula of a substance in questions 5 and 6 means *concentration of*. Square brackets around the symbol of a noble gas, such as [Ne], means the electron configuration of that noble gas (see Chapter 3). In Chapter 10 (Higher Level only), you will meet a third use of square brackets in complex ions.

> **TIP**
>
> The answer should be given to the same number of significant figures as the fewest number of significant figures used in data in the question.

> **TIP**
>
> The answer to question 1b is not 300 cm³, as H_2O molecules contain more atoms than either H_2 or O_2 molecules. Look at the relative number of moles of H_2O formed, as shown by the coefficients (numbers in front of each formula) in the equation.

2 What volume of oxygen is required to react with the following?

    a 25 cm³ of methane in the reaction
$$CH_4(g) + 2O_2(g) \rightarrow CO_2(g) + 2H_2O(g)$$

    b 0.50 dm³ of butane in the reaction
$$2C_4H_{10}(g) + 13O_2(g) \rightarrow 8CO_2(g) + 10H_2O(g)$$

    c 200 cm³ of hydrazine in the reaction
$$N_2H_4(g) + O_2(g) \rightarrow N_2(g) + 2H_2O(g)$$

3 2 dm³ of hydrogen sulfide is burned in 7 dm³ of oxygen, which is an excess according to the following equation:

$$2H_2S(g) + 3O_2(g) \rightarrow 2H_2O(g) + 2SO_2(g)$$

    a What volume of oxygen actually reacts with the 2 dm³ of hydrogen sulfide used?

    b What is the volume of each gas at the end of the reaction?

    c What is the final volume of the mixture?

4 In an experiment, 25 cm³ of methane was reacted with 25 cm³ of oxygen. What was the total volume of all gases at the end? State how much there was of each gas.

$$CH_4(g) + 2O_2(g) \rightarrow CO_2(g) + 2H_2O(l)$$

> **TIP**
>
> Look closely at the state symbol of H_2O in question 4.

EXAM-STYLE QUESTIONS

1 What is the molar mass of $Na_2B_4O_7 \cdot 10H_2O$?

    A 278 g mol⁻¹

    B 381 g mol⁻¹

    C 146 g mol⁻¹

    D 238 g mol⁻¹

2 What is the mass of 0.5 mol of C_3H_8?

    A 44 g

    B 24 g

    C 22 g

    D 26 g

3 Which substance contains the highest number of moles of hydrogen atoms?

    A 0.05 mol of CH_4

    B 0.04 mol of $(NH_4)_2SO_4$

    C 0.03 mol of H_2O_2

    D 0.1 mol of H_2

CONTINUED

4 How many moles of Cl^- ions are there in 9.5 g of $MgCl_2$?

  A 0.1 mol

  B 0.2 mol

  C 0.3 mol

  D 0.4 mol

5 What is the approximate percentage of calcium in calcium carbonate, $CaCO_3$?

  A 10%

  B 20%

  C 30%

  D 40%

6 How many atoms are there in 4.4 g of carbon dioxide?

  A 9.03×10^{24}

  B 1.81×10^{23}

  C 6.02×10^{22}

  D 3.01×10^{22}

7 A hydrocarbon was found to have a composition by mass of 24 g carbon and 8 g hydrogen. What is its empirical formula?

  A CH

  B CH_2

  C CH_3

  D CH_4

8 What mass of solute is needed to make 100 cm^3 of 0.100 mol dm^{-3} of $MgSO_4$?

  A 1.2 g

  B 12 g

  C 120 g

  D 1200 g

9 What volume of oxygen is required to completely react with 40 cm^3 of pentane?

  $2C_5H_{12}(g) + 16O_2(g) \rightarrow 10CO_2(g) + 12H_2O(g)$

  A 320 cm^3

  B 160 cm^3

  C 80 cm^3

  D 40 cm^3

10 What volume of carbon dioxide is produced when 65 cm^3 of butane is burnt in 65 cm^3 of oxygen?

  $2C_4H_{10}(g) + 13O_2(g) \rightarrow 8CO_2(g) + 10H_2O(l)$

  A 260 cm^3

  B 130 cm^3

  C 65 cm^3

  D 40 cm^3

CONTINUED

11 In an experiment to deduce the formula of $MgSO_4 \cdot xH_2O$, a sample of the solid was heated to constant mass in a crucible to remove the water of crystallisation. The following data were obtained.

mass of crucible, empty crucible = 18.27 g

mass of crucible and hydrated magnesium sulfate (before heating) = 21.19 g

mass of crucible and anhydrous magnesium sulfate (after heating) = 19.70 g

  a Describe what is meant by 'heated to constant mass'. [1]

  b Use the data to find the value of x in the formula. [4]

  c The balance used had an uncertainty of ±0.01 g. Calculate the percentage uncertainties in the masses of both the hydrated and anhydrous magnesium sulfate. [2]

  d The contents of the crucible were then transferred into a 250 cm^3 volumetric flask, along with any washings, and distilled water was added to make up the solution to the mark on the flask. Assuming that none of the anhydrous magnesium sulfate was spilt or lost, calculate the concentration of the solution. [1]

  e Calculate what mass of hydrated magnesium sulfate would need to be used to make the same volume of solution with the same concentration. [1]

12 In an experiment, a 0.500 g sample of a volatile liquid with a molar mass of 132.18 g mol^{-1} was analysed by burning it in an excess of oxygen. 0.999 g of carbon dioxide and 0.409 g of water were formed. There were no other products. Deduce the empirical formula and the molecular formula of the substance. [7]

Chapter 5

Ideal gases

CHAPTER OUTLINE

In this chapter you will:

- understand the assumptions of the ideal gas model

- understand under what conditions a real gas is most different from an ideal gas

- describe the relationships between pressure, volume and temperature for an ideal gas

- carry out calculations using $\dfrac{P_1 V_1}{T_1} = \dfrac{P_2 V_2}{T_2}$

- carry out calculations involving the ideal gas equation

- understand what is meant by the molar volume of a gas.

KEY TERMS

Make sure you understand the following key terms before you do the exercises.

ideal gas: a theoretical model that approximates the behaviour of real gases. It can be defined in terms of macroscopic properties (a gas that obeys the equation $PV = nRT$) or in terms of microscopic properties (the main assumptions that define an ideal gas on a microscopic scale are that the molecules are point masses – their volume is negligible compared with the volume of the container – and that there are no intermolecular forces except during a collision)

standard temperature and pressure (STP): 273 K, 100 kPa pressure

standard ambient temperature and pressure (SATP): 298 K and 100 kPa

KEY EQUATIONS

$PV = nRT$

where

P = pressure, Pa (1 Pa = 1 Nm^{-2})

V = volume, m^3

n = number of moles, mol

R = gas constant = 8.31 J K^{-1} mol^{-1}

T = temperature, K

CONTINUED
Alternatively, pressure can be measured in kPa and volume in dm³. $\dfrac{P_1 V_1}{T_1} = \dfrac{P_2 V_2}{T_2}$

where
 	
  P = pressure
  V = volume
  T = temperature, K
  Subscripts 1 and 2 denote different conditions.
  Any units for pressure and volume can be used as long as they are the same for conditions 1 and 2. Temperature must be measured in K.

$n = \dfrac{\text{volume}}{\text{molar volume under the same conditions}}$

where
 	
  n = number of moles, mol
  Units of volume must be the same as the units for the molar volume.

Exercise 5.1 Real gases and ideal gases

In this exercise, you will explore the behaviour of **ideal gases**, what is meant by this term and how real gases differ from ideal gases.

The assumptions made about an ideal gas allow us to predict the behaviour of real gases when conditions such as temperature, pressure and volume are changed. Later in this chapter, you will practise applying mathematical equations to make these predictions.

1   One of the assumptions about an ideal gas is that the collisions between the particles are perfectly elastic. What is meant by the term *perfectly elastic*?

2   What are the other assumptions about ideal gases, apart from the one mentioned in question 1?

3   One of the assumptions about ideal gases is that the particles themselves occupy zero volume. Considering just this assumption,

    a   would a real gas behave more or less like an ideal gas at high pressure?

    b   would a real gas behave more or less like an ideal gas at high temperatures?

    c   would a gas with larger particles be more or less like an ideal gas than one with smaller particles?

> TIP
>
> You may be expected to know the assumptions of the ideal gas model in an exam.

> TIP
>
> Consider how pressure, temperature and size affect the distances between the particles. How will this affect the proportion of the total volume occupied by the particles themselves? In an ideal gas, this is assumed to be zero.

4   Another assumption about ideal gases is that there are no forces between the particles of a gas. Considering just this assumption,

   a   would a real gas behave more or less like an ideal gas at high pressure?

   b   would a real gas behave more or less like an ideal gas at high temperatures?

   c   would a gas with polar particles be more or less like an ideal gas than one with non-polar particles?

5   Give the name of the gas that is closest to having the properties of an 'ideal' gas.

6   The differences between real gases and ideal gases are greatest at high pressure, low temperature and for large, polar molecules.

   Choose whether statement A or statement B correctly finishes each sentence of the observed differences in the behaviour of a real gas and that of an ideal gas.

   Statement A: …the volume of the particles themselves relative to the total volume of the gas becomes more significant.

   Statement B: …the forces of attraction between the particles are stronger and hold the particles closer together.

   a   At high pressure, the volume of a real gas is slightly larger than the volume predicted by the ideal gas model because…

   b   At high pressure, the volume of a real gas is slightly smaller than the volume predicted by the ideal gas model because…

   c   At low temperatures, the volume of a real gas is slightly smaller than the volume predicted by the ideal gas model because…

   d   For gases containing large molecules, the volume of a real gas is slightly larger than the volume predicted by the ideal gas model because…

   e   For gases containing more polar molecules, the volume of a real gas is slightly smaller than the volume predicted by the ideal gas model because…

> **TIP**
>
> Think about the effect on the intermolecular forces that, in an ideal gas, are assumed to be zero.

Exercise 5.2 Macroscopic properties of ideal gases

In this exercise, you will explore how the relationships between the pressure, temperature and volume of an ideal gas can all be described mathematically.

1 Sketch graphs for the following relationships between pressure and volume at constant temperature:

  a P and V

  b P and $\dfrac{1}{V}$

  c V and $\dfrac{1}{P}$

  d PV and V

  e PV and P

2 Sketch graphs for the following relationships between volume and temperature at constant pressure:

  a V and T (in kelvin)

  b V and T (in °C)

3 Sketch graphs for the following relationships between pressure and temperature at constant volume:

  a P and T (in kelvin)

  b P and T (in °C)

> **TIP**
>
> Memorising the shapes of these graphs is difficult, so it is better if you can work them out by imagining a balloon containing a fixed amount of gas and what happens to it when the temperature, pressure or volume is changed.

Exercise 5.3 Calculations involving ideal gases

In this exercise you will use the expressions $\dfrac{P_1 V_1}{T_1} = \dfrac{P_2 V_2}{T_2}$ and $PV = nRT$ to solve calculations involving gases. In all these calculations, assume that all the gases are ideal gases and $R = 8.31$ J K^{-1}.

The final few questions are based on Avogadro's law. This states that the volume of a gas is directly proportional to the number of moles of gas at a specified temperature and pressure. The most common set of conditions used are STP and standard ambient temperature and pressure (SATP). These are given in the IB data book. You will use both of these in this exercise, so be sure to read the questions carefully.

One of the most challenging aspects of these types of calculations is using the correct units, so the exercise starts with some simple conversions.

1   Calculate the volume when 100 cm³ of an ideal gas at a pressure of 100 kPa and a temperature of 330 K is cooled to a temperature of 250 K at the same pressure.

2   Calculate the pressure if a fixed volume of gas occupying a volume of 1 dm³ is sealed in a flask at a pressure of 200 kPa and a temperature of 25 °C and then heated to a temperature of 100 °C.

3   At what temperature (in °C) would 200 cm³ of an ideal gas at **standard temperature and pressure (STP)** occupy 400 cm³ at a pressure of 150 kPa?

4   A fixed mass of gas occupies 250 cm³ at a temperature of 75 °C and a pressure of 125 kPa. What volume will it occupy if the temperature is raised to 400 K and the pressure is halved?

5   Convert the following into the units shown:

   a   2.25 dm³ into m³

   b   100 cm³ into m³

   c   0.5 dm³ into cm³

   d   0.075 m³ into cm³

   e   0.034 m³ into dm³

   f   250 cm³ to dm³

6   Calculate the pressure of a gas if 0.25 mol occupies 1×10^{-3} m³ at a temperature of 300 K.

7   Calculate the number of moles of gas that would occupy 0.4 dm³ at a temperature of 298 K and a pressure of 1.5×10^2 kPa.

8   Calculate the pressure exerted by 2.40 g of carbon dioxide with a volume of 1000 cm³ at 25 °C.

9   A mixture containing 10 g of oxygen and 40 g of helium was mixed together. What volume in m³ would the mixture occupy at 200 kPa and 350 K?

10 If 73.07 g of an ideal gas occupies 35.0 dm³ at 50.0 °C and a pressure of 200 kPa, calculate the molar mass of the gas.

11 Using the expression $n = \dfrac{\text{volume}}{\text{molar volume under the same conditions}}$ and given

   that the volume of one mole of gas at STP is 22.7 dm³ mol⁻¹, calculate the amount in mol in each of the following at STP:

   a   2.45 dm³ of NO_2

   b   200 cm³ of Ar

   c   0.75 m³ of Cl_2

TIP

The most important consideration when using this expression is the units. The units of pressure and volume must be consistent on both sides of the equation, but the units of temperature must be in kelvin.

TIP

The conversion of kPa to Pa is 10^3 and from dm³ to m³ is 10^{-3}. These cancel each other out, so kPa and dm³ can be used in $PV = nRT$ instead of converting the units into Pa and m³.

TIP

Note that questions 5a and b ask for the units in m³. What units of pressure need to be used to give the volume in m³?

TIP

First calculate n and then use $n = \dfrac{m}{M}$, or this expression can be substituted into the ideal gas equation to give $M = \dfrac{mRT}{PV}$.

12 Calculate the volume of the following at STP:

    a   1.5 mol of H_2

    b   0.25 mol CH_4

    c 3.5×10^{-5} mol of N_2H_4

13 What volume would 2.50 g of carbon dioxide occupy at STP?

14 a   Using the expression $\dfrac{P_1 V_1}{T_1} = \dfrac{P_2 V_2}{T_2}$, calculate the volume of 1 mol of a gas at SATP.

    b   Calculate the number of moles of gas that would occupy 150 cm³ at SATP.

> **TIP**
>
> Check the units you are using!
> $1\ m^3 = 10^3\ dm^3 = 10^6\ cm^3$

> **TIP**
>
> The relationship between the mass of a substance and the number of moles is
> $n = \dfrac{m}{M}$ (see Chapter 4).

EXAM-STYLE QUESTIONS

In all questions, assume that all gases behave as ideal gases. The value of the gas constant is 8.31 J K⁻¹ mol⁻¹. The molar volume of an ideal gas at STP is 22.7 dm³ mol⁻¹. STP is 273 K and 100 kPa.

1 If 1 mol of a gas occupies 22.7 dm³ at STP, what volume would be occupied by 2.5 mol of an ideal gas at the same temperature and pressure?

    A 56.75 dm³

    B 567.5 cm³

    C 567.5 dm³

    D 5.675 m³

2 If 1 mol of a gas occupies 22.7 dm³ at STP, what amount of an ideal gas would occupy 500 cm³?

    A 0.011 mol

    B 0.022 mol

    C 0.11 mol

    D 22 mol

3 A 100 cm³ sample of an ideal gas at 25 °C and a pressure of 100 kPa was compressed to a volume of 40 cm³. What will the pressure of gas be if the temperature remains constant?

    A 125 kPa

    B 200 kPa

    C 250 kPa

    D 2500 kPa

CONTINUED

4 A helium balloon containing 6 dm³ of gas at 27 °C and 100 kPa was released into the atmosphere. As it rose, the temperature and pressure both decreased. Assuming the balloon did not burst, and its volume stayed the same, what was the pressure inside the balloon when the temperature in the atmosphere had fallen by 30 °C?

   A 60 kPa

   B 70 kPa

   C 90 kPa

   D 95 kPa

5 Which of the following would halve the volume of an ideal gas?

   A Changing the temperature from 100 to 200 °C at constant pressure.

   B Changing the pressure from 100 to 200 kPa at constant temperature.

   C Changing the number of moles of gas from two to four at constant pressure.

   D Changing the pressure from 300 to 150 kPa and the number of moles of gas from 4 to 2 at constant temperature.

6 Which of the following would behave most like an ideal gas?

   A 10 mol of H_2 at STP

   B 1 mol of CH_4 at 400 K and 50 kPa

   C 100 mol of H_2 at 400 K and 50 kPa

   D 10 g of CH_4 at 400 K and 50 kPa

7 The graphs in Figures **5.1–5.4** show the different relationships between pressure, volume and temperature of an ideal gas. Identify each graph correctly from the options in the table.

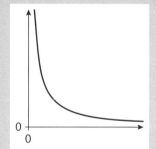 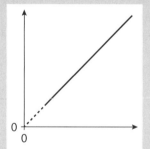 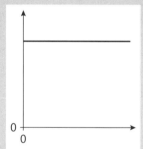 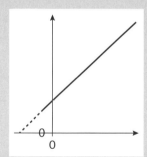

	Figure 5.1	Figure 5.2	Figure 5.3	Figure 5.4
A	x-axis: V / cm³ y-axis: P / Pa	x-axis: $(1/V)$ / cm⁻³ y-axis: P / Pa	x-axis: P / Pa y-axis: PV / cm³ Pa	x-axis: T / °C y-axis: V / cm³
B	x-axis: T / °C y-axis: V / cm³	x-axis: V / cm³ y-axis: P / Pa	x-axis: $(1/V)$ / cm⁻³ y-axis: P / Pa	x-axis: V / cm³ y-axis: P / Pa
C	x-axis: V / cm³ y-axis: P / Pa	x-axis: $(1/V)$ / cm⁻³ y-axis: P / Pa	x-axis: P / Pa y-axis: PV / cm³ Pa	x-axis: T / K y-axis: V / cm³
D	x-axis: $(1/V)$ / cm⁻³ y-axis: P / Pa	x-axis: T / K y-axis: V / cm³	x-axis: P / Pa y-axis: PV / cm³ Pa	x-axis: V / cm³ y-axis: P / Pa

CONTINUED

8   Calculate the amount of an ideal gas that occupies 10 dm^3 at a temperature of 400 K and a pressure of 166 kPa.

   A   2.5 mol

   B   0.3 mol

   C   4.5 mol

   D   0.5 mol

9   Which of the following is **not** an assumption about ideal gases?

   A   There are no forces of attraction between the particles.

   B   The total volume occupied by the particles is negligible compared to the total volume of the gas.

   C   The particles are not moving.

   D   The particles collide elastically.

10   Suggest the identity of a gas if 30 g of it occupies 15.5 dm^3 at STP.

   A CO_2

   B H_2

   C NH_3

   D C_4H_{10}

11 a   State Avogadro's law.   [1]

   b   Gases differ most from ideal gas behaviour at high pressure and low temperature.
      Give two assumptions about ideal gases that explain the difference in the behaviour
      of real gases from that of an ideal gas.   [2]

   c   50 cm^3 of an organic compound containing only carbon and hydrogen was burnt in 250 cm^3
      of oxygen (an excess). At the end of the reaction, the volume of the products and unused
      oxygen was found to have reduced by 100 cm^3; some liquid water was also formed. The gaseous
      products were treated with sodium hydroxide, which reacts with carbon dioxide, and a further
      reduction in volume of 100 cm^3 occurred. Assuming that all measurements were made at 298 K
      and 1.0×10^5 Pa, deduce the formula of the compound, and give the balanced equation for
      its combustion.   [6]

Bonding and structure

Chapter 6

The ionic model

CHAPTER OUTLINE

In this chapter you will:

- understand the formation of anions and cations
- deduce the charges on ions from their position in the periodic table
- know the charges of commonly encountered ions
- deduce the formulas of ionic compounds
- understand ionic bonding
- describe the structure of ionic compounds
- explain the properties of ionic compounds in terms of structure and bonding
- discuss the connection between the lattice enthalpy and the strength of ionic bonding.

KEY TERMS

Make sure you understand the following key terms before you do the exercises.

ionic bonding: the electrostatic attraction between oppositely charged ions

covalent bond: the electrostatic attraction between a shared pair of electrons and the nuclei of the atoms making up the bond

anion: a negative ion. It is formed when an atom gains (an) electron(s) so that the ion has more electrons (−) than protons (+)

cation: a positive ion. It is formed when an atom loses (an) electron(s) so that the ion has more protons (+) than electrons (−)

volatility: a measure of how easily a substance evaporates

lattice: usually used when describing crystals; a structure with a regular, repeating 3D arrangement

standard lattice enthalpy ($\Delta H^{\ominus}_{latt}$): the enthalpy change when one mole of ionic compound is broken apart into its constituent gaseous ions under standard conditions, e.g. for NaCl:

$$NaCl(s) \rightarrow Na^{+}(g) + Cl^{-}(g) \qquad \Delta H^{\ominus}_{latt} = +771 \text{ kJ mol}^{-1}$$

lattice enthalpy can be defined in either direction, i.e. as the making or breaking of the lattice, but in the IB syllabus it is usually defined in terms of breaking apart the lattice

Exercise 6.1 Ionic and covalent bonding

In simple terms, **ionic bonding** and **covalent bonding** can be thought of as opposites of one another. The reality is that it is not so simple; the distinction between ionic and covalent is a sliding scale. Chapters 7 and 8 cover covalent and metallic bonding respectively. In Chapter 9 all three bonding types are combined to give an overall model.

In this first exercise you will explore ions and how they are formed.

1   Complete the paragraph below, which describes ionic compounds:

Ionic substances are made of both **cations** and **anions**. Cations have a

.... charge, whereas anions have a .... charge.

Cations are formed when metal atoms .... one or more electrons.

Anions are formed when non-metals .... one or more electrons.

As oppositely charged ions are attracted to each other, ionic compounds are

normally formed between metallic elements and .... elements,

although there are exceptions.

2   a   Explain why ionic bonding only occurs in compounds and not in elements.

   b   Suggest which of the following substances are probably ionic:

     i K_2O

     ii NO_2

     iii CH_4

     iv H_2O_2

     v   NaClO

     vi HCl

3   a   Describe how a metal atom, such as sodium, forms an ion.

   b   Draw a diagram to represent this process in sodium.

   c   Write an equation to represent this process in sodium.

   d   Give the electron configuration of the sodium ion.

4   a   Describe how a non-metal atom, such as chlorine, forms an ion.

   b   Draw a diagram to represent this process in chlorine.

   c   Write an equation to represent this process in chlorine.

   d   Give the electron configuration of the ion.

   e   Give the name of the ion formed.

5 Give the electron configurations of the following ions:

    a Li^+

    b S^{2-}

    c Be^{2+}

    d Mn^{2+}

    e Zn^{2+}

> **TIP**
>
> In transition metals, the 4s electrons are lost before the 3d electrons.

Exercise 6.2 Formation of ions

The formula of an ion depends on its position in the periodic table. In this exercise, you will meet some common ions.

1 What is the relationship between the number of electrons in the outer shell of an atom and the charge on its ion?

2 What is the relationship between the charge on an ion and its group number in the periodic table?

> **TIP**
>
> The relationship is different in different blocks of the periodic table.

3 Complete Table **6.1** to show the relationship between the charge on a simple ion and its position in the periodic table.

Group number	1	2	d-block elements	13	14	15	16	17	18
charge on ion									

Table 6.1: Periodicity of the charge on simple ions.

4 How is the charge on a d-block element indicated in the name of a compound?

Exercise 6.3 The formation of ionic compounds

In this exercise, you will look at the formation of ionic compounds and their formulas.

1 In terms of their electrons, describe what happens when atoms bond ionically.

2 Draw a diagram to show the bonding in sodium chloride.

3 Draw a diagram to show the formation of the ionic bonding in sodium oxide.

> **TIP**
>
> There is no such thing as an ionic *bond*, as this implies that one thing is joined by a bond to another. Electrostatic forces of attraction extend in all directions, and so, the oppositely charged ions in an ionic substance are *all* joined to each other. The correct term is ionic *bonding*.

> **TIP**
>
> Remember that Roman numerals are used after the name of a transition metal to indicate the charge on the metal ion.

4   Complete Table **6.2** to identify the ions in the following ionic compounds.

Name or formula of compound	Formula of the cation	Formula of the anion
$MgBr_2$		
Fe_2O_3		
iron(III) hydroxide		
potassium sulfate		
magnesium sulfide		
copper(II) carbonate		
ammonium nitrate		

Table 6.2: Identifying ions.

> **TIP**
>
> Ions that contain more than one atom, such as nitrate, should be treated as whole ions and not broken down into the separate elements. The nitrate ion is NO_3^- and is not made of N^{3-} and O^{2-}.

5   Look at the list of ions below. Use them to work out the formula of compounds **a–i**.

sodium, Na^+

magnesium, Mg^{2+}

iron(II), Fe^{2+}

copper(II), Cu^{2+}

chromium(III), Cr^{3+}

aluminium, Al^{3+}

fluoride, F^-

chloride, Cl^-

oxide, O^{2-}

nitride, N^{3-}

a   sodium fluoride

b   sodium oxide

c   sodium nitride

d   iron(II) fluoride

e   copper(II) oxide

f   magnesium nitride

g   aluminium chloride

> **TIP**
>
> Compounds are neutral, so the total number of positive and negative charges must be equal. Although the charges on the ions are used to work out the formula, the charges are not written as part of the formula. For example, sodium chloride is made up of Na^+ ions and Cl^- ions, but the formula is written NaCl and not Na^+Cl^-.

h   chromium(III) oxide

i   aluminium nitride

6   Look at the list of ions below, and the ions listed in question **5**. Use them to work out the formula of compounds **a–i**.

sulfate, SO_4^{2-}

nitrate, NO_3^-

hydroxide, OH^-

phosphate, PO_4^{3-}

carbonate, CO_3^{2-}

hydrogencarbonate, HCO_3^-

ammonium, NH_4^+

a   ammonium nitrate

b   sodium sulfate

c   magnesium hydrogencarbonate

d   iron(II) sulfate

e   sodium phosphate

f   aluminium nitrate

g   aluminium sulfate

h   copper(II) phosphate

i   ammonium carbonate

> **TIP**
>
> Do not think of ions as separate atoms. Think of them as whole ions with a single charge.
> For example, do not think of nitrate as one nitrogen atom and three oxygen atoms, think of it as an ion with a single charge $(X)^-$ where $X = NO_3$.

> **TIP**
>
> Never change the formula of an ion by changing the number of atoms in it. If more than one ion is needed, use brackets. For example, two NH_4^+ ions combine with one SO_4^{2-} ion to form ammonium sulfate, so the formula is $(NH_4)_2SO_4$.

Exercise 6.4 Ionic bonding and the structure of ionic compounds

Bonding is the term used to describe the way that particles such as atoms or ions are joined together. Structure describes the way in which the particles are arranged in space. In this exercise, you will explore the structure of substances that have ionic bonding.

1   What is ionic bonding?

2   The term **lattice** is often used to describe the structure of ionic substances. What does this word mean?

3   a   Describe the structure of sodium chloride.

   b   Draw a diagram to show the structure of sodium chloride.

TIP

A common error with a question like question 1 is to describe how ionic bonding is formed and not what it actually is.

TIP

Include labels in your diagram.

Exercise 6.5 Physical properties of ionic compounds

Ionic substances have a giant lattice structure with strong forces of attraction between the oppositely charge ions. The physical properties of ionic compounds can be explained in terms of this structure. In this exercise, you will link these properties with the aspect of the structure that explains them.

1   Link the following properties of ionic compounds to their correct reason. The reasons can be used more than once.

Property
- Usually have high melting and boiling points
- Usually have low **volatility**
- Do not conduct electricity when solid
- Conduct electricity when molten or dissolved

Reason
- Ions are free to move
- Electrostatic forces of attraction are strong and exerted in all directions through the 3D lattice
- Ions are held in a fixed lattice and cannot move

2   Describe why ionic substances are often soluble in polar solvents, such as water, but are not usually soluble in non-polar solvents.

3   Ionic substances conduct electricity when molten and when dissolved in water.

When drawing an electrical circuit, we often include an arrow to show the direction of the flow of the electrons through the wires. Figure **6.1** shows a simple circuit, which includes a solution of an ionic compound.

Name the particles that move in the solution and describe in which direction they travel.

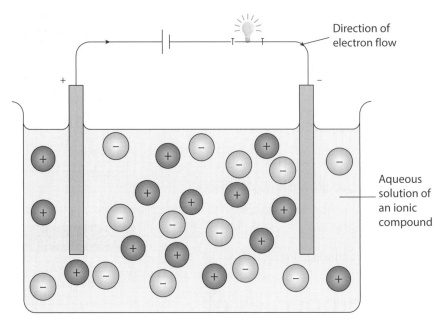

Direction of electron flow

Aqueous solution of an ionic compound

Figure 6.1: A simple circuit, which includes a solution of an ionic compound.

Exercise 6.6 Lattice enthalpy and the strength of ionic bonding

Melting points are an indicator of the strength of the electrostatic forces of attraction between the oppositely charged ions in an ionic compound. The weakness in using melting points is that the electrostatic forces of attraction still exist in the liquid state. A better measure is to use **lattice enthalpy**, which is discussed in more detail in Chapter 13 (Higher Level only).

1   Lattice enthalpy depends on the sizes of the ions and on the charges of the ions. Complete Table **6.3**.

	Effect on lattice enthalpy
increasing anion radius	
increasing cation radius	
increasing anion charge	
increasing cation charge	

Table 6.3: Effect of ion size and charge on lattice enthalpy.

2 For each pair of compounds below, suggest which has the larger lattice enthalpy and give a reason for your answer.

   a   NaBr or KBr

   b   KF or KCl

   c $MgCl_2$ or NaCl

   d   CaO or $CaCl_2$

3 Considering your answers to question **2**, which substance in each pair is likely to have the higher melting point?

   a   NaBr or KBr

   b   KF or KCl

   c $MgCl_2$ or NaCl

   d   CaO or $CaCl_2$

EXAM-STYLE QUESTIONS

1 What is the correct description of *ionic bonding*?
   A The transfer of electrons from one atom to another.
   B 3D lattice of oppositely charged ions.
   C The electrostatic force of attraction between oppositely charged ions.
   D A metal atom bonded to a non-metal atom.

2 In which of the following compounds is the bonding probably ionic?
   A HCl
   B NaI
   C F_2O
   D SO_2

3 Which statement is correct about the formation of cations?
   A Cations are formed when a metal atom gains electrons.
   B Cations are formed when a non-metal atom gains electrons.
   C Cations are formed when a metal atom loses electrons.
   D Cations are formed when a non-metal atom loses electrons.

4 Which of the following statements are **true**?
   I   Group 1 elements tend to form ions with a +1 charge.
   II Group 7 elements tend to form ions with a −1 charge.
   III d-block elements can form more than one ion.
      A I and II only
      B I and III only
      C II and III only
      D I, II and III

5 Which is the correct formula for the hydrogencarbonate ion?

  A HCO_3^-

  B HCO_2^-

  C HCO_3^{2-}

  D HCO_4^-

6 Which is the correct formula for the compound formed between calcium and phosphorus?

  A CaP

  B Ca_2P_3

  C Ca_3P_2

  D Ca_4P

7 Which property is **not** typical of ionic compounds?

  A Conduct electricity when molten.

  B Often soluble in non-polar solvents.

  C Have high melting points.

  D Conduct electricity when dissolved in water.

8 Lattice enthalpy is a measure of how much energy is required to break apart one mole of an ionic substance into its gaseous ions.

In which of the following are the compounds listed in increasing lattice enthalpy?

  A $LiCl < NaCl < KCl$

  B $MgO < MgCl_2 < MgS$

  C $KF < KCl < KBr$

  D $K_2O < CaO < MgO$

9 The statements below are about the particles in an aqueous solution of an ionic compound. Which statement is **not** correct?

  A The ions are surrounded by water molecules.

  B The ions are free to move.

  C The ions are hydrated.

  D There are very strong forces between the ions and the water molecules.

10 Which of the options in the table below is correct?

	Factor	Lattice enthalpy	Melting point
A	decreasing cation radius	increases	increases
B	increasing anion radius	decreases	increases
C	decreasing charge on cation	increases	increases
D	increasing charge on anion	decreases	increases

CONTINUED

11 When metals react with oxygen, they typically form ionic compounds.

a Give the formula of the compounds formed when potassium, calcium and aluminium each react separately with oxygen. [3]

b Draw a diagram to show the formation of aluminium oxide from aluminium and oxygen atoms. [3]

12 Magnesium oxide is an ionic solid with the same structure as sodium chloride.

a Describe the structure of magnesium oxide and include a diagram to show the arrangement of the particles. [4]

b State the typical properties of solids with this type of structure. [4]

Magnesium oxide has a very high lattice enthalpy of +3791 kJ mol^{-1}.

c Describe the factors that affect lattice enthalpy. [2]

d Suggest how this very high lattice enthalpy may affect the melting point of magnesium oxide. [1]

Chapter 7

The covalent model

CHAPTER OUTLINE

In this chapter you will:

- explain the term *covalent bond*
- explain the relationship between bond strength and length for multiple bonds
- explain what a coordination bond is
- deduce Lewis formulas (structures) for covalent molecules
- understand what is meant by the *octet rule*
- deduce the shapes of molecules/ions with up to four electron domains
- understand what makes a molecule polar
- describe and explain the bonding and structure of substances with covalent network structures
- explain the formation of intermolecular forces
- explain the influence of intermolecular forces on the melting/boiling point of covalent substances
- explain the physical properties of covalent substances
- explain how mixtures can be separated using paper chromatography and thin-layer chromatography.

> explain resonance and delocalisation of electrons

> deduce Lewis formulas and shapes for molecules and ions with expanded octets of electrons

> use formal charge to distinguish between possible Lewis formulas

> explain the formation of σ and π bonds

> explain hybridisation

> describe and explain the structure of benzene.

KEY TERMS

Make sure you understand the following key terms before you do the exercises.

adsorption: the tendency of atoms/molecules/ions to 'bond' to a surface either through a chemical or a physical interaction

pi (π) bond: bond formed by the sideways overlap of parallel p orbitals; the electron density in the pi bond lies above and below the internuclear axis

sigma (σ) bond: bond formed by the axial (head-on) overlap of atomic orbitals; the electron density in a sigma bond lies mostly along the axis joining the two nuclei

valence-shell electron-pair repulsion (VSEPR) theory: the theory by which the shapes of molecules and ions can be deduced

Lewis (electron dot) formula: a diagram showing all the valence (outer-shell) electrons in a molecule (or ion). Also called a Lewis structure

valence electrons: outer-shell electrons

coordination bond: a type of covalent bond in which both electrons come from the same atom. Also called a dative bond or coordinate covalent bond

electron domain: a lone pair, the electron pair that makes up a single bond or the electron pairs that together make up a multiple bond. Each single, double or triple bond counts as one electron domain when working out shapes of molecules

electron domain geometry: the arrangement of the electron domains around a central atom

electronegativity: a measure of the attraction of an atom in a molecule for the electron pair in the covalent bond of which it is a part. A more electronegative atom attracts electrons more strongly

polar: a bond or molecule in which there is an uneven distribution of charge

intermolecular forces: forces between different molecules. These include London forces, permanent dipole–permanent dipole interactions and hydrogen bonding

non-polar: a bond or molecule in which charge is distributed evenly

dipole: the separation of charge due to its uneven distribution

dipole–dipole forces: intermolecular forces between molecules with a permanent dipole

dipole–induced dipole forces: intermolecular forces between a polar molecule with a permanent dipole inducing a dipole in a neighbouring non-polar molecule

hydrogen bonding: an intermolecular force resulting from the interaction of a lone pair on a very electronegative atom (N/O/F) in one molecule with an H atom attached to N/O/F in another molecule. These forces may also occur between atoms in different parts of the same molecule

intramolecular forces: forces within a molecule – usually covalent bonding

CONTINUED

London (dispersion) forces: intermolecular forces arising from temporary (instantaneous) dipole–induced dipole interactions

van der Waals forces: the collective name given to the forces between molecules and includes London (dispersion) forces, dipole–dipole interactions and dipole–induced dipole interactions but not hydrogen bonding and ion–dipole interactions

solubility: a measure of the maximum amount of a solute that can dissolve in a given volume of solvent

paper chromatography: a separation technique that separates different solutes according to how the solutes are partitioned between water on the fibres of the paper and the solvent

stationary phase: in chromatography, the phase that does not move; this may be the water coating the fibres in paper chromatography or the solid adsorbent in thin-layer chromatography

partition: the tendency of a solute to distribute itself between two immiscible solvents due to its solubility in each

mobile phase: the phase that moves in chromatography, e.g. the solvent moving up the paper in paper chromatography

R_f (retardation factor) value: in chromatography:

$$R_f = \frac{\text{distance solute moves}}{\text{distance solvent front moves}}$$

thin-layer chromatography (TLC): a separation technique similar to paper chromatography that separates different solutes according to how strongly they are adsorbed onto the stationary phase

covalent network structure: the structure of substances such as diamond and graphite that contain an extended network of covalently bonded atoms and not individual molecules. This is also called a giant covalent structure

formal charge: the charge that an atom in a molecule/ion would have if we assumed that the electrons in a covalent bond were equally shared between the atoms that are bonded – i.e., we assume that all atoms have the same electronegativity. Formal charge arises when there is a charge on an ion and when coordination bonds are formed. The two electrons in a coordination bond are shared equally between the donating atom (which, therefore, has a formal charge of +1) and the receiving atom (which then has a formal charge of −1)

expanded octet: when a central atom in a molecule or ion can have more than eight electrons in its outer shell

hybridisation: the mixing of atomic orbitals when a compound forms to produce a new set of orbitals (the same number as originally), which are better arranged in space for covalent bonding

resonance hybrid: the actual structure of a molecule/ion for which resonance structures can be drawn can be described as a resonance hybrid made up of contributions (not necessarily equal) from all possible resonance structures

CONTINUED

resonance structure: one of several Lewis formulas that can be drawn for some molecules/ions

bond order: the number of covalent bonds between two atoms. A single bond has a bond order of 1. A double bond has a bond order of 2, and a triple bond has a bond order of 3. When molecules/ions are best described as resonance hybrids, the bond orders will involve fractions

allotropes: different forms of the same element; e.g. diamond, graphite and fullerene are allotropes of carbon

miscible: able to mix to form a homogeneous mixture

delocalisation: the sharing of a pair of electrons between three or more atoms

KEY EQUATIONS

$$FC = v - \frac{b}{2} - n$$

where

v = number of valance electrons in the uncombined atom

b = number of bonding electrons

n = number of non-bonding electrons

formal charge	=	number of valence electrons on the un-combined atom	−	$\frac{1}{2}$ number of bonding electrons	−	number of non-bonding electrons

$$R_f = \frac{\text{distance solute moves}}{\text{distance solvent front moves}}$$

Exercise 7.1 Covalent bonds

The focus of this chapter is on **covalent bonds**, which are created by the sharing of electrons. The arrangement of electrons in simple molecules is represented by a **Lewis formula**, also known as an electron dot structure. In this exercise, you will practise drawing Lewis structures. Electron pairs can be shown as dots, crosses or a dash.

1   Draw the Lewis structures for each of the following molecules:

   a F_2

   b H_2O_2

   c NH_3

   d CH_4

TIP

Lewis formulas show all the **valence electrons**, both bonding and non-bonding pairs in a covalently bonded species. Do not forget to show the non-bonding pairs.

2 Single, double and triple bonds involve one, two and three shared pairs of electrons respectively. Draw the Lewis structures for the following molecules:

    a O_2

    b N_2

    c CO_2

    d C_2H_4

3 Draw the Lewis structures for each of the following ions:

    a OH^-

    b CO_3^{2-}

    c HCO_3^-

4 Some molecules do not follow the octet rule, and so, have fewer than eight electrons in their valence shell. Draw the Lewis structures for each of the following molecules:

    a BCl_3

    b $BeCl_2$

    c $AlCl_3$

5 State the relationship between the number of bonds, bond strength and bond length between two atoms.

6 Explain the relationship between the number of bonds, bond strength and bond length.

7 In what way do **coordination bonds** differ from covalent bonds in terms of bond length, bond strength and reactivity?

8 Draw Lewis structures for the following molecules and ions, which all include coordination bonds. Use an arrow to represent the coordinate bond.

    a NH_4^+

    b H_3O^+

    c CO

    d NH_3BF_3

    e NO_3^-

TIP

The molecule in question 2d is ethene, which is an organic compound. As a hydrogen atom can only form one covalent bond, the two carbon atoms must be next to each other.

TIP

Note the different command terms used in questions 5 and 6.

TIP

Coordination bonds should be shown by using two dots or two crosses, rather than a line, because this then shows the origin of the electrons.

Exercise 7.2 Shapes of molecules: VSEPR theory

The valence-shell electron-pair repulsion (VSEPR) theory is used to predict the shape of a molecule or ion. In this exercise, you will practise working out the shape of a molecule. The first task is always to draw the correct Lewis structure, so make sure you can do this before continuing.

1   Describe the VSEPR theory.

2   Complete Table **7.1** to show the relationship between the number of **electron domains** and the shape and bond angles in a molecule or ion that does not have any non-bonding pairs of electrons around the central atom.

Number of electron domains	Shape	Bond angle
2		
3		
4		

Table 7.1: The relationship between the number of electron domains and the shape of a molecule.

> **TIP**
>
> A common mistake is to focus on the repulsion between different types of electron pairs. Remember to include the fundamental principle of the theory.

Exercise 7.3 Lone pairs and bond angles

Different types of electron domain around a central atom can affect the bond angles in a molecule. In this exercise, you will practise predicting the bond angles of molecules with lone pairs of electrons on the central atom.

1   Describe the relative strength of repulsion between different types of electron domain.

2   The VSEPR theory uses the idea of the number of electron domains in a molecule or ion, rather than the number of electron pairs. This means that the **electron domain geometry** is not the same as the geometry/shape of the molecule. Give an example of a simple molecule or ion where the number of electron domains is not the same as the number of electron pairs around the central atom.

> **TIP**
>
> You should include the terms *bonding* and *non-bonding* in your answer to question 2.

3 Complete Table **7.2** to show the Lewis structure, shape and bond angles for the following species:

Species	Lewis structure	Sketch showing the shape	Bond angle	Name of the shape
H_2S				
PCl_3				
CCl_4				
NH_2^-				

Table 7.2: The shapes of various species.

TIP

The shape of a molecule should always be drawn using 3D notation. Use a solid line for a bond in the plane of the page, a dashed line indicating a bond that goes into the page and a wedge to show a bond coming towards the viewer.

Exercise 7.4 Multiple bonds and bond angles

Multiple bonds can also affect the bond angles in a molecule. This exercise includes examples of molecules with multiple bonds.

1 Explain why the repulsion between a single bond and a double bond is greater than the repulsion between two single bonds.

2 Complete Table **7.3** to show the Lewis structure, shape and bond angles for the species shown.

Species	Lewis structure	Sketch showing the shape	Bond angle	Name of the shape
NO_2^-				
CS_2				
NO_3^-				

Table 7.3: The shapes of various species.

Exercise 7.5 Polarity and Exercise 7.6 Pauling electronegativities

Bond polarity depends on the difference in the **electronegativity** values of the bonded atoms.

1 Suggest a reason why the IB data book does not give electronegativity values for the elements in Group 18 of the periodic table.

2 Using the electronegativity values in the IB data book, rank the bonds listed below in order of increasing polarity.

N—H, O—H, C—H, C—Cl, H—S, F—F, O—Cl, P—Cl, C—Br, P—H

3 Molecular polarity depends on both bond polarity and on the shape of a molecule. Deduce whether the following molecules are **polar**:

a CCl$_4$

b CH$_4$

c NH$_3$

d H$_2$O

e CO$_2$

Exercise 7.7 Intermolecular forces

In this exercise, you will consider the nature of **intermolecular forces** that hold molecules together in the solid or liquid state.

1 The intermolecular forces in **non-polar** molecules are known as **London forces**. How do these forces arise?

2 Dipole–dipole interactions occur between molecules with permanent **dipoles**.

    a Which of the following substances has the strongest **dipole–dipole forces**?

       H—Cl, H—Br, H—I

    b Explain your answer to part **a**.

3 **Dipole–induced dipole forces** occur between a molecule that has a permanent dipole and a different non-polar molecule. Can this type of intermolecular force be found in the following pairs of liquids?

    a C$_6$H$_{12}$(l) and Br$_2$(l)

    b C$_8$H$_{18}$(l) and CH$_3$Cl(l)

    c HBr(l) and Br$_2$(l)

4 Draw a diagram to show the **hydrogen bonding** between water molecules.

5 Explain why some substances can form hydrogen bonds.

6 Does hydrogen bonding occur between molecules in each of the following substances?

    a H$_2$O$_2$

    b

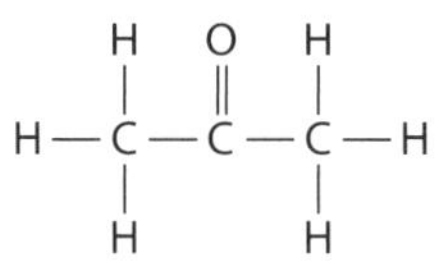

    c

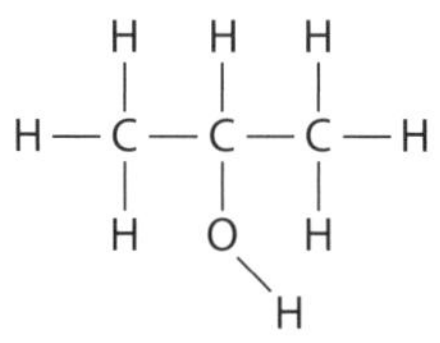

    d

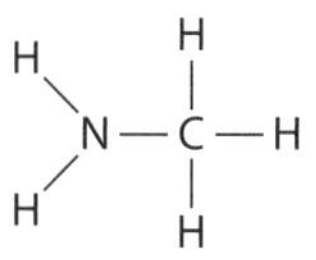

> **TIP**
>
> Include at least two molecules, at least one hydrogen bond, dipoles and lone pairs in your diagram for question 4.

7 Comment on the relative strength of dipole–dipole forces, London (dispersion) forces and hydrogen bonding.

8 In terms of the relative strength of the different types of intermolecular force, suggest a reason why ion–dipole forces and hydrogen bonding are not classed as **van der Waals forces**.

Exercise 7.8 Melting points and boiling points

The intermolecular forces met in Exercise 7.7 are the forces that are overcome when a solid melts or a liquid boils. In this exercise, you will explore how the strength of these forces affects the melting and boiling points of these substances.

1 Describe the relationship between the strength of the forces between molecules and the melting/boiling point of a substance.

2 Explain the following statements:

   a Generally, non-polar substances with higher relative molecular masses have higher melting/boiling points.

   b Generally, substances with only London forces between the molecules have the lowest melting/boiling points.

   c Generally, molecular substances with hydrogen bonding between the molecules have higher melting/boiling points.

3 The graph in Figure **7.1** shows the trend in the melting points of Group 17 elements. Explain this trend.

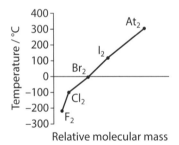

Figure 7.1: Trend in the melting points of Group 17 elements.

4 Predict which of the following pairs of molecules will have the higher boiling point and explain your answer in each case:

   a Br_2 and I_2

   b C_4H_{10} and CH_3OCH_3

   c H_2O and H_2S

> **TIP**
>
> Always use the phrase, *between molecules* when discussing intermolecular forces, as, although intermolecular means between molecules, you need to make it clear that you understand that the bonds that hold the atoms together in the molecule are not broken during melting or boiling and the molecules remain whole.

Exercise 7.9 Solubility

Solubility depends on a number of different factors. In this exercise, we will focus on the intermolecular forces. If more energy is released by the formation of intermolecular forces between the solvent and the solute than is required to overcome the intermolecular forces in the solid, then the substance is probably soluble. This is most likely to occur if the type of intermolecular forces in the solute and in the solvent are similar; 'like dissolves like'.

1 State whether the following substances are likely to be soluble in water:

a C_4H_8

b CH_3OH

c CCl_4

d
$$H-\underset{\underset{H}{|}}{\overset{\overset{H}{|}}{C}}-\underset{}{\overset{\overset{O}{\|}}{C}}-\underset{\underset{H}{|}}{\overset{\overset{H}{|}}{C}}-H$$

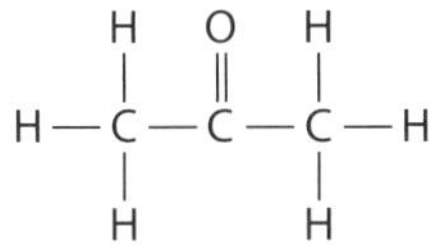

2 Explain why fatty acids, such as the one shown in Figure **7.2**, are not soluble in water but are soluble in non-polar solvents, despite the ability of the —COOH group to form hydrogen bonds.

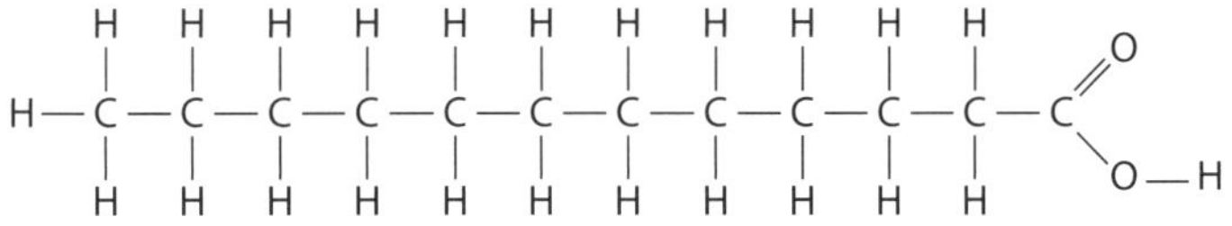

$$H-\overset{H}{\underset{H}{C}}-\overset{H}{\underset{H}{C}}-\overset{H}{\underset{H}{C}}-\overset{H}{\underset{H}{C}}-\overset{H}{\underset{H}{C}}-\overset{H}{\underset{H}{C}}-\overset{H}{\underset{H}{C}}-\overset{H}{\underset{H}{C}}-\overset{H}{\underset{H}{C}}-\overset{H}{\underset{H}{C}}-\overset{H}{\underset{H}{C}}-C\overset{\overset{O}{\|}}{\underset{O-H}{}}$$

Figure 7.2: A fatty acid.

3 In **paper chromatography**, water trapped within the cellulose fibres of the paper is the **stationary phase**. In an experiment using a non-polar solvent as the **mobile phase**, two mixtures, A and B, were spotted on the same piece of chromatography paper, and the chromatogram in Figure **7.3** was obtained.

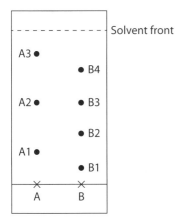

Figure 7.3: A chromatogram.

a Which of the components in mixture B was the least polar?

b Which component was common to both mixture A and mixture B?

c Calculate the R_f **value** of component A3.

d A second experiment was done using the same mixtures A and B, again using a non-polar solvent, but, instead of using chromatography paper, a **thin-layer chromatography (TLC)** plate was used; this plate was coated with a fine layer of silica, which is polar.

    i Suggest how this second chromatogram would differ from the one shown in Figure **7.3**.

    ii What name is given to the way that the solute particles stick to the silica coating?

Exercise 7.10 Covalent network structures

Some covalent substances form giant structures rather than discrete molecules. Common examples include silicon, silicon dioxide and some **allotropes** of carbon.

1 What is the meaning of the term *allotrope*?

2 Do allotropes of an element have the same chemical and physical properties?

3 Figure **7.4a–d** shows four common allotropes of carbon. Name these common allotropes.

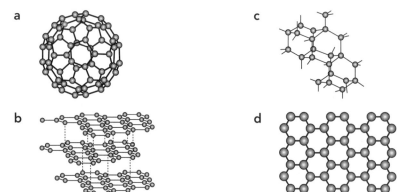

Figure 7.4: Four common allotropes of carbon.

> **TIP**
>
> C_{60} has a molecular structure, and it does not have a covalent network structure because it has a fixed formula.

4 Silicon and silicon dioxide both have **covalent network structures**. Which of the structures shown in Figure **7.4** do they most closely match?

5 Explain the difference in the electrical conductivity of graphite and diamond.

6 Explain why graphite and diamond have high melting points whereas that of buckminsterfullerene (C_{60}) is much lower.

Exercise 7.11 The expanded octet and Exercise 7.12 Formal charge

Some atoms are large enough to fit more than four electron domains around the central atoms. This is known as expanding the octet. In this exercise, you will practise drawing Lewis structures with **expanded octets** and then go on to use **formal charge** as a tool to choose between alternative structures.

1   Elements from which period of the periodic table are most likely to have expanded octets?

2   Draw the Lewis structure of the following molecules, which have expanded octets:

   a PCl_5

   b SF_6

3   The ability of an atom to expand its octet can sometimes make deducing the Lewis structure difficult. Formal charge is a concept that can be used to deduce the most likely Lewis structure for a molecule or ion. Deduce the formal charge on each atom in the following species:

   a

   b

   c

4   Using the concept of formal charge, suggest which of the structures below is the most likely.

   a   **i**

       ii

   b   **i** $:N\equiv N-\ddot{O}:$

       ii $\ddot{N}=N=\ddot{O}$

       iii $:\ddot{N}-N\equiv O:$

5   Deduce two possible Lewis structures for each of the following species and use the concept of formal charge to decide which structure is more likely:

   a ClO_3^-

   b SCN^-

> **TIP**
>
> The formula for formal charge is given at the start of this chapter.

> **TIP**
>
> In general, the preferred Lewis structure is the one in which the formal charges are closest to zero.

> **TIP**
>
> Make sure that your Lewis structures are different from each other and are not simply **resonance structures** of each other. The number of double and single bonds in the structures should be different.

Exercise 7.13 Shapes of molecules and ions with an expanded octet

The presence of non-bonding pairs affects the shapes and bond angles in molecules and ions with more than four electron domains in a similar way to those examples met in Exercise 7.2. In this exercise, you will practise drawing molecules and ions with five or six electron domains.

1   For each of the molecules or ions below, sketch the shape and state the approximate bond angles:

    a PF_5 **e** SbF_5

    b SF_6 **f** $PtCl_6^{2-}$

    c IF_3 **g** IBr_2^{-}

    d $BrCl_5$

2   Figure **7.5** shows two possible structures for XeF_4. Suggest which structure is more likely and give a reason for your choice.

a   **b**

Figure 7.5: Two possible structures for XeF_4.

3   Draw a diagram to show the shape of $TeCl_4$ and estimate the bond angles in this molecule.

Exercise 7.14 Hybridisation

The formation of covalent bonds releases energy, so the more bonds formed, the more stable the products of a reaction are, relative to the reactants. To increase the number of unpaired electrons, and so, ultimately form more bonds, electrons can be promoted to slightly higher energy levels and hybrid orbitals are formed. This is known as **hybridisation**. This exercise explores examples of hybridisation and how it can be used to explain the shape of a molecule.

1   How does the number of hybrid orbitals formed compare to the number of original atomic orbitals from which they were made?

2   How does the maximum number of electrons that can occupy a group of hybrid orbitals compare to the maximum number of electrons that could be held by the atomic orbitals from which the hybrid orbitals have been made?

3   How does the total energy of a group of hybrid orbitals compare to the total energy of the atomic orbitals from which they were made?

4 Complete Table **7.4**, which summarises the relationship between the number of atomic orbitals, the number of hybrid orbitals, the type of hybridisation and the electron domain geometry.

Name of hybrid orbital	Number of hybrid orbitals formed	Type and number of original atomic orbitals	Bond angle of the hybrid orbitals
sp			
sp^2			
sp^3			

Table 7.4: Relationship between atomic orbitals and hybrid orbitals.

5 Identify the type of hybridisation that occurs in the central atom of the following species:

a H_2S c C_2H_4 e HCO^-

b NI_3 d SCN^-

Exercise 7.15 Sigma and pi bonds

Covalent bonds are formed by the overlap of atomic orbitals. There are two different ways that the atomic orbitals can overlap: they can overlap along the axis of the bond (σ) or by the sideways (lateral) overlap of parallel p orbitals (π). In this exercise, you will practise identifying the type of bonds formed.

1 What name is given to the type of bond formed by the overlap of the following atomic orbitals?

a   Two s orbitals

b   An s orbital and a p orbital

c   Two p orbitals overlapping end-to-end along an axis

d   Two p orbitals overlapping side-by-side

e   An s orbital with an sp^2 hybrid orbital

f   Two sp^3 hybrid orbitals

2 Fill in the gaps in the following summary:

A single bond is formed from the .... overlap of atomic orbitals.

These are called .... bonds.

A double bond is made up of a .... bond and a pi bond.

A pi bond is formed by the .... overlap of two p orbitals.

A .... bond is made up of one sigma and two pi bonds.

The pi bonds are at .... degrees to each other.

TIP

To find the bond angle between the hybrid orbitals, consider each orbital as an electron domain. The shapes and bond angles follow the ideas of the VSEPR theory.

TIP

First draw the Lewis structure and use the geometry/shape to identify the type of hybridisation. For example, if there are four electron domains, then there must be four hybrid orbitals, so the hybridisation must be sp^3.

TIP

A common mistake is to think that, as π bonds involve p orbitals, then σ bonds involve only s orbitals. This is not correct.

3 Identify the number of σ and π bonds in the substances in Table **7.5**.

	Number of σ bonds	Number of π bonds
H_2O		
CO_2		
N_2		
HCN		

Table 7.5: Sigma and pi bonding in a variety of simple molecules.

TIP

Start by drawing the Lewis structure for each compound. Do not forget that a double bond is made up of both a sigma and a pi bond.

Exercise 7.16 Resonance and delocalisation

Resonance structures occur when there is more than one possible position for a double bond in a molecule. In this exercise, you will look at some examples of this. Again, the first step is drawing the Lewis structure, which is why this is an important skill. The idea of **delocalisation** is a much better explanation for the experimental observations of bond lengths. The classic example of delocalisation is benzene, C_6H_6. The reactions of benzene are described in more detail in Chapter 22.

1 Draw the Lewis structure for the following:

   a O_3

   b NO_3^-

   c SO_3^{2-}

2 Draw the two resonance structures of O_3.

3 Draw the three resonance structures of NO_3^-.

4 Draw all the resonance structures of SO_3^{2-}.

5 Molecules and ions that have resonance structures do not really exist in a number of different interchangeable forms with bonds changing from single to double. They are more accurately described as **resonance hybrids** and the bonds described by a **bond order**. Deduce the bond order for the following:

   a O_3

   b NO_3^-

   c SO_3^{2-}

6   Using data from Table **7.6**, suggest the length and strength of the oxygen–oxygen bonds in ozone.

Bond	Bond strength/kJ mol⁻¹	Bond length/pm
O—O	144	148
O=O	498	121

Table 7.6: Oxygen bond length and strength data.

7   Define the term *delocalisation*.

8   Identify in which of the following species delocalisation can occur.

a
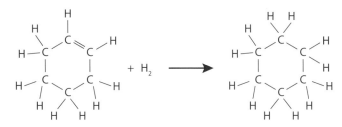

c CO_2

d

b NO_3^-

9   State two pieces of physical evidence for the delocalised structure of benzene.

10 One piece of chemical evidence for the delocalised structure of benzene comes from the enthalpy of hydrogenation.

a   Give an equation for the hydrogenation of benzene.

b   The enthalpy change for the reaction in Figure **7.6** is −120 kJ mol⁻¹.

Figure 7.6: Hydrogenation of cyclohexene.

If benzene were considered to have three double bonds, what would the predicted enthalpy change for the hydrogenation of benzene be?

c   The enthalpy change for the hydrogenation of benzene differs from the predicted value by approximately 155 kJ mol⁻¹. Is the actual value more or less exothermic than the predicted value, and what does this suggest about the stability of benzene?

11 The reactions of benzene also provide chemical evidence for the delocalisation of benzene. Describe this evidence using the reaction with bromine as an example.

EXAM-STYLE QUESTIONS

1 Which substance has the shortest carbon to oxygen bond?

 A CO_3^{2-}

 B CO

 C CH_3OH

 D CO_2

2 Which of the following molecules is polar?

 A H_2S

 B CH_4

 C CO_2

 D CCl_4

3 Which of the options shows the correct order of relative bond length and relative bond strength?

	Relative bond length	Relative bond strength
A	single > double > triple	single > double > triple
B	single < double < triple	triple < double < single
C	triple > double > single	single > double > triple
D	single > double > triple	triple > double > single

4 Which of the following allotropes of carbon does not have a giant structure?

 A graphene

 B graphite

 C diamond

 D buckminsterfullerene

5 What is the shape of the CO_2 molecule?

 A linear

 B bent

 C trigonal planar

 D tetrahedral

6 Which of the following molecules does not form hydrogen bonds?

 A $CH_3CH_2NH_2$

 B CH_3OH

 C CH_2F_2

 D NH_2F

7 Which of the following statements about the molecular compound BF_3 is **not** true?

 A The bond angles are 120°.

 B The molecule is non-polar.

 C The intramolecular bonding is covalent.

 D The molecule has a pyramidal shape.

CONTINUED

8   What is the approximate bond angle in KrF_4?

A   90°

B   104.5°

C   109.5°

D   120°

9   How many σ and π bonds are there in an NO_2^- ion?

	Number of σ bonds	Number of π bonds
A	2	0
B	1	1
C	2	1
D	2	2

10   The Lewis structure of SO_2 can be drawn as shown in Figure **7.7**.

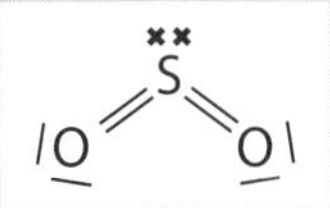

Figure 7.7: Lewis structure of SO_2.

What is the type of hybridisation of the sulfur atoms and oxygen atoms in this molecule?

	Sulfur	Oxygen
A	sp³	both sp³
B	sp²	both sp²
C	sp³	sp² and sp³
D	sp	both sp³

11 a   Draw the Lewis structures for the following molecules:

   i C_2H_6

   ii CH_3OH

   iii CH_3Cl [3]

   b   Name the type of forces between the molecules in part **a** in their liquid states. [3]

   c   Explain why CH_3OH is miscible with water whereas CH_3Cl is not. [1]

12 The valence-shell electron-pair repulsion (VSEPR) theory can be used to predict the shape of a molecule or ion.

  a What is meant by the VSEPR theory? [2]

  b Draw a diagram to show the shape of the SO_3^{2-} ion and estimate the likely O—S—O bond angle. [2]

  c H_2S and SO_2 are both bent shaped molecules.

    i Estimate the bond angles in these molecules and explain why they are not the same. [4]

    ii Suggest whether these molecules are polar or non-polar. [1]

  d The boiling point of H_2S is 60 °C, whereas the boiling point of H_2O is 100 °C, despite H_2S having a higher relative molecular mass than H_2O. Explain the reasons for this difference. [1]

13 Nitrogen forms a number of different oxides, including NO, N_2O, NO_2 and N_2O_4. NO and NO_2 both have an unpaired electron.

  a Draw the Lewis structures of NO_2 and N_2O_4. [2]

  b Phosphorus also forms a number of oxides and, unlike nitrogen, can expand its octet. One oxide of phosphorus has the formula P_4O_{10} and is shown in Figure 7.8.

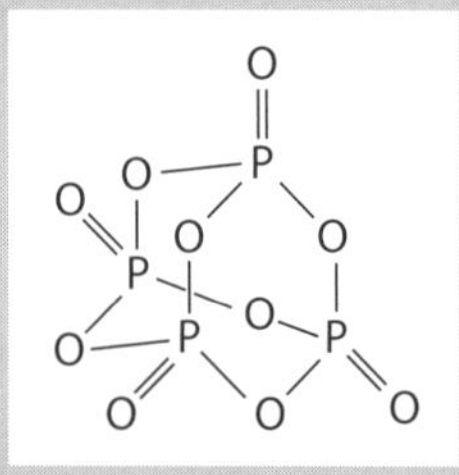

Figure 7.8: Structure of P_4O_{10}.

    i State the hybridisation of the phosphorus atoms. [1]

    ii Estimate the P—O—P bond angle. [1]

  c Another compound of phosphorus is phosphorus oxytrichloride, $POCl_3$. The Lewis structure of this molecule can be drawn in a number of ways as shown in Figure 7.9.

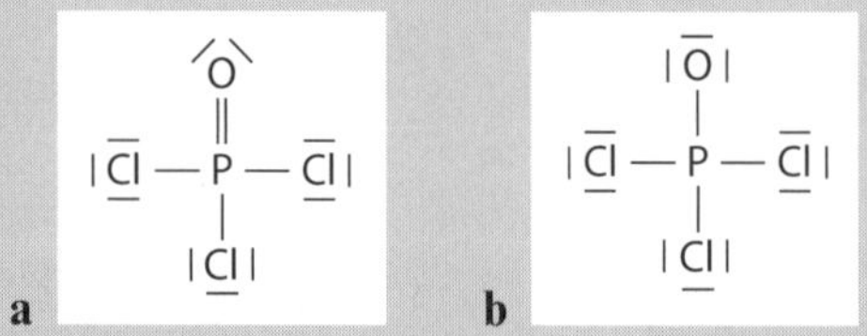

Figure 7.9: Alternative Lewis structures for $POCl_3$.

    i What name is given to the type of bond between the phosphorus and the oxygen atom in Figure **7.9b**? [1]

    ii Using the idea of formal charge, deduce which structure is more likely and justify your choice. [3]

CONTINUED

d   Phosphorus also forms a number of compounds and ions with halogens. Draw a diagram to show the shape of the following, clearly indicating the bond angles around the phosphorus atom in each case:

i PCl_3 [2]

ii PCl_5 [2]

iii PF_6^- [2]

iv PF_4^+ [2]

Chapter 8

The metallic model

CHAPTER OUTLINE

In this chapter you will:

- explain metallic bonding

- explain the factors that affect the strength of metallic bonding

- explain the variation in the melting point of main group metals down a group and across a period

- describe and explain the characteristic properties of metals

- understand the connection between the properties of a metal and its uses.

> understand that transition metals have delocalised d electrons

> explain the melting points and electrical conductivity of transition metals.

KEY TERMS

Make sure you understand the following key terms before you do the exercises.

metallic bonding: the electrostatic attraction between the positive ions and the delocalised electrons in a metallic lattice

malleable: can be hammered into different shapes

ductile: can be drawn out into wires

lustrous: shiny

Exercise 8.1 Classifying elements as metals, Exercise 8.2 Metallic bonding and Exercise 8.3 Properties of metals and their uses

In this exercise, you will begin by exploring the physical and chemical properties of metals and then go on to explore these properties in terms of the bonding and structure of metals.

1 Where in the periodic table are the metals located?

2 Many metals share the common physical properties listed below.

Give the meaning of each of these properties:

a **lustrous**

b good electrical conductor

c good thermal conductor

d **ductile**

e **malleable**.

3 The chemical properties of metals vary widely, but there are some characteristic chemical properties; list these.

4 This question is about **metallic bonding**.

a What is the meaning of the term *delocalised*?

b Draw a diagram to show the structure of a typical metal.

c Describe the movement of delocalised electrons in a metal.

5 Give two factors that affect the strength of metallic bonding.

6 Explain the trend in the melting points down Group 2 of the periodic table.

7 Explain the trend in the melting points of the metals in Period 3 of the periodic table.

8 Explain the following properties of metals:

a electrical conductivity

b thermal conductivity

c malleable/ductile.

TIP

Characteristic properties means the general properties of metals.

TIP

Try to show that metals have a 3D structure. Do not forget to include labels.

TIP

In questions 6 and 7, the command term is *explain*, so you need to do more than just describe the trend; you need to explain why the trend is as described.

9 Suggest why the following metals are suitable for the use described:

a Gold is used in jewellery.

b Aluminium is used for aeroplanes.

c Iron is used for car body panels.

Exercise 8.4 Transition metals

In this exercise, you will explore the properties of transition metals in more detail.

1 Compare the melting points of transition metals to metals in the s and p blocks of the periodic table.

2 Which electrons are delocalised in the first-row transition metals?

3 As the number of d electrons increases across the first-row transition elements, why do the melting points of the elements not increase sequentially?

4 How does the electrical conductivity of the first-row transition metals provide evidence that d electrons tend to be less delocalised than the valence electrons in sodium, magnesium and aluminium?

> TIP

You are not expected to know specific details about electrical conductivity, just how this applies to s and p block elements.

EXAM-STYLE QUESTIONS

1 Which of the following is **not true** for all metals?
   A good electrical conductors
   B solid at 298 K
   C form cations
   D good thermal conductors

2 Which statement correctly explains why metals are malleable?
   A The layers of atoms can slide over each other when a force is applied.
   B The layers of molecules can slide over each other when a force is applied.
   C The layers of cations can slide over each other when a force is applied.
   D The layers of anions can slide over each other when a force is applied.

3 Which statements explain why the melting point of potassium is lower than that of calcium?
   I Calcium ions have a higher charge than potassium ions.
   II Potassium ions have a larger radius than calcium ions.
   III Potassium has a lower first ionisation energy than calcium.
   A I and II
   B II and III
   C I and III
   D I, II and III

CONTINUED

4 What property of copper best explains why it is often used for pots and pans?

A good electrical conductor

B lustrous

C ductile

D good thermal conductor

5 Transition metals often have higher melting points than metals in the s-block of the periodic table. Which statement best explains the reason for this?

A Transition metals have delocalised d electrons.

B Transition metals have higher first ionisation energies than the s-block metals.

C Transition metals have smaller and more highly charged ions than s-block elements.

D Transition metals can form ions with different charges.

6 Aluminium has a wide range of uses, including drinks cans and high-performance racing cars, due to its strength and malleability. Describe the bonding in aluminium. [4]

7 Figure **8.1** shows the electrical conductivity of the elements sodium, magnesium and aluminium and the first-row d-block elements scandium to copper.

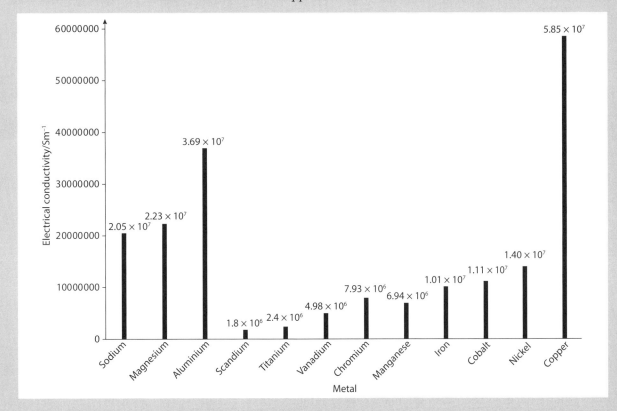

Figure 8.1: Electrical conductivity of selected elements.

a Explain why metals conduct electricity. [1]

b Explain why there is an increase in conductivity from sodium to aluminium. [1]

c Explain why the electrical conductivity of scandium is much lower than that of aluminium. [1]

Chapter 9

From models to materials

CHAPTER OUTLINE

In this chapter you will:

- understand the continuum between ionic, covalent and metallic bonding

- use electronegativity values to place substances in a bonding triangle

- relate the position of a compound in the bonding triangle to its properties

- understand the term *alloy*

- explain the properties of alloys

- understand the term *polymer*

- explain the properties of polymers (plastics) in terms of structure and bonding

- explain how addition polymers are formed

- deduce the structure of the repeating unit and equations for the formation of addition polymers.

> explain how condensation polymers are formed

> deduce the structure of the repeating unit of a condensation polymer

> understand that biological macromolecules form by condensation polymerisation and break down by hydrolysis

KEY TERMS

Make sure you understand the following key terms before you do the exercises.

alloy: homogeneous mixtures of two or more metals or of a metal with a non-metal

plastic: the common term for synthetic polymers

polymers: long-chain molecules, usually based on carbon, which are formed when smaller molecules (monomers) join together

polymerisation: the process of joining together a large number of monomers to form a long chain molecule (polymer). There are two types of polymerisation: addition and condensation

CONTINUED

addition polymerisation: a large number of monomers are joined together into a polymer chain; no other groups are lost in the process. Alkenes (containing C=C) undergo addition polymerisation

condensation polymerisation: monomers, each containing two functional groups, join together to form a long chain, with the elimination of a small molecule, such as water or hydrogen chloride, each time two monomers join together

monomer: a molecule from which a polymer chain may be built up, e.g. ethene is the monomer for polyethene

hydrolysis: a reaction in which a covalent bond in a molecule is broken by reaction with water; most commonly, hydrolysis reactions occur when a molecule is reacted with aqueous acid or aqueous alkali

macromolecule: a very large molecule

biodegradable: can be broken down by microorganisms in the environment

Exercise 9.1 Bonding and electronegativity

This exercise looks at bonding triangles as a more flexible model of bonding types. (A bonding triangle is given in the IB data book.) The exercise finishes with a consideration of their limitations.

1   The bonding triangle is based on electronegativity values. Define the term *electronegativity*.

2   What are the axes on the bonding triangle?

3   What types of substance do the vertices of the triangle represent?

4   Using the bonding triangle in the IB data book, suggest the type of bonding in the following substances:

a TiO_2

b   Cu

c Al_2O_3

d   Ge

e H_2O

f $AlCl_3$

g $MgBr_2$

> **TIP**
>
> When a question asks for *types* of substance, specific names or examples are not required.

5   Bonding triangles can only be used for elements and binary compounds.

   a   What is meant by a *binary compound*?

   b   What other limitations are there to the use of bonding triangles?

Exercise 9.2 Alloys

Alloys are first mentioned in Chapter 1 when considering ideas about mixtures.
In this exercise, you will look at alloys in more detail and consider why they are
classed as mixtures.

1   What is the difference between a mixture and a compound?

2   Although there is chemical bonding between the atoms in an alloy, why are they
   considered to be mixtures?

3   Alloys are classed as homogeneous mixtures. What does the term *homogeneous
   mixture* mean?

4   A mixture usually has the properties of the substances that it is made from.
   To what extent is this true for alloys?

5   What effect does the introduction of different-sized atoms into a metal have on the
   ability of the planes of metal ions to slide over one another?

6   What effect does the introduction of different-sized atoms into a metal have on the
   physical properties of a metal?

Exercise 9.3 Polymers

The name **plastic** comes from a common property of **polymers**, as they can be
moulded into shape. Polymers can be formed by two different types of reactions:
addition polymerisation and **condensation polymerisation** (Exercise 9.4). Most
natural polymers are formed by condensation reactions. In this exercise, you will
consider the general properties of polymers and then go on to look at **addition
polymerisation** reactions.

1   List the desirable properties of a typical plastic such as polyethene.

2   Describe two major environmental concerns about the use of plastics.

3   Plastics are more correctly called polymers. What is meant by the term *polymer*?

4   Figures **9.1** and **9.2** show two different types of bonding between polymer chains.

What effect do these differences have on the properties of the materials?

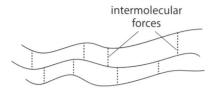

Figure 9.1: Intermolecular forces in a thermoplastic.

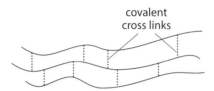

Figure 9.2: Cross-linking in a thermoset plastic.

5   The properties of a polymer can be affected by a number of factors.
What effect would the following have on the strength and flexibility of a polymer?

a   chain length

b   degree of chain branching

c   degree of crystallinity

d   addition of a plasticiser

e   type of intermolecular forces between the polymer chains.

6   Explain why polymers are poor electrical and thermal conductors.

7   What functional group do the **monomers** used in addition polymerisation all contain?

8   During an addition polymerisation reaction, what other products, apart from the polymer itself, are formed?

9   Figure **9.3** shows a section of a polymer chain.

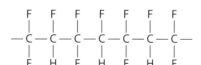

Figure 9.3: A section of a polymer chain.

a   Draw the repeating unit.

b   Draw the monomer.

> **TIP**
>
> In question 6, electrical and thermal conductivity should be discussed separately.

> **TIP**
>
> The functional group is the part of the molecule that gives the substance its characteristic properties.

> **TIP**
>
> A repeating unit should be drawn in square brackets with the bonds at both ends extending through the brackets.

10 Figure **9.4** shows the structure of 1,1-dichloropropene.

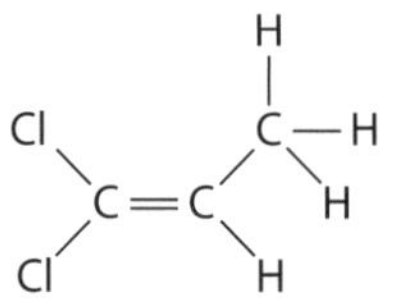

Figure 9.4: 1,1-dichloropropene.

Give an equation to show the polymerisation of 1,1-dichloropropene, and give the name of the polymer formed.

Exercise 9.4 Condensation polymers

Polymers can also be formed from condensation reactions. The links between monomers in the polymers met in the IB syllabus are formed by the reaction of two different classes of organic compounds. In this exercise you will meet two different condensation polymers; polyesters and polyamides.

1 Describe what is meant by a *condensation* reaction.

2 Draw the functional group that links the monomer units in a polyester.

3 Which two functional groups react together to form an ester?

4 Draw the monomers used to form the polyester in Figure **9.5**.

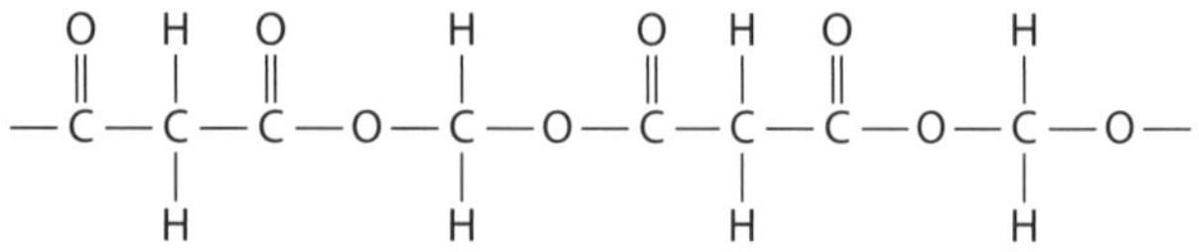

Figure 9.5: A section of a polyester.

5 Draw the functional group that links the monomer units in a polyamide.

6 Which two functional groups react together to form an amide?

7 Draw the monomers used to form the polyamide in Figure **9.6**.

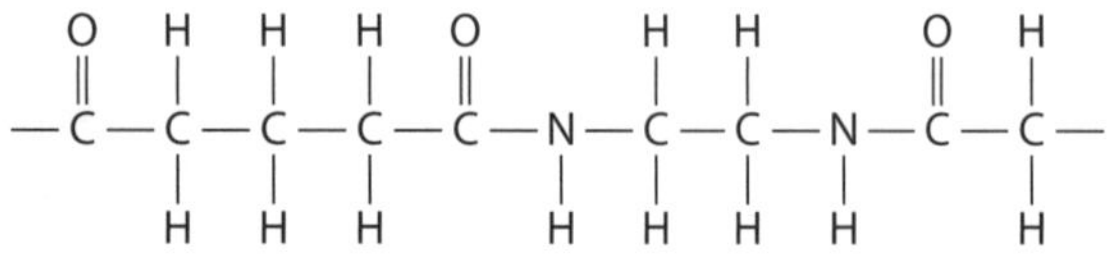

Figure 9.6: A section of a polyamide.

8 How is it possible to form a polyester or polyamide from a single monomer?

TIP
Condensation polymers are usually formed when two different functional groups join together. How can this happen if there is only one monomer?

9   Draw the monomer used to form the polymer shown in Figure **9.7**.

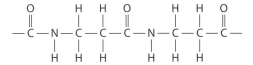

Figure 9.7: A section of a condensation polymer.

10   Condensation polymers can be broken down by **hydrolysis**. What is meant by the term *hydrolysis*?

11   Hydrolysis reactions usually occur in the presence of an acid, alkali or, in the case of biological molecules, what other substance?

EXAM-STYLE QUESTIONS

1   Which statement best describes an alloy?

   A   a homogeneous mixture

   B   a heterogeneous mixture

   C   an element

   D   a compound

2   Brass is an alloy made of 75% copper and 25% zinc. The melting point of copper is 1085 °C and the melting point of zinc is 907 °C. Which statement about the melting point of the alloy is correct?

   A   The melting point of the alloy will be between 907 and 1085 °C.

   B   The melting point of the alloy will be higher than 1085 °C.

   C   The melting point of the alloy will be lower than 907 °C.

   D   The melting point of the alloy cannot be determined from the information in the question.

3   The addition of differently sized atoms to a metal to produce an alloy prevents the layers sliding over one another. What property of the metal is most affected by this?

   A   malleability

   B   electrical conductivity

   C   thermal conductivity

   D   melting point

4   Which of the following is **not** a property of a typical plastic?

   A   low density

   B   poor thermal insulator

   C   low reactivity

   D   poor conductor of electricity

5   Which statement best describes addition polymers?

   A   They are formed by the joining of monomers, which are alkenes.

   B   The double bond breaks when the monomer units join together.

   C   Water is also produced during the formation of addition polymers.

   D   Addition polymers are long-chain molecules containing carbon–carbon double bonds.

6 Some polymers have covalent bonds between the polymer chains. What is the likely effect of these covalent bonds on the properties of the polymer?

A increased flexibility

B less dense

C more rigid

D better insulator

7 Bonding triangles can be used to predict the properties of an element or binary compound. What data are used to determine a compound's position in a bonding triangle?

I the difference in the electronegativities of the elements

II the % ionic character of the compound

III the average electronegativity of the elements

A I and II

B II and III

C I and III

D I, II and III

8 Biological macromolecules, such as proteins, are formed by what type of reaction?

A addition polymerisation

B condensation polymerisation

C hydrolysis

D substitution polymerisation

9 Figure **9.8** shows a section of a polymer. What name is given to this type of polymer?

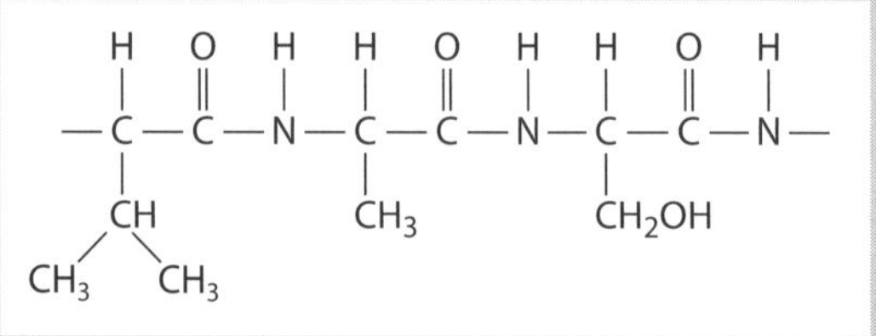

Figure 9.8: A section of a polymer.

A polyester

B polyamine

C polyamide

D polysaccharide

10 Which statement is **not** true?

A Addition polymers are not biodegradable.

B All natural polymers are condensation polymers.

C Condensation polymers are broken down by hydrolysis.

D Only natural condensation polymers can be broken down by hydrolysis.

CONTINUED

11 Table **9.1** describes the composition, hardness, tensile strength and ductility of various types of brass relative to the same properties of pure copper, which is assigned a value of 100.

% Copper	% Zinc	Relative hardness	Relative ductility
100	0	100	100
90	10	103	125
80	20	109	150
70	30	112	152
64	36	121	121
60	40	138	97
55	45	155	69

Table 9.1: The composition of some different types of brass.

a   What name is given to a mixture of metals? [1]

b   Hardness is related to the malleability of a metal. Explain why the addition of zinc increases the hardness of the metal. [2]

c   The ductility of a metal also depends on the crystal structure of the metal, and so, does not always follow the same trend as hardness. Plot a graph to show how the ductility of the metal varies with the percentage of copper in the mixture and use the graph to find the composition that is most ductile. [4]

12 Draw the repeating units for polymers made from the following monomers:

a

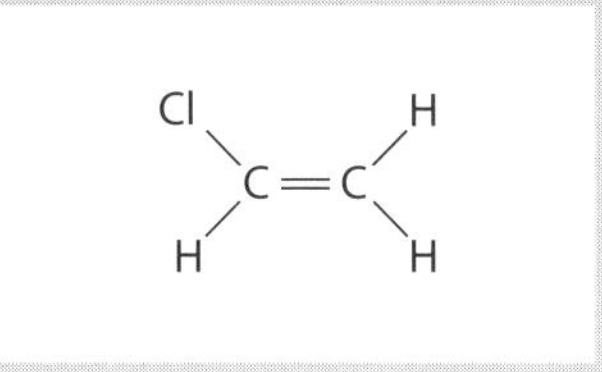

b

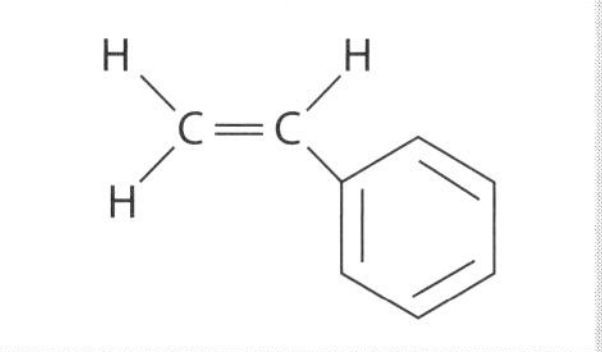

c

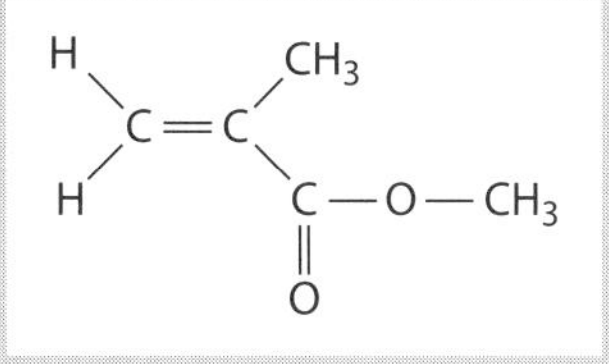

CONTINUED

13 Kevlar® is a polyamide that is used in bulletproof vests and protective clothing.
Its monomers are shown in Figure **9.9**.

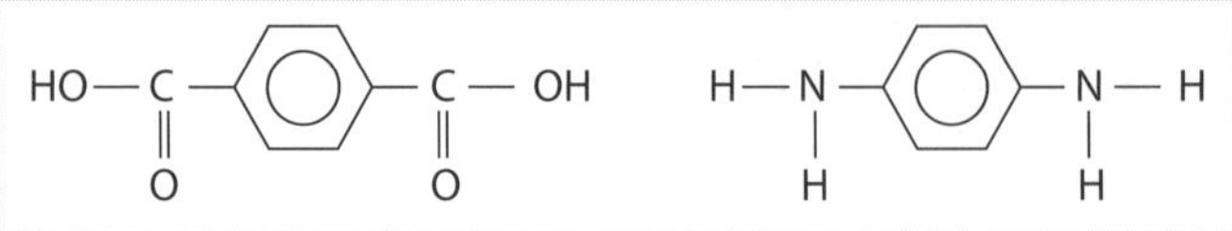

Figure 9.9: The monomers of Kevlar®.

a Give a balanced equation to show the formation of Kevlar®. [2]

b Explain why Kevlar® is strong enough for use in bulletproof materials. [1]

c Condensation polymers can be degraded by strong acids and strong alkalis.
   What name is given to this reaction? [1]

14 a Using the bonding triangle in the IB data book, determine the percentage ionic character of the
   Group 13 oxides. [3]

   b Considering your answers to part **a**, predict the trend in the following for the Group 13 oxides,
   giving a reason for your answers.

   i melting point [3]

   ii electrical conductivity [2]

Classification of matter

Chapter 10

The periodic table

In this chapter you will:

- describe the structure of the periodic table

- deduce the electron configuration of an element from its position in the periodic table

- explain the trends in the properties of elements down a group and across a period

- describe and explain the reactions of Group 1 elements with water

- describe and explain the reactions of Group 17 elements with halide ions

- describe the trends in the acid–base behaviour of oxides

- write equations for the reactions with water of the oxides of Group 1 and 2 metals, carbon and sulfur

- explain acid rain and ocean acidification

- deduce oxidation states for elements in molecules and ions

- name compounds using oxidation states.

> describe and explain the characteristic properties of transition metals

> explain why transition metal complexes are coloured

> explain the factors that affect the colours of transition metal ions.

KEY TERMS

Make sure you understand the following key terms before you do the exercises.

first electron affinity: the enthalpy change when one electron is added to each atom in one mole of gaseous atoms under standard conditions: $X(g) + e^- \rightarrow X^-(g)$. The first electron affinity is exothermic for virtually all elements

periodicity: the repetition of properties

group: vertical column in the periodic table. These are numbered from 1 to 18, including the transition metal groups

period: horizontal row in the periodic table. Hydrogen and helium are in Period 1

CONTINUED

displacement reaction: a reaction in which one element in a compound is replaced by another

acid: a substance that reacts with a base/alkali to form a salt

amphoteric: a substance that can act as an acid and a base

base: a substance that reacts with an acid to form a salt

oxidation state (oxidation number): the degree of oxidation of an atom in terms of counting electrons. It is a purely formal concept that regards all compounds as ionic and assigns charges to the components accordingly; it provides a guide to the distribution of electrons in covalent compounds

acid rain: rain with a pH less than would be expected from dissolved atmospheric carbon dioxide (5.6). It is caused by dissolved oxides of nitrogen and sulfur

acid deposition: a more general term than acid rain that refers to any process in which acidic substances (particles, gases and precipitation) leave the atmosphere to be deposited on the surface of the Earth – it can be divided into wet deposition (acid rain, fog and snow) and dry deposition (acidic gases and particles)

reduction: gain of electrons or decrease in oxidation state. Reduction can also be defined in terms of the loss of oxygen or the gain of hydrogen, but these are less general definitions

oxidation: loss of electrons or increase in oxidation state. Oxidation can also be defined in terms of the gain of oxygen or the loss of hydrogen, but these are less general definitions

complex: a species consisting of a central atom or ion surrounded by a number of ligands to which it is bonded by dative covalent bonds

ligand: negative ion or neutral molecule that uses lone pairs of electrons to bond to a transition metal ion to form a complex ion. Coordination bonds are formed between the ligand and the transition metal ion

transition metals/elements: the elements in the central part (d-block) of the periodic table. There are various ways of defining a transition metal. IUPAC definition: 'an element whose atoms have an incomplete (partially filled) d subshell or forms positive ions with an incomplete (partially filled) d subshell'

metalloid: elements, such as Si, Ge and Sb, that have some of the properties of both metals and non-metals or properties that are intermediate between those of a metal and non-metal

Exercise 10.1 The periodic table

The periodic table is one of the most easily recognised emblems of chemistry. Its form is not fixed, however – there are a large number of different representations of the elements. In this exercise, you will start by looking at a basic overview of the arrangement of the elements in the more familiar form of the periodic table. You will then go on to look at the relationships between an element's position and its electron configuration.

1 In what order are the elements in the periodic table arranged?

2 Name the elements that are liquid at 298 K.

3 What is meant by **group**?

4 What is meant by **period**?

5 a There is an approximately diagonal divide from boron to astatine in the periodic table. What is this the divide between?

b What term is used to describe the elements close to this dividing line?

6 The periodic table is divided into four blocks. What are these blocks called and why?

7 What names are given to the following sections of the periodic table?

a Group 1 elements

b Group 17 elements

c Group 18 elements

d first row of the f-block

e second row of the f-block

f the d-block

8 Which element does not fit well in any group of the periodic table?

9 The location of an element can be described by its block, period and group number.

Give the location of the following elements and give their electron configurations:

a arsenic

b copper

c tungsten (electron configuration not required).

> **TIP**
>
> You are only expected to give the electron configuration of elements with an atomic number of up to 36. Do not forget that two of these elements do not follow the electron filling rules.

10   Work out the identity of the elements in the following positions of the periodic table and give their electron configurations:

a   Period 2, Group 14

b   Period 4, Group 1

c   Period 5, Group 9 (electron configuration not required).

Exercise 10.2 Periodicity

Periodicity is the term used to describe the trends in properties that occur in the periodic table. It was the similarities and patterns in the properties of substances that led early scientists to the idea that there was order to be found amongst the elements. In this exercise, you will look at some of these patterns: atomic radius, ionic radius, ionisation energy, **electron affinity** and electronegativity. You will start by exploring the foundation ideas on which all of these properties are based.

1   Describe the trend in the charge of the nucleus of an atom across and down the periodic table.

2   Describe the trend in the shielding of outer-shell electrons by inner complete shells of electrons across and down the periodic table.

3   Considering your answers to questions 1 and 2, describe the trend in the strength of the forces of attraction between the positive nucleus of an atom and the outer-shell electrons across a period.

4   Considering your answers to questions 1 and 2, describe the trend in the strength of the forces of attraction between the positive nucleus of an atom and the outer-shell electrons down a group.

5   Define both *electronegativity* and *electron affinity*.

6   Define what is meant by *first ionisation energy*.

7   Describe and explain the general trend in the following properties across a period:

a   atomic radius

b   first ionisation energy

c   electronegativity.

8   Describe and explain the general trend in the following properties down a group:

a   atomic radius

b   first ionisation energy

c   first electron affinity

d   electronegativity.

> **TIP**
>
> The terms *electronegativity* and *electron affinity* are often confused; make sure you know the difference and always use the correct one.

> **TIP**
>
> When answering question 4, you should also consider the change in the atomic radius down a group.

> **TIP**
>
> The command term *explain* is used in questions 7 and 8 to make sure you understand the reasons for the patterns, and you do not just try to memorise them.

Exercise 10.3 The chemistry of Group 1 and Group 17

Chemical and physical properties depend on the bonding and structure of a substance. This is covered in more detail in Chapters 6, 7 and 8. In this exercise, you will describe the trends in the Group 1 elements and some of the typical reactions that can be used to illustrate them. You will also look at the patterns in the physical and chemical properties of the elements in Group 17. This includes **displacement reactions**, which can be used to demonstrate the trend in the reactivity down the group.

The questions at the end of this exercise return to ideas about the trends in the properties of the oxides and in metallic properties across the periodic table.

1   In terms of their electron configurations, what do the Group 1 elements have in common with each other?

2   Name the type of bonding in the Group 1 elements.

3   The melting point of the Group 1 elements decreases down the group; explain this trend.

4   Give equations for the reactions of potassium with the following:

   a   oxygen

   b   chlorine

   c   water.

5   Explain the trend in the reactivity down Group 1, and so, the increasing metallic character of the elements.

6   In terms of their electron configurations, what do the Group 17 elements have in common with each other?

7   Describe the bonding in the Group 17 elements.

8   The melting point of the Group 17 elements increases down the group. Explain this trend.

9   Displacement reactions can be used to demonstrate the trend in the reactivity in Group 17.

   a   Design a simple experiment that could be performed in a school laboratory to show the trends for chlorine, bromine and iodine. Include observations and equations.

   b   These reactions are described as *redox reactions*. What does this term mean? Use the reaction of bromine with potassium iodide to explain your answer.

> **TIP**
>
> Start by considering the type of bonding and structure of these elements.

> **TIP**
>
> The Group 1 elements form ionic compounds by losing their outer-shell electron; how easily does this happen?

> **TIP**
>
> Consider the type of bonding in the Group 17 elements and the factors that affect the strength of this.

10 Which Period 3 oxides are considered to be

   a   basic?

   b   **amphoteric**?

   c   acidic?

11 Give equations for the reactions of the following oxides with water. In each case, suggest whether the solution formed is acidic or alkaline. Include state symbols in your answer.

   a Na_2O

   b MgO

   c CO

   d CO_2

   e NO_2

   f SO_2

   g SO_3

> **TIP**
>
> The equations for these non-metal oxides may seem difficult at first. In Exercise 10.5, you will learn about **oxidation states**; these will help you to remember these equations as the non-metal does not change its oxidation state, apart from in the reaction of NO_2.

Exercise 10.4 Oxides

Acidic and basic oxides have been present in the atmosphere for tens of thousands of years. In this exercise, you will look at the environmental impact of the changes in the amounts of some of these oxides caused by recent human activity.

1   Carbon dioxide is a slightly soluble gas that forms an acidic solution. The increased concentration of carbon dioxide in the atmosphere has led to *ocean acidification*. Describe what this term means and the possible consequences on aquatic life.

2   As carbon dioxide dissolves to form an acidic solution, all rain is **acid rain**. Why is this statement incorrect?

3   What are the main causes of acid rain?

4   What are the main environmental problems associated with acid rain?

Exercise 10.5 Oxidation state

Scientists often use classification as a way of finding order and patterns in the things they are studying. Reactions are often classified into types.

Reduction/oxidation reactions can sometimes be difficult to identify, especially as they can be defined in a number of different ways. Oxidation states, also known as oxidation numbers, are a useful tool to help in determining whether a reduction/oxidation (redox) reaction has happened. You will meet them again in Chapter 20. In this exercise, you will begin by checking that you are confident about the definitions of *oxidation* and *reduction*. You will then practise devising formulas from names and vice versa.

Before the widespread use of oxidation states, the name of a compound gave little clue as to its formula; $Fe(ClO_4)_2$ was previously known as ferrous perchlorate, but iron(II) chlorate(VII) is much more informative. It is true, however, that lots of common names are still in use, it will probably be a long time before carbon dioxide becomes commonly known as carbon(IV) oxide.

1 Identify whether the following definitions describe oxidation or reduction:

    a   gain of oxygen

    b   gain of electrons

    c   loss of oxygen

    d   loss of electrons

    e   gain of hydrogen

    f   increase in oxidation number

    g   loss of hydrogen

    h   decrease in oxidation number.

> **TIP**
>
> The mnemonic *OIL RIG* is often used:
>
> *Oxidation Is Loss* of electrons, *Reduction Is Gain* of electrons.

2 Deduce the oxidation number of the following atoms and complete the table. The first row has been completed for you.

Substance	Oxidation states		
KBr	K: +1	Br: −1	
PCl_5	P:	Cl:	
Fe_2O_3	Fe:	O:	
$NaNO_2$	Na:	N:	O:
K_2CrO_4	K:	Cr:	O:
H_2	H:		
SO_4^{2-}	S:	O:	
HCO_3^-	H:	C:	O:
NO_3^-	N:	O:	

> **TIP**
>
> Oxidation numbers are always written as a charge followed by a number, e.g. +2 and not 2+.

3   Deduce the oxidation number of the atoms in the following substances:

a $LiAlH_4$

b Na_2O_2

c C_3H_8

4   Name the following compounds using IUPAC rules:

a   CuI

b V_2O_5

c $Cr_2(SO_4)_3$

d NH_4VO_3

e K_2CrO_4

f $NaNO_2$

g $Sc_2(SO_3)_3$

5   Work out the formulas of the following compounds:

a   iron(II) oxide

b   sodium chlorate(I)

c   potassium bromate(V)

d   iron(II) sulfate(VI)

e   sulfuric(IV) acid

f   potassium manganate(VII)

g   chromium(III) nitrate(V)

h   nitrogen(I) oxide

i   nitrogen(II) oxide

j   nitrogen(IV) oxide.

Exercise 10.6 Exceptions to the general increase in first ionisation energy across a period

TIP

The trend in the ionisation energies down a group is not due to an increase in the shielding, as this is offset by an increase in the nuclear charge.

Exercise 10.2 looked at the general trends in ionisation energies across a period and down a group. This exercise begins with a reminder of the general trends and then it looks at the explanation for the discontinuities in the trend across a period.

1   Describe the trend in nuclear charge down a group.

2   Describe the trend in the amount of shielding down a group.

3   Explain the general trend in the first ionisation energies down a group.

4   Describe the trend in nuclear charge across a period.

5   Describe the trend in the amount of shielding across a period.

6   Explain the general trend in the first ionisation energies across a period.

7   Explain the slight discontinuities in the first ionisation energies between magnesium and aluminium and between phosphorus and sulfur, as shown in **Figure 10.1**.

TIP

Note the use of the command term *explain* in question 6. To explain the trend, you will need to link the ideas described in questions 4 and 5.

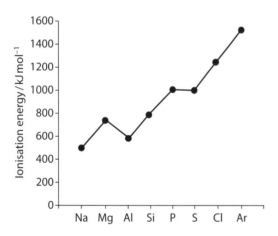

Figure 10.1: First ionisation energies.

Exercise 10.7 The transition elements (d-block)

Not all first-row d-block elements are **transition metals/elements**. The term *transition element* can be defined in a number of ways. In this exercise, you will begin by considering its definition and then look at some of the properties of transition elements.

1   What is meant by a *d-block* element?

2   What is meant by the term *transition element*?

3   List the characteristic properties of transition elements.

4   Explain why zinc is **not** considered a transition element.

5   Give the electron configurations of the following elements and ions:

   a   Zn

   b   Sc

   c   Ti

   d   Cr

   e   Ni

   f   Cu

   g Fe^{3+}

   h Mn^{2+}

   i V^{3+}

   j Co^{2+}

6   Explain why transition elements show variable oxidation states.

7   Describe the type of bond between a central metal ion in a **complex** and a **ligand**.

8   What does the term *coordination number* mean in reference to complexes?

9   Draw diagrams to show the shape and bond angles in four- and six-coordinate complexes.

10   Give the formula of a complex consisting of a central Cr^{3+} ion and six SCN^- ligands.

> **TIP**
>
> Read the wording of an exam question carefully; is it looking for properties that characterise metals or those that are special to transition metals?

> **TIP**
>
> Remember the 4s subshell is both filled first in the elements and lost first when ions are formed.

> **TIP**
>
> Drawings showing shape must use 3D notation (solid, dashed and wedged lines). Do not forget to label the bond angles. Remember that for four-coordinate complexes, there are two possible shapes.

11 Determine the oxidation state of the transition element in the following complexes:

    a $[Ag(NH_3)_2]^+$

    b $[Fe(H_2O)_5Cl]^{2+}$

    c $[Pt(CO)_2(NH_3)Br]^+$

    d $[Ni(CN)_4]^{2-}$

12 Explain why transition metal complexes are often coloured.

13 A complex ion absorbs light of wavelengths between 650 and 700 nm. Deduce what colour the substance will appear. (The colour wheel can be found in the IB data book.)

14 List five factors that affect the colour of complexes.

15 How does an increase in the splitting of the d orbitals affect the wavelength of light absorbed in a transition metal complex?

EXAM-STYLE QUESTIONS

1 Which of the following elements could be described as a metalloid?

    A S

    B Sb

    C Sc

    D Sn

2 Which is the correct electron configuration for chromium?

    A $1s^2\ 2s^2\ 2p^6\ 3s^2\ 3p^6\ 4s^2\ 3d^4$

    B $1s^2\ 2s^2\ 2p^6\ 3s^2\ 3p^6\ 3d^6$

    C $1s^2\ 2s^2\ 2p^6\ 3s^2\ 3p^6\ 4s^1\ 3d^5$

    D $1s^2\ 2s^2\ 2p^6\ 3s^2\ 3p^6\ 4s^2\ 4p^4$

3 Which of the following properties increases down Group 17?

    I melting point

    II first ionisation energy

    III electronegativity

    A I only

    B II only

    C I and II

    D II and III

CONTINUED

4   The graph shows the variation in a property around the periodic table.
Which property and for which elements?

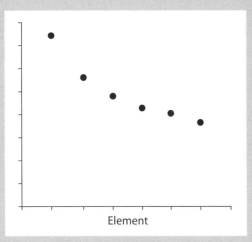

Element

Figure 10.2: Periodic trends.

A   Melting point of elements across Period 3 from Na to S.

B   Electronegativity of elements down Group 18 from He to Rn.

C   First ionisation energies of elements up Group 2 from Ra to Be.

D   Atomic radius of elements across Period 2 from Li to O.

5   In a series of experiments between various halogen solutions with aqueous halides, the following results were obtained.

	Halide X^-(aq)	Halide Y^-(aq)	Halide Z^-(aq)
Halogen X_2(aq)	no reaction	reaction	no reaction
Halogen Y_2(aq)	no reaction	no reaction	no reaction
Halogen Z_2(aq)	reaction	reaction	no reaction

Which is the correct likely identity of X, Y and Z?

A   X = fluorine, Y = chlorine, Z = iodine

B   X = bromine, Y = iodine, Z = chlorine

C   X = iodine, Y = bromine, Z = chlorine

D   X = fluorine, Y = iodine, Z = bromine

CONTINUED

6   What is the oxidation number of chlorine in a ClO_3^- ion?

   A   −1

   B   0

   C   +3

   D   +5

7   What would be observed when a small piece of lithium is dropped into a large volume of water?

   A   A lilac flame.

   B   The solution turns purple.

   C   The metal melts into a ball.

   D   The metal floats on the surface.

8   Which list shows elements in order of increasing first ionisation energy?

   A   O < F < Ne

   B   Na < Mg < Al

   C   Si < P < S

   D   Cl < Ar < K

9   Which d-block element is **not** normally considered a transition metal?

   A   copper

   B   zinc

   C   titanium

   D   vanadium

10   In which complex is the metal ion in oxidation state +2?

   A $[Fe(CN)_6]^{3-}$

   B $[Fe(H_2O)_5CO]^{3+}$

   C $[Fe(NH_3)_4Cl_2]^+$

   D $[Fe(H_2O)_3(CN)_6]^{4+}$

11   Which of the following compounds is likely to be coloured?

   A   CuI

   B TiO_2

   C $ScCl_3$

   D V_2S_3

12   Explain the following:

   a   why Mg^{2+} has a smaller radius than Mg.   [4]

   b   why metallic character increases down Group 1.   [3]

   c   why there are no electronegativity values assigned to Group 18 elements.   [1]

13   Explain the trend in the following properties across Period 3 using equations where appropriate:

   a   the acid–base properties of the oxides   [5]

   b   first ionisation energy   [4]

   c   metallic character.   [3]

CONTINUED

14 a   Define the term *transition element* and explain why not all d-block elements are described as transition elements.   **[2]**

   b   One of the characteristic features of transition elements is that they have variable oxidation states.

     i   Explain why the transition elements show this property.   **[2]**

     ii   Describe three other properties that are characteristic of the transition elements.   **[3]**

   c   Give the electron configurations of the Cu^+ and Cu^{2+} ions. Suggest the effect these different electron configurations have on some of the properties in your answer to **b ii**.   **[3]**

15   Many transition metal compounds are coloured. When concentrated hydrochloric acid is added slowly to a solution containing $[Cu(H_2O)_6]^{2+}$ ions, the solution turns from pale blue to green to yellow as $[CuCl_4]^{2-}$ ions are formed.

   a   Give the balanced equation for the reaction.   **[1]**

   b   Suggest why the solution changes to green before turning yellow.   **[1]**

   c   Draw diagrams to show the shapes of these complexes and give the bond angles and oxidation states of the copper in both cases.   **[4]**

   d   Using the colour wheel in the IB data book, give the range of wavelengths of light absorbed by the two complexes.   **[2]**

Chapter 11

Classification of organic compounds

CHAPTER OUTLINE

In this chapter you will:

- understand how the structures of organic molecules can be represented by different types of formula
- understand what a homologous series is
- recognise different homologous series
- understand the term *functional group* and how they influence properties
- recognise different functional groups
- understand the terms *saturated* and *unsaturated*
- understand how to name saturated or mono-unsaturated organic molecules containing up to six carbon atoms in the longest carbon chain
- understand what structural isomers are
- draw structural isomers of compounds
- understand the classification of groups as primary, secondary or tertiary.

> understand the term *stereoisomerism*

> understand *cis–trans* isomerism

> understand what chirality is

> draw enantiomers using stereochemical formulas

> understand how mass spectrometry can be used to provide information about the structure of an organic compound

> understand how infrared (IR) spectroscopy can be used to provide information about the structure of an organic compound

> understand what greenhouse gases are

> understand how ^{1}H nuclear magnetic resonance (NMR) can be used to provide information about the structure of an organic compound

> use spectroscopic data to deduce the structure of an organic compound.

KEY TERMS

Make sure you understand the following key terms before you do the exercises.

structural formula: a representation of a molecule that shows the arrangement of the atoms

condensed structural formula: shows how the atoms are joined together in a molecule but does not show all of the bonds, e.g. $CH_3CH_2CH_2OH$

stereochemical formula: a diagram of a molecule that shows the spatial arrangement of the atoms/groups. Solid wedges show a bond coming out of the plane of the paper/screen and dashed wedges show bonds going into the plane

skeletal formula: a representation of the structure of a molecule that shows only the bonds in the carbon skeleton and any groups joined to the carbon skeleton. The carbon atoms are not shown explicitly nor are hydrogen atoms joined to carbon

homologous series: a series of compounds with the same functional group, in which each member differs from the next by $—CH_2—$

functional group: an atom or group of atoms that gives an organic molecule its characteristic chemical properties. A functional group also influences the physical properties of a compound

general formula: the formula of a family of molecules that can be used to determine the molecular formula of any member of the series

hydrocarbon: a compound containing carbon and hydrogen only

aliphatic: organic compounds not containing a phenyl group

aromatic: in organic chemistry, aromatic compounds are those that contain a phenyl group

structural isomers: two or more compounds that have the same molecular formula but different structural formulas, i.e., the atoms are joined together in a different way

stereoisomers: molecules with the same molecular formula and structural formula, but the atoms are arranged differently in space; *cis–trans* isomers and optical isomers are stereoisomers

optical isomerism: optical isomers rotate the plane of plane-polarised light in opposite directions (by the same amount as long as concentrations are equal). Optical isomers have the same molecular and structural formula, but groups are arranged differently in space and the individual optical isomers are non-superimposable mirror images of each other

***cis–trans* isomerism:** where two compounds have the same structural formula, but the groups are arranged differently in space around a double bond or a ring

enantiomers: the non-superimposable mirror images of a chiral molecule

> **CONTINUED**
>
> **infrared spectroscopy:** an analytical technique used to identify the functional groups in an organic molecule due to their absorption of radiation in the infrared region of the electromagnetic spectrum
>
> **proton (^{1}H) nuclear magnetic resonance spectroscopy:** an analytical technique used for structural determination. It is used to identify the hydrogen atoms (protons) in a molecule

Exercise 11.1 The structures of organic molecules

The focus of this exercise is on becoming more familiar with organic formulas and the different ways of representing organic molecules. The type of formula used needs to be one that gives the information required by the reader in a simple form that can only be interpreted in one way. You will practise drawing different types of organic structures from a model and then look at molecules containing phenyl groups.

> **TIP**
>
> Always read the question carefully to help you decide which type of formula you need to provide.

1   Write out the full **structural formulas** of the following molecules:

   a $CH_3CH_2CH(OH)CH_3$

   b CH_3OCOCH_3

   c $CH_2CClCH_2CH_2Cl$

2   Write the **condensed structural formulas** of the following molecules:

   a

$$H-\overset{\overset{\displaystyle H}{|}}{\underset{\underset{\displaystyle Br}{|}}{C}}-\overset{\overset{\displaystyle H}{|}}{\underset{\underset{\displaystyle H}{|}}{C}}-\overset{\overset{\displaystyle H}{|}}{\underset{\underset{\displaystyle H}{|}}{C}}-O-H$$

   b

$$H-\overset{\overset{\displaystyle H}{|}}{\underset{\underset{\displaystyle H}{|}}{C}}-\overset{\overset{\displaystyle H}{\|}}{\underset{\underset{\displaystyle O}{}}{C}}-\overset{\overset{\displaystyle H}{|}}{\underset{\underset{\displaystyle H}{|}}{C}}-C\overset{\displaystyle O-H}{\underset{\displaystyle O}{}}$$

   c

$$H-\overset{\overset{\displaystyle H}{|}}{\underset{\underset{\displaystyle H}{|}}{C}}-\overset{\overset{\displaystyle H}{|}}{C}=\overset{\overset{\displaystyle H}{|}}{C}-\overset{\overset{\displaystyle H}{|}}{\underset{\underset{\displaystyle H}{|}}{C}}-\overset{\overset{\displaystyle H}{|}}{\underset{\underset{\displaystyle H}{|}}{C}}-\overset{\overset{\displaystyle H}{|}}{\underset{\underset{\displaystyle H}{|}}{C}}-\overset{\overset{\displaystyle H}{|}}{\underset{\underset{\displaystyle H}{|}}{C}}-H$$

> **TIP**
>
> Be careful not to confuse chlorine, Cl, with carbon and iodine, CI, as in some fonts this can be tricky.

3 Give the **stereochemical formulas** of the following molecules:

a CH_3OH

b C_2H_6

c C_2H_4

4 Draw the following molecules as **skeletal formulas**:

a

$$H-\underset{\underset{H}{|}}{\overset{\overset{H}{|}}{C}}-\underset{\underset{H}{|}}{\overset{\overset{H}{|}}{C}}=\overset{\overset{H}{|}}{C}-\underset{\underset{O-H}{|}}{\overset{\overset{H}{|}}{C}}-\underset{\underset{H}{|}}{\overset{\overset{H}{|}}{C}}-H$$

b $CH_3CHBrCH(CH_3)CH_2CHO$

c

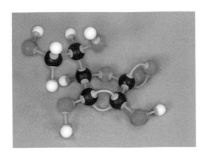

5 Give the condensed structural formulas of the following molecules:

a

b

c

6 Figure **11.1** is a photograph of an organic compound. Carbon is black, hydrogen is white and oxygen is grey.

Figure 11.1: Photograph of an organic compound.

   a   What is its molecular formula?

   b   What is its empirical formula?

   c   Draw its full structural formula.

   d   Draw its skeletal formula.

7   Give the molecular and empirical formulas of the following molecules:

   a

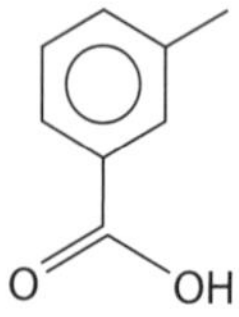

   b

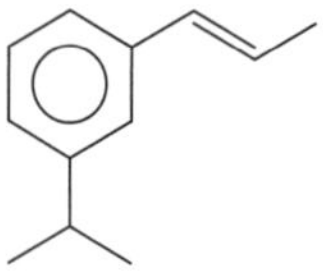

   c

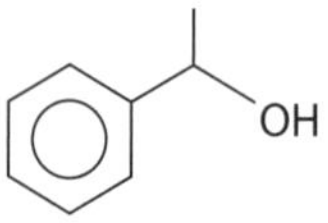

> **TIP**
>
> These molecules all contain a benzene ring. You may have met the structure of benzene, and why it is represented with a circle in the centre of the hexagon, at Higher Level in Chapter 7. Molecules that contain a benzene ring are called **aromatic**.

Exercise 11.2 Homologous series and functional groups

Organic molecules are often grouped into different classes or **homologous series**, depending on the **functional group** that they contain. This exercise looks at three examples of homologous series: the alkanes, alkenes and alcohols.

It also looks at hydrocarbons and other functional groups. **Hydrocarbons** include alkanes, alkenes and alkynes, which are classed as **aliphatic** compounds, and some aromatic compounds.

1   Organic molecules can be described by a **general formula**. Give the general formula of the following:

   a   alkanes

   b   alkenes

   c   alcohols.

2   Why do members of a homologous series have similar chemical properties?

3   Why do members of a homologous series show a gradual trend in their physical properties?

4 Draw the functional group in alkenes.

5 Draw and name the functional group in alcohols.

6 Complete Table **11.1**. The grey boxes can be left blank.

Homologous series	Functional group	Name of functional group
		hydroxyl
aldehyde		
		alkyl
	$C{=}C$	
alkyne		
amide		
	$-NH_2$ $-NHR$ $-NR_2$	
		carboxyl
ester		
	$C{-}O{-}C$	
halogenoalkane		
ketone		

Table 11.1: Names and functional groups of different homologous series.

TIP

Take care to distinguish between the name of a homologous series and the name of the functional group; these are the same for some classes of organic compounds, but not for all.

7 Give the general formula of the following:

a alkynes

b halogenoalkanes

c aldehydes

d ketones

e carboxylic acids

f esters.

TIP

What do you notice about the general formulas of aldehydes and ketones and of carboxylic acids and esters?

8 Name the functional groups in the following molecules:

a

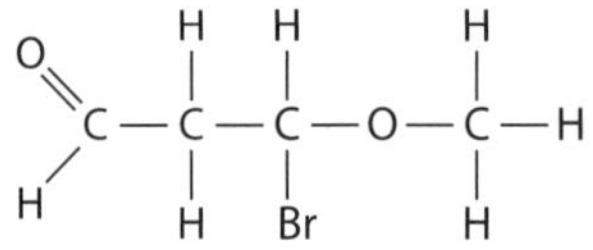

b

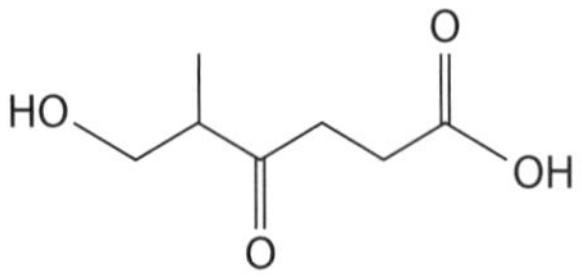

c

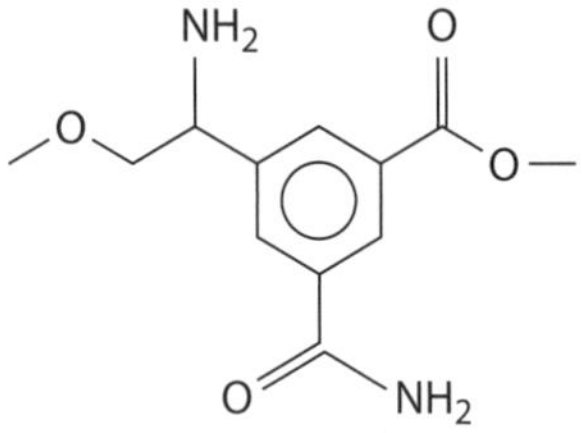

9 Explain the following:

a The boiling points of the members of a homologous series increase as the number of carbon atoms increases.

b The trend in the boiling points of the members of a homologous series is not linear.

10 Figure **11.2** shows three molecules with similar molar mass, but each belongs to a different homologous series.

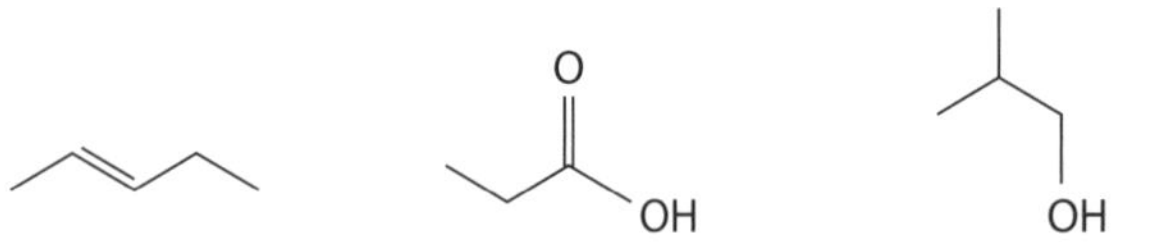

$M = 70.15\ \text{gmol}^{-1}$ $M = 74.09\ \text{gmol}^{-1}$ $M = 74.14\ \text{gmol}^{-1}$

molecule A molecule B molecule C

Figure 11.2: Molecules A, B and C.

a Place the molecules in order of boiling point, lowest first.

b Place the molecules in order of solubility in water, lowest first.

c Explain your answers to parts **a** and **b**.

Exercise 11.3 Naming organic molecules

Organic molecules can be named using the International Union of Pure and Applied Chemistry (IUPAC) system. For example, the pain killer ibuprofen has the IUPAC name of (*RS*)-2-[4-(2-methylpropyl)phenyl]propanoic acid. In this exercise, you will practise naming simple molecules using the IUPAC system.

1   Name the following compounds.

a

$$H-\underset{\underset{H}{|}}{\overset{\overset{H}{|}}{C}}-\underset{\underset{H}{|}}{\overset{\overset{H}{|}}{C}}-\underset{\underset{H}{|}}{\overset{\overset{H}{|}}{C}}-\underset{\underset{H}{|}}{\overset{\overset{H}{|}}{C}}-H$$

b

$$H-\underset{\underset{H}{|}}{\overset{\overset{H}{|}}{C}}-\underset{\underset{Br}{|}}{\overset{\overset{H}{|}}{C}}-\underset{\underset{H}{|}}{\overset{\overset{H}{|}}{C}}-H$$

c

$$H-\underset{\underset{H}{|}}{\overset{\overset{H}{|}}{C}}-\underset{\underset{H}{|}}{\overset{\overset{H}{|}}{C}}-\underset{|}{\overset{\overset{H}{|}}{C}}-\underset{\underset{H}{|}}{\overset{\overset{H}{|}}{C}}-H$$

$$H-\underset{|}{\overset{|}{C}}-H$$

$$H-\underset{\underset{H}{|}}{\overset{|}{C}}-H$$

d

$$H-\underset{\underset{H}{|}}{\overset{\overset{H}{|}}{C}}-\underset{\underset{H}{|}}{\overset{\overset{H}{|}}{C}}-\underset{\underset{H}{|}}{\overset{\overset{CH_3}{|}}{C}}-C\overset{\diagup O}{\diagdown O-H}$$

e

$$H-\underset{\underset{H}{|}}{\overset{\overset{H}{|}}{C}}-\underset{\underset{O}{||}}{C}-\underset{\underset{H}{|}}{\overset{\overset{H}{|}}{C}}-\underset{\underset{H}{|}}{\overset{\overset{H}{|}}{C}}-\underset{\underset{H}{|}}{\overset{\overset{H}{|}}{C}}-H$$

f

$$H-\underset{\underset{H}{|}}{\overset{\overset{H}{|}}{C}}-C\overset{\diagup O}{\diagdown H}$$

g

$$\underset{H}{\overset{H}{\diagdown}}C=\underset{\underset{H}{|}}{\overset{\overset{H}{|}}{C}}-\underset{\underset{H}{|}}{\overset{\overset{CH_3}{|}}{C}}-\underset{\underset{H}{|}}{\overset{\overset{H}{|}}{C}}-H$$

h

i

j

2 Draw the following molecules as instructed:

    a   displayed formula of hex-1-ene

    b   skeletal formula of 3-methylbut-1-yne

    c   condensed formula of methyl propanoate

    d   stereochemical formula of a tertiary bromoalkane with four carbon atoms

    e   skeletal formula of an ester containing four carbon atoms.

3 In organic chemistry, what do the terms *saturated* and *unsaturated* mean?

4 Name two homologous series of unsaturated hydrocarbons.

5 In which homologous series can the molecules be classified as primary, secondary or tertiary?

6 Identify which of the molecules in question **1a–j**

    a   are saturated hydrocarbons

    b   are unsaturated hydrocarbons

    c   contain a primary group

    d   contain a secondary group

    e   contain a tertiary group.

7 Identify which homologous series the molecules shown in question **1d–f** belong to.

Exercise 11.4 Isomers

There are a number of different types of isomerism. In this exercise, you will begin by looking at three different types of **structural isomerism**: straight-chain/branched (also called skeletal or chain isomerism), position and functional group isomerism. You will then focus on two more types of isomerism, which are only needed at Higher Level: **stereoisomerism** and **optical isomerism**.

1 Draw and name the chain isomers of C_5H_{12}.

2 Draw and name the position isomers of C_4H_8 that are alkenes.

3 Draw and name the position isomers of C_3H_7Br.

4 Draw the position isomers of $C_6H_4(OH)_2$.

5 Draw a functional group isomer of pentene, C_5H_{10}.

6 Draw a functional group isomer of propan-1-ol.

7 Draw a functional group isomer of propanone with only one functional group.

8 Draw a functional group isomer of ethanoic acid with only one functional group.

9 Compare the boiling point of a straight-chain and a branched alkane with the same molecular mass.

10 Describe what structural feature of a molecule causes ***cis–trans* isomerism**.

11 Identify which of the following molecules can exhibit *cis–trans* isomerism:

a

b $CH_3CH_2CH_2CHCH_2$

c 2,3-dibromohex-2-ene

d 1,3-dichlorocyclobutane.

12 Draw the following molecules:

a *cis*-pent-2-ene

b *trans*-1,3-dichlorobut-1-ene

c *cis*-1,2-dichlorocyclopropane.

13 Name the following molecules:

a

b
![Br structure with double bond]

c
![Br Br structure with double bond]

> **TIP**
>
> The molecule in question 4 contains a benzene ring.

> **TIP**
>
> When deciding if a molecule has *cis–trans* isomers or not, we say that there have to be *two different groups on each side of the double bond*. It would be much clearer in this situation to say that there have to be *two different groups on both carbons of the double bond*.

> **TIP**
>
> As stereoisomerism is about special arrangement, accurate drawings are especially important.

14 Optical isomers are usually drawn as mirror images of each other. Which of the following upper-case letters have non-superimposable mirror images?

a A

b B

c C

d M

e N

f S

g W

h H

i E

j Z

15 How can you determine if a molecule is chiral from its structural formula without having to draw it using any 3D notation?

16 Determine which of the following compounds are chiral and, for those that are, draw both isomers.

a

b

c

d

17 What name is given to isomers that are non-superimposable mirror images of each other?

18 Explain why *cis*-1,2-dimethylcyclobutane is not chiral, despite having two chiral carbon atoms.

19 Chiral molecules show optical activity. Explain the term *optical activity*.

20 What name is given to an equimolar mix of optical isomers.

21 What are the differences in physical and chemical properties of **enantiomers**?

Exercise 11.5 Spectroscopic identification of organic compounds

There are a number of different spectroscopic techniques that can be used to help identify an organic molecule. In this exercise, you will explore three of these: **infrared spectroscopy**, mass spectrometry and **proton (^{1}H) nuclear magnetic resonance spectroscopy**.

1   Why do some bonds absorb infrared radiation?

2   Can infrared spectroscopy be used to definitively identify a molecule, or can it only be used to identify the presence/absence of functional groups?

3   Using the IB data book, describe the regions in which you would expect to see key absorption bands for the following molecules:

a   pentan-1-ol

b   cyclohexene

c   ethanoic acid

d   ethylpropanoate.

4   Identify the key peaks present in the IR spectra shown in Figures **11.3** and **11.4**.

a

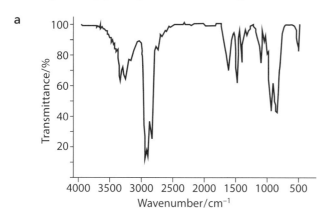

Figure 11.3

> **TIP**
>
> You do not need to know the difference between spectroscopy and spectrometry.

> **TIP**
>
> As well as the absorption bands, you should also indicate if a signal is broad or sharp.

b

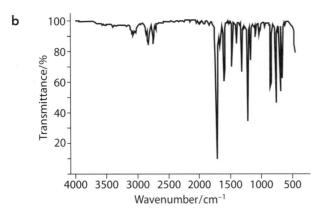

Figure 11.4

5 What structural feature must a molecule have to be able to act as a greenhouse gas?

6 Which of the following molecules will absorb infrared radiation?

   a SO_2

   b Cl_2

   c CH_3Cl

7 What changes happen to a greenhouse gas when it absorbs infrared radiation?

8 Table **11.2** lists a number of greenhouse gases, their relative abundance in the atmosphere and their relative effectiveness at absorbing infrared radiation.

Gas	Relative abundance / %	Relative effectiveness
H_2O	0.10	0.1
CO_2	0.036	1
CH_4	0.0017	26

Table 11.2: Greenhouse gas data.

Why are carbon dioxide and methane of more concern than water vapour, despite their lower relative abundances?

9 State what is meant by the *fragmentation pattern* in mass spectrometry.

10 What is the scale on the *x*-axis of a mass spectrum?

11 What name is given to the peak with the highest value on the *x*-axis of a mass spectrum?

> **TIP**
>
> This peak may not necessarily be the tallest on the spectrum, but it should be clearly visible in an exam paper. In reality, the peak with the highest value in the spectrum will be due to the presence of ^{13}C isotopes, but, as the abundance of these is relatively low, tiny peaks can be ignored.

12 In the mass spectrum of a hydrocarbon, a number of peaks were observed. Suggest the formulas of the species that could be responsible for peaks at *m/z* values of

a   15

b   27

c   29.

13 Figure **11.5** shows the mass spectrum of propan-1-ol. Suggest the identity of the species giving rise to the peaks at *m/z* values of 29, 31, 59 and 60.

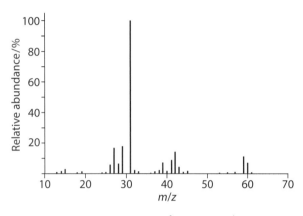

Figure 11.5: Mass spectrum of propan-1-ol

14 Given that bromine has two common isotopes, ^{79}Br and ^{81}Br, which occur in approximately equal proportions, suggest the most likely peaks that could be formed in the mass spectrum of 1-bromoethane.

15 The signals in an NMR spectrum are due to the presence of atoms of which element?

16 Energy in which region of the electromagnetic spectrum is used to produce the signals in an NMR spectrum?

17 What information can be deduced from the following aspects of an NMR spectrum?

a   the number of signals

b   the integration trace of the signals

c   the splitting pattern

d   the chemical shift of a signal.

18 What is the role of tetramethylsilane (TMS) in NMR?

19 Complete Table **11.3** to show the number of signals, splitting patterns, the ratio of the integration trace and chemical shifts in the NMR spectra of the following molecules:

Compound	Number of signals	Splitting pattern	Ratio of integration trace	Chemical shift / ppm
propanone				
1-chlorobutane				
2-chlorobutane				

Table 11.3: NMR signals.

20 Figure **11.6** gives the NMR spectrum of a compound containing carbon, hydrogen and oxygen with a molar mass of 88 g mol^{-1}. Suggest an identity for this compound.

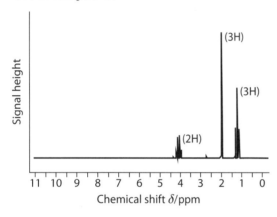

Figure 11.6: NMR of an unknown compound.

21 Limonene is a hydrocarbon with the molecular formula $C_{10}H_{16}$. Its structure is shown in Figure **11.7**

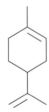

Figure 11.7: Structure of limonene.

a Give the empirical formula of limonene.

b Figure **11.8** shows the infrared spectrum of limonene.

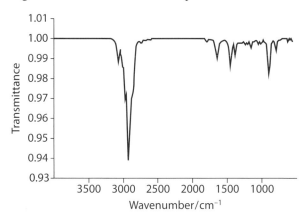

Figure 11.8: Infrared spectrum of limonene.

Identify the peaks at 1630 and 2900 cm⁻¹.

c Suggest identities and *m/z* values of likely fragments in the mass spectrum of limonene.

d Suggest how many signals might be seen in the proton NMR spectrum of limonene.

EXAM-STYLE QUESTIONS

1 Which compound could be in the same homologous series as ethane?

A C_3H_6

B C_4H_{10}

C C_8H_{16}

D C_5H_{10}

2 Which compound is an isomer of heptane, C_7H_{16}?

A $CH_3(CH_2)_4CH_3$

B $CH_3CH_2CH(CH_3)CHCHCH_3$

C $(CH_3)_3CCH(CH_3)CH_3$

D $(CH_3)_2CHCHCHCH(CH_3)CH_3$

3 Which is the correct molecular formula for this compound?

A $C_9H_{13}O_2N$

B $C_9H_{10}O_2N$

C $C_8H_{11}O_2N$

D $C_8H_9O_2N$

4 Which is the correct name for this molecule?

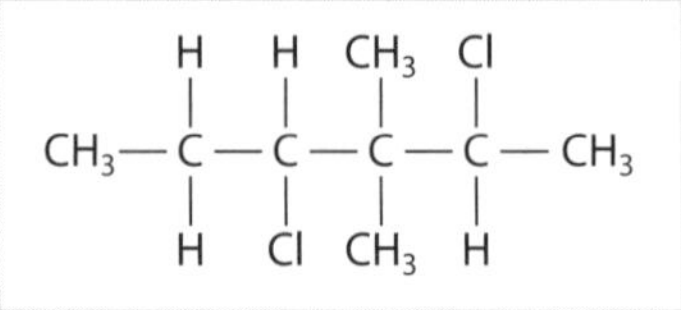

A 1,3-dichloro-1,2,2,4-tetramethylbutane

B 2,4-dichloro-3-dimethylhexane

C 2,4-dichloro-3,3-dimethylhexane

D 3,5-dichloro-4,4-dimethylhexane

5 Which of the following molecules is a tertiary alcohol?

A 2,4-dimethylpentan-2-ol

B 2-methylpentan-3-ol

C 2,2-dimethylpentan-1-ol

D 2,2-dimethylpentan-3-ol

6 Identify the names of the functional groups present in the molecule below.

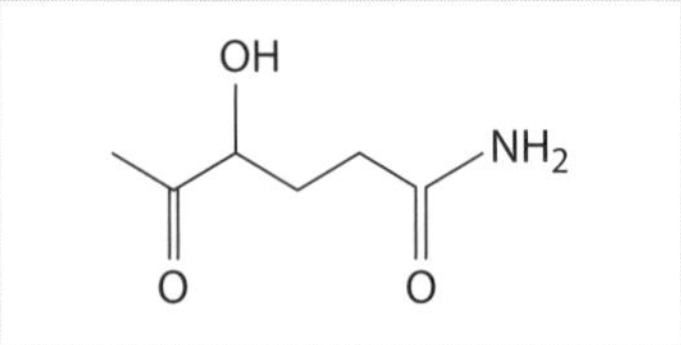

A ketone, alcohol, amide

B carbonyl, hydroxyl, carbonyl, amino

C carboxyl, amido

D carbonyl, hydroxyl, amido

7 What is the correct order of increasing boiling point?

A butanoic acid > hexane > 2,2-dimethylbutane > pentanal

B hexane > 2,2-dimethylbutane > pentanal > butanoic acid

C 2,2-dimethylbutane > hexane > pentanal > butanoic acid

D 2,2-dimethylbutane > hexane > butanoic acid > pentanal

8 Which is the correct name for this molecule?

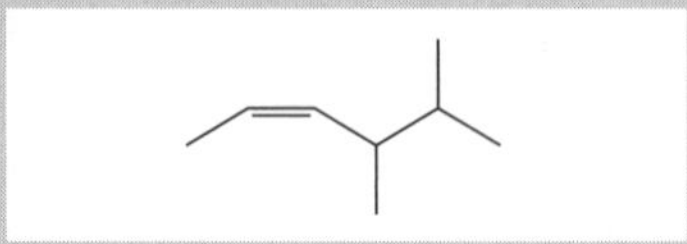

A *cis*-2,3-dimethylhex-4-ene

B *cis*-4,5-dimethylhex-2-ene

C *trans*-4,5,5-trimethylpent-2-ene

D *trans*-4,5-dimethylhex-2-ene

CONTINUED

9 Which of the following molecules exhibits optical isomerism?

A butane

B 1-chlorobutane

C 2-chlorobutane

D 2-chloro-2-methylbutane

10 Which technique can be used to determine the functional groups in a compound?

A infrared spectroscopy

B NMR spectroscopy

C mass spectroscopy

D colorimetry

11 The high-resolution NMR spectrum of ethanol is made up of three signals.

The ratio of the areas under each peak is 3 : 2 : 1. Which of the following correctly describes the splitting pattern in the same order?

A triplet : doublet : singlet

B doublet : triplet : doublet

C triplet : quartet : singlet

D triplet : quartet : triplet

12 How many proton environments are there in the following molecule?

A 3

B 4

C 5

D 6

CONTINUED

13 Figure **11.9** shows the trend in the boiling points of three different homologous series: straight-chain alkanes, straight-chain primary chloroalkanes and straight-chain primary alcohols.

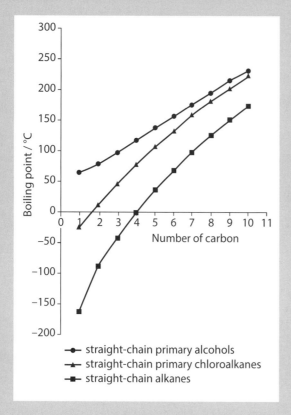

Figure 11.9: Boiling points in three homologous series.

a   Explain the general trend in the boiling points of the alkanes. [2]

b   Explain why the relationship between boiling point and the number of carbon atoms is not linear. [1]

c   Explain why it would not be fair to compare the boiling points of molecules from each series with the same number of carbon atoms, for example, comparing the boiling points of ethane, chloroethane and ethanol. [1]

d   Choose one molecule from each homologous series to illustrate the effect of the nature of the functional group on boiling point. [5]

14 There are a number of different compounds with the molecular formula C_4H_8.

a   Draw and name all the straight-chain unsaturated isomers with the molecular formula C_4H_8. [4]

b   What name is given to the homologous series to which the answers to part **a** belong? [1]

c   Draw a branched isomer with the molecular formula C_4H_8. [1]

d   Draw a cyclic compound with the molecular formula C_4H_8. [1]

e   Give the IUPAC name of the compound of your answer to part **d**. [1]

CONTINUED

15 It is possible to distinguish between optical isomers of a particular compound by comparing their effect on plane-polarised light using a polarimeter.

   a   Describe the effect of optical isomers on plane-polarised light and how a polarimeter can be used to distinguish them.   [4]

   b   The first member of the homologous series of alkanes that is optically active has the molecular formula C_7H_{16}. Draw both enantiomers of this molecule.   [2]

   c   Cyclic compounds can also exhibit optical isomerism. The first cyclic alkane to do so has the molecular formula C_5H_{10}. Draw the enantiomers and name this molecule.   [2]

What drives chemical reactions?

Chapter 12

Measuring enthalpy change

CHAPTER OUTLINE

In this chapter you will:

- understand the difference between heat and temperature

- understand the difference between exothermic and endothermic reactions

- understand what is meant by the term *stability*

- sketch and interpret potential energy profiles

- understand the term *standard enthalpy change* for a reaction

- calculate standard enthalpy changes from experimental data.

KEY TERMS

Make sure you understand the following key terms before you do the exercises.

heat: the energy that flows from something at a higher temperature to something at a lower temperature because of the temperature difference between them

exothermic reaction: a chemical reaction that results in the release of heat to the surroundings – the reaction vessel gets hotter; ΔH for an exothermic reaction is negative

endothermic reaction: a chemical reaction in which heat is taken in from the surroundings – the reaction vessel gets colder; ΔH for an endothermic reaction is positive

enthalpy change (ΔH): the heat energy exchanged with the surroundings at constant pressure

system/surroundings: system refers to the chemicals themselves, whereas the surroundings refers to the solvent, the air and the apparatus – all that surrounds the chemicals

internal energy (sometimes called chemical energy): the name given to the total amount of energy (kinetic and potential) in a sample of a substance

potential energy profile diagram: a diagram showing the change in the potential energy (*y*-axis) of a system as a reaction proceeds (*x*-axis is the reaction coordinate)

CONTINUED

calorimetry: experimental determination of the heat given out/taken in during chemical reactions/physical processes

specific heat capacity: the energy required to raise the temperature of 1 g of substance by 1 K (1 °C). It can also be defined as the energy to raise the temperature of 1 kg of substance by 1 K. Specific heat capacity has units of $J\ g^{-1}\ K^{-1}$ or $J\ g^{-1}\ °C^{-1}$. Units that are also encountered are $kJ\ kg^{-1}\ K^{-1}$ or $J\ kg^{-1}\ K^{-1}$

standard enthalpy change of neutralisation (ΔH_n): the enthalpy change when one mole of H_2O molecules is formed when an acid (H^+) reacts with an alkali (OH^-) under standard conditions, i.e

$H^+(aq) + OH^-(aq) \rightarrow H_2O(l)$

the enthalpy change of neutralisation is always exothermic

KEY EQUATIONS

$Q = mc\Delta T$
where
Q = heat energy, J
m = mass, g
c = specific heat capacity, $J\ g^{-1}K^{-1}$
ΔT = temperature change, K or °C
$\Delta H = \dfrac{-Q}{n}$
where
ΔH = enthalpy change, $J\ mol^{-1}$
Q = heat energy, J
n = number of moles, mol

Exercise 12.1   Heat and temperature

In this exercise, you will explore the difference between **heat** and temperature. Temperature was first introduced in Chapter 1.

1   What is temperature a measure of?

2   What is the SI unit of temperature?

3   What is the SI unit of heat energy?

4   What is the usual unit of heat energy used in chemistry?

5 Which has a higher amount of chemical energy:

   a a block of silver with a mass of 50 g at a temperature of 300 K or a block of copper with a mass of 50 g at a temperature of 300 K?

   b 150 g of water at a temperature of 350 K or a block of copper with a mass of 150 g at a temperature of 300 K?

   c a block of nickel with a mass of 100 g at a temperature of 300 K or a block of aluminium with a mass of 50 g at a temperature of 300 K?

Exercise 12.2 Exothermic and endothermic reactions

Some reactions, like combustion and respiration, are easily recognised as being **exothermic**. Some reactions are easily recognised as being **endothermic**, such as thermal decomposition and photosynthesis. In this exercise, these terms are explored and ideas about the exchange of heat energy (the **enthalpy change**) between the **system** and the surroundings, are introduced. In this exercise, you will also practise drawing and labelling **potential energy profile diagrams**, which are a useful way of representing energy changes during a chemical reaction.

1 During a chemical reaction, there is an interchange between the **internal energy** of the substances and heat energy. Identify which statement describes an endothermic reaction and which describes an exothermic reaction.

   a During the reaction, chemical energy is converted into heat energy.

   b During the reaction, heat energy is converted into chemical energy.

2 H is the symbol used for enthalpy. What symbol is used to represent enthalpy *change*?

3 Explain why the sign for the enthalpy change of an exothermic reaction is negative, even though the temperature increases.

4 Which of the following statements are **true** about exothermic reactions?

   a The products are more stable than the reactants.

   b Total energy is conserved.

   c The temperature of the surroundings will increase.

   d There will be a flow of energy from the system to the surroundings.

   e The sign of the enthalpy change will be positive.

5 Suggest whether the following reactions are exothermic or endothermic:

   a $C(s) + O_2(g) \rightarrow CO_2(g)$

   b $H_2O(l) \rightarrow H_2O(g)$

   c $HCl(aq) + NaOH(aq) \rightarrow NaCl(aq) + H_2O(l)$

6   Sort the following statements into those that are true for exothermic reactions and those that are true for endothermic reactions.

a   Temperature increases during the reaction.

b   Temperature decreases during the reaction.

c $\Delta H > 0$

d $\Delta H < 0$

e   The products are more stable than the reactants.

f   The reactants are more stable than the products.

g   Total energy is conserved.

7   Sketch the potential energy profile (energy level diagram) for an endothermic reaction. Include the following in your diagram:

a   labels on both axes

b   the energy of the reactants and the products

c   the overall enthalpy change for the reaction

d   the activation energy of the reaction.

8   Sketch the potential energy profile (energy level diagram) for an exothermic reaction. Include the following in your diagram:

a   labels on both axes

b   the energy of the reactants and the products

c   the overall enthalpy change for the reaction

d   the activation energy of the reaction.

Exercise 12.3 Enthalpy changes and standard conditions

Enthalpy changes have different values, depending on the conditions under which they are measured. Standard conditions are used to make these energy changes more easily compared. In this syllabus, you do not need to calculate the difference in enthalpy changes under different conditions; you only need to be aware that there are differences. In this exercise, you will look at what is meant by *standard conditions*.

1   What are *standard conditions*?

2   What symbol is used to denote that a value has been measured or calculated under standard conditions?

3 Given the standard enthalpy change for the reaction

$$2H_2(g) + O_2(g) \rightarrow 2H_2O(l) \qquad \Delta H^\ominus = -572 \text{ kJ mol}^{-1}$$

calculate the standard enthalpy changes for the following reactions:

a $2H_2O(l) \rightarrow 2H_2(g) + O_2(g)$

b $H_2(g) + \frac{1}{2}O_2(g) \rightarrow H_2O(l)$

c $H_2O(l) \rightarrow H_2(g) + \frac{1}{2}O_2(g)$

Exercise 12.4 Measuring enthalpy changes

In this exercise, you will practise calculating enthalpy changes from experimental **calorimetry** data. The exercise begins with practise using the expression $Q = mc\Delta T$. This expression is used to calculate enthalpy of combustion, and then it is applied to enthalpy changes in solution, such as neutralisation reactions. In all of the questions, you can assume that the density of any solution is 1.00 g cm^{-3} and the **specific heat capacity** of a solution is $4.18 \text{ J g}^{-1} \text{ K}^{-1}$.

1 A block of copper of mass 20.0 g was heated using an electric heating element. 384 J were required to raise the temperature of the block by 50.0 °C. Calculate the specific heat capacity of copper.

2 Calculate the temperature change for the reactions below.

specific heat capacity of water = $4.18 \text{ J g}^{-1} \text{ K}^{-1}$, of Ag = $0.240 \text{ J g}^{-1} \text{ K}^{-1}$, of Al = $0.900 \text{ J g}^{-1} \text{ K}^{-1}$

a 2000 J of heat energy is transferred to 100 g of water

b 2000 J of heat energy is transferred to 100 g of silver

c 7.5 kJ of heat energy is transferred to 100 g aluminium.

> **TIP**
>
> The formula $Q = mc\Delta T$ should be used here.

> **TIP**
>
> Pay attention to the units.

3   The apparatus in Figure **12.1** was used to determine the enthalpy change of combustion of a liquid fuel with the formula $C_5H_{11}OH$.

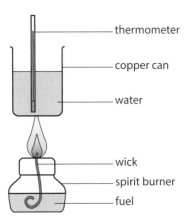

Figure 12.1: Apparatus to determine the enthalpy of combustion of a liquid fuel.

The following results were obtained:

mass of empty copper can = 212.3 g

mass of can and water before heating = 326.5 g

temperature of water before heating = 21.5 °C

mass of spirit burner before lighting = 104.0 g

mass of spirit burner at the end of experiment = 99.3 g

temperature of water after heating = 77.5 °C

specific heat capacity of the water = 4.18 J g⁻¹ K⁻¹

a   Calculate the enthalpy change of combustion of the fuel in kJ mol⁻¹.

b   Explain why copper is a good choice of material for the can.

c   Suggest two possible sources of experimental error in the experiment.

d   Suggest ways to reduce the experimental errors suggested in part **c**.

e   Other than experimental errors, suggest two reasons why the value for the enthalpy change of combustion of this fuel differs from the values quoted in data books.

4   20.0 cm³ of 1.00 mol dm⁻³ hydrochloric acid was added to 20.0 cm³ of 1.00 mol dm⁻³ sodium hydroxide solution. The temperature rose by 6.8 °C. Calculate the amount of energy released by this reaction.

5   50.0 cm³ of 1.00 mol dm⁻³ hydrochloric acid was added to 40.0 cm³ of 1.00 mol dm⁻³ sodium hydroxide solution. The temperature rose by 6.1°C. Calculate the **enthalpy change of neutralisation** for this reaction.

6   30.0 cm³ of 1.00 mol dm⁻³ hydrochloric acid was added to 20.0 cm³ of 1.00 mol dm⁻³ calcium hydroxide solution. The temperature rose by 8.2 °C. Calculate the enthalpy change of neutralisation.

TIP

In question 5, note that one substance is in excess, so you will need to calculate the number of moles of water formed.

TIP

Always include the equation for the reaction, as you need to check that the ratio of the number of moles of each substance matches their ratio in the equation to find out if one is in excess.

7 Calculate the temperature change when 2.00 g of sodium hydrogencarbonate is dissolved in 25.0 cm^3 of water if the standard enthalpy change of solution for sodium hydrogencarbonate is +18 kJ mol^{-1}.

8 50.0 cm^3 of 0.200 mol dm^{-3} silver nitrate solution was put in a calorimeter and 0.400 g of zinc powder added. The equation for the reaction is as follows:

$$2AgNO_3(aq) + Zn(s) \rightarrow Zn(NO_3)_2(aq) + Ag(s)$$

The temperature of the solution rose by 8.6 °C. Calculate the enthalpy change for the reaction per mole of zinc that reacts. Ignore the heat capacity of the metals.

9 In question 8, you are told to ignore the heat capacity of the metals. What are the exact contents of the calorimeter at the end of this experiment, and hence, why are the specific heat capacities of the metals ignored?

10 A significant source of error in calorimetry experiments is due to heat losses, particularly if the reaction occurs slowly.

   a Classify heat loss as a systematic or random error.

   b How can calorimetry experiments be modified to estimate a more accurate and quantifiable temperature change?

> TIP
>
> The mass of the solution formed in the reaction in question 7 could be debated; is it 25.0 g or 27.0 g?
>
> Most past IB papers have allowed either answer, although the answer that excludes the mass of the solid is usually the primary answer.

EXAM-STYLE QUESTIONS

1 Deduce the heat energy supplied if 50 g of water with a specific heat capacity of 4.2 J g^{-1} K^{-1} increases in temperature by 10 °C.

   A 210 J

   B 420 J

   C 2.1 kJ

   D 4200 J

2 What will be the temperature change if 100 g of copper with a specific heat capacity of 0.385 J g^{-1} K^{-1} is supplied with 770 J of heat energy?

   A 50 K

   B 20 K

   C 10 K

   D 5 K

3 Which statement is correct?

   A Temperature is a measure of the amount of heat energy something has.

   B Heat energy is a measure of the average kinetic energy of the particles.

   C Temperature is a measure of the average kinetic energy of the particles.

   D Heat and temperature have the same meaning.

CONTINUED

4   In an experiment, 0.50 g of ethanol was used to raise the temperature of 100 g of water by 35 °C. Which calculation shows how to find the correct enthalpy of combustion of ethanol?

specific heat capacity of water = 4.18 J g^{-1} K^{-1}

specific heat capacity of ethanol = 2.46 J g^{-1} K^{-1}

molar mass of ethanol = 46.08 g mol^{-1}

A $\Delta H = \dfrac{100.50 \times 4.18 \times 35 \times 0.50}{46.08}$

B $\Delta H = -\dfrac{46.08 \times 4.18 \times 35}{100}$

C $\Delta H = \dfrac{100 \times (4.18 + 2.46) \times 35}{46.08}$

D $\Delta H = -\dfrac{100 \times 4.18 \times 35 \times 46.08}{0.50}$

5   In an experiment, 50 cm^3 of a solution of HCl with a concentration of 1 mol dm^{-3} was reacted with 50 cm^3 of a solution of NaOH with a concentration of 1 mol dm^{-3}. The temperature of the solution increased by 12 °C. Calculate the temperature rise if 50 cm^3 of the same HCl solution was reacted with 50 cm^3 of a solution of NaOH with a concentration of 0.5 mol dm^{-3}.

A   6 °C

B   12 °C

C   24 °C

D   3 °C

6   Which of the following statements is **not** correct about endothermic reactions?

A   The surroundings lose energy.

B   The enthalpy change will be positive.

C   The enthalpy change will be negative.

D   The temperature of the surroundings decreases.

7   Which statement is correct about the energy profile diagram in Figure **12.2**?

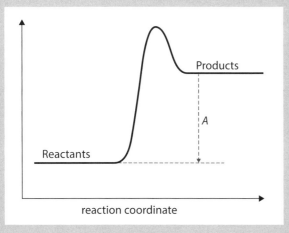

Figure 12.2: Energy profile diagram.

CONTINUED

A The reaction is exothermic.

B The products are more stable than the reactants.

C The *y*-axis shows the potential energy of the system.

D Arrow A is the enthalpy change for the reaction.

8 In an experiment to determine the enthalpy change of a reaction, 50.0 cm³ of a solution of copper(II) sulfate with a concentration of 0.100 mol dm⁻³ was placed in a polystyrene cup and the temperature recorded every 30 s. After 3 min, 2.00 g of magnesium powder was added to the cup, and the temperature was measured every 30 s for a further 7 min.

$$Mg(s) + CuSO_4(aq) \rightarrow MgSO_4(aq) + Cu(s)$$

The data shown in Figure **12.3** were obtained.

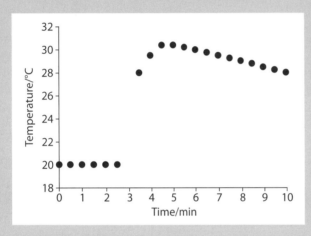

Figure 12.3: Temperature change for the reaction between $CuSO_4$ and Mg.

a Use the graph to find the temperature change for the reaction.   [1]

b Calculate the heat energy produced by the reaction.   [1]

Assume that the specific heat capacity of the mixture is the same as water: 4.18 J g⁻¹ K⁻¹

c Calculate the number of moles of magnesium and the number of moles of copper(II) sulfate present and state which reactant was the limiting reactant.   [2]

d Calculate the enthalpy change for the reaction.   [2]

e What is the advantage of obtaining the temperature change for the reaction graphically, rather than simply measuring the initial temperature and the maximum temperature?   [1]

f Estimate the temperature change for the reaction if the reaction were repeated using 100 cm³ of copper(II) sulfate of concentration 0.100 mol and 2.0 g of magnesium powder. Justify your answer.   [3]

Chapter 13

Energy cycles in reactions

CHAPTER OUTLINE

In this chapter you will:

- understand the term *average bond enthalpy*

- calculate enthalpy changes using bond enthalpies

- use Hess's law to calculate enthalpy changes.

> calculate enthalpy changes using standard enthalpy changes of combustion

> understand the term *standard enthalpy change of formation*

> calculate enthalpy changes using standard enthalpy changes of formation

> use a Born–Haber cycle to calculate enthalpy changes for ionic compounds.

KEY TERMS

Make sure you understand the following key terms before you do the exercises.

bond enthalpy: the enthalpy change when one mole of covalent bonds, in a gaseous molecule, is broken under standard conditions. Bond breaking requires energy (endothermic), ΔH is positive; bond making releases energy (exothermic), ΔH is negative

Hess's law: the enthalpy change accompanying a chemical reaction is independent of the pathway between the initial and final states

average bond enthalpy: the average amount of energy required to break one mole of covalent bonds, in a gaseous molecule under standard conditions; 'average' refers to the fact that the bond enthalpy is different in different molecules and, therefore, the value quoted is the average amount of energy to break a particular bond in a range of molecules

standard enthalpy change of combustion ($\Delta H^{\ominus}_c$): the enthalpy change (heat given out) when one mole of a substance is completely burnt in oxygen under standard conditions

standard enthalpy change of formation ($\Delta H^{\ominus}_f$): the enthalpy change when one mole of a substance is formed from its elements in their standard states under standard conditions. $\Delta H^{\ominus}_f$ for any element in its standard state is zero

CONTINUED

Born–Haber cycle: an enthalpy level diagram breaking down the formation of an ionic compound into a series of simpler steps

standard enthalpy change of atomisation ($\Delta H^\ominus_{at}$): the enthalpy change when one mole of gaseous atoms is formed from an element in its standard state under standard conditions

first electron affinity: enthalpy change when one electron is added to each atom in one mole of gaseous atoms under standard conditions:

$X(g) + e^- \rightarrow X^-(g)$

The first electron affinity is exothermic for virtually all elements

second electron affinity: the enthalpy change for the following process:

$X^-(g) + e^- \rightarrow X^{2-}(g)$

KEY EQUATIONS

$\Delta H^\ominus = \Sigma$(bond enthalpy of bonds broken) $- \Sigma$(bond enthalpy of bonds made)
$\Delta H^\ominus = \Sigma \Delta H^\ominus_c$(reactants) $- \Sigma \Delta H^\ominus_c$(products)
$\Delta H^\ominus = \Sigma \Delta H^\ominus_f$(products) $- \Sigma \Delta H^\ominus_f$(reactants)

Exercise 13.1 Bond enthalpies

A covalent bond is the electrostatic force of attraction between a shared pair of electrons and the nuclei of the atoms in the bond. The strength of that force of attraction can be described by the **bond enthalpy** (although, strictly, bond enthalpy is the energy required to break the bond in a gaseous diatomic molecule). As most molecules are not diatomic, **average bond enthalpy** is far more useful. In this exercise, you will start by exploring the difference between bond enthalpy and average bond enthalpy.

1   Which of the following data represents bond enthalpy and which average bond enthalpy?

    a   C—H, 414 kJ mol^{-1}

    b   C—Cl, 324 kJ mol^{-1}

    c   H—H, 436 kJ mol^{-1}

    d   O=O, 498 kJ mol^{-1}

    e   O—O, 144 kJ mol^{-1}

2   If bond enthalpy and average bond enthalpy both represent the energy required to break a covalent bond, what is the difference between them?

3   Bond enthalpy/average bond enthalpy calculations can only be used for substances in which state?

Exercise 13.2 Hess's law

In this exercise, you will practise using bond enthalpy values to calculate the enthalpy change of a reaction. This is an application of **Hess's law**. Calculations using Hess's law can be approached using two different methods: either by manipulating the equations or by using an energy cycle. Some of the questions in this exercise ask you to use a particular method so that you can practise both approaches. In an exam, you can generally choose the method you prefer.

1   Look at Table **13.1**.

Bond	Bond enthalpies at 298 K / kJ mol^{-1}	Bond	Bond enthalpies at 298 K / kJ mol^{-1}
C—C	346	O—H	463
C—H	414	O=O	498
C=O	804	N—N	158
C=C	614	N≡N	945
C—O	358	N—H	391
C—Cl	324	H—H	436
Cl—Cl	242		

Table 13.1: Bond enthalpies.

a   Using the average bond enthalpy values from Table **13.1**, calculate the enthalpy change for the reaction shown in Figure **13.1**.

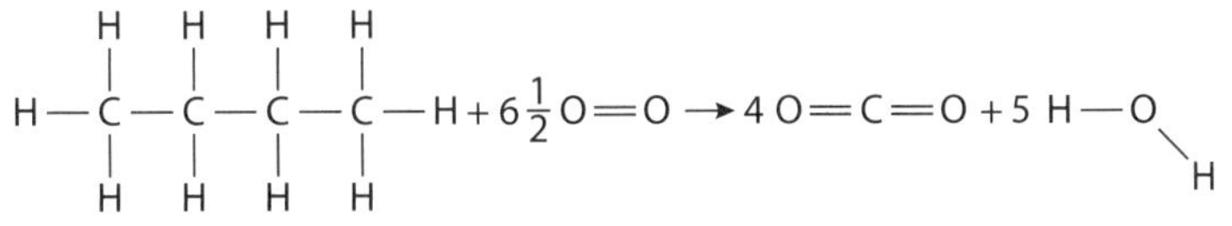

Figure 13.1: Combustion of butane.

b   The data book value for the **standard enthalpy change of combustion** of butane is –2878 kJ mol^{-1}. Suggest a reason why this value is different from that calculated in part **a**.

2   Using data from Table **13.1**, calculate the enthalpy change for the following reactions:

a $C_2H_5OH(g) \rightarrow C_2H_4(g) + H_2O(g)$

b $N_2H_4(g) + O_2(g) \rightarrow N_2(g) + 2H_2O(g)$

c $C_3H_6(g) + Cl_2(g) \rightarrow C_3H_6Cl_2(g)$

3   Using data from Table **13.1**, and given the enthalpy change for the following reaction:

$CO(g) + 2H_2(g) \rightarrow CH_3OH(g)$ $\Delta H = -114$ kJ mol^{-1}

calculate the bond enthalpy of the carbon–oxygen triple bond in carbon monoxide.

TIP

Always draw out the molecules showing all of the bonds, as has been done for you in this question. A common mistake is to miscount the bonds.

TIP

Question 1b is not about a practical experiment, so the difference is not due to experimental errors. Think about the definitions of *average bond energy* and of the term *standard*.

4   Using the energy cycle in Figure **13.2**, calculate the enthalpy change for the following reaction:

$2NO(g) + O_2(g) \rightarrow 2NO_2(g)$

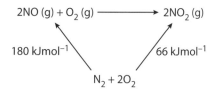

Figure 13.2: Energy cycle for $2NO(g) + O_2(g) \rightarrow 2NO_2(g)$

5   Given that

$P_4(s) + 6Cl_2(g) \rightarrow 4PCl_3(g)$ $\Delta H_1 = -2438$ kJ mol^{-1}

$4PCl_5(g) \rightarrow P_4(s) + 10Cl_2(g)$ $\Delta H_2 = 3438$ kJ mol^{-1}

manipulate the equations to calculate the enthalpy change for the following reaction:

$PCl_5(g) \rightarrow PCl_3(g) + Cl_2(g)$

6   Given that

$C_2H_6(g) + Cl_2(g) \rightarrow C_2H_5Cl(g) + HCl(g)$ $\Delta H_1 = -99$ kJ mol^{-1}

$H_2(g) + Cl_2(g) \rightarrow 2HCl(g)$ $\Delta H_2 = -185$ kJ mol^{-1}

$C_2H_4(g) + H_2(g) \rightarrow C_2H_6(g)$ $\Delta H_3 = -136$ kJ mol^{-1}

calculate the enthalpy change for the following reaction:

$C_2H_4 + HCl \rightarrow C_2H_5Cl$

7   a   Complete the diagram in Figure **13.3** by adding the data below into the correct spaces.

$C_6H_6(l) + 7\frac{1}{2}O_2(g) \rightarrow 6CO_2(g) + 3H_2O(l)$ $\Delta H = -3268$ kJ mol^{-1}

$C_6H_{12}(l) + 9O_2(g) \rightarrow 6CO_2(g) + 6H_2O(l)$ $\Delta H = -3920$ kJ mol^{-1}

$H_2(g) + \frac{1}{2}O_2(g) \rightarrow H_2O(l)$ $\Delta H = -286$ kJ mol^{-1}

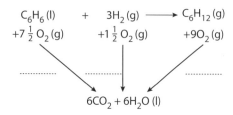

Figure 13.3: Energy cycle for the hydrogenation of benzene.

b   Calculate the enthalpy change for the reaction.

8 Given the following data:

$$Mg(s) + 2Ag^+(aq) \rightarrow Mg^{2+}(aq) + 2Ag(s) \qquad \Delta H = -145 \text{ kJ mol}^{-1}$$

$$Zn(s) + 2Ag^+(aq) \rightarrow Zn^{2+}(aq) + 2Ag(s) \qquad \Delta H = -85 \text{ kJ mol}^{-1}$$

construct an energy cycle and calculate the enthalpy change for the following reaction:

$$Mg(s) + Zn^{2+}(aq) \rightarrow Mg^{2+}(aq) + Zn(s)$$

9 Given the following data:

$$N_2H_4(l) + CH_3OH(l) \rightarrow HCHO(g) + N_2(g) + 3H_2(g) \qquad \Delta H_1 = -37 \text{ kJ mol}^{-1}$$

$$N_2(g) + 3H_2(g) \rightarrow 2NH_3(g) \qquad \Delta H_2 = -46 \text{ kJ mol}^{-1}$$

$$CH_3OH(l) \rightarrow HCHO(g) + H_2(g) \qquad \Delta H_3 = -65 \text{ kJ mol}^{-1}$$

calculate the value of the enthalpy change for the following reaction:

$$N_2H_4(l) + H_2(g) \rightarrow 2NH_3(g)$$

> **TIP**
>
> You can use your preferred method for this question. It is worth trying both for practice. They should both give the same answer!

Exercise 13.3 Standard enthalpy change of combustion data

In this exercise, you will use the standard enthalpy change of combustion to calculate other enthalpy changes. The advantage of using defined enthalpy changes, such as the enthalpy change of combustion, is that they provide universally understood data. Another advantage is that we can use a mathematical equation to calculate an enthalpy change. This exercise starts by examining the meaning of enthalpy change of combustion and derivation of the mathematical equation.

1 Give the balanced chemical equation for the standard enthalpy of combustion of the following substances:

  a $CH_4(g)$

  b $C_5H_{10}(g)$

  c $C_3H_7OH(l)$

2 Given the data in Table **13.2**,

  a draw an energy cycle and calculate the enthalpy change for the following reaction:

  $$2C(s) + O_2(g) \rightarrow 2CO(g)$$

> **TIP**
>
> Data given are combustion data. Combustion is the reaction of a substance with oxygen. In these reactions, the products will be carbon dioxide, so this is the substance that should be written in the third corner/bottom line of the energy cycle.

Substance	$\Delta H^\ominus_c$/kJ mol^{-1}
C(s)	−394
CO(g)	−283

Table 13.2: Standard enthalpy changes of combustion.

b Use the energy cycle you drew in part **a** to derive a mathematical equation for calculating the enthalpy change of a reaction from standard enthalpy change of combustion data.

3 Given the data in Table **13.3**, calculate the enthalpy change for the hydrogenation of cyclohexene:

$$C_6H_{10}(l) + H_2(g) \rightarrow C_6H_{12}(l)$$

Substance	$\Delta H^{\ominus}_c$/kJ mol^{-1}
$C_6H_{10}(l)$	−3800
$H_2(g)$	−286
$C_6H_{12}(l)$	−3920

Table 13.3: Standard enthalpy changes of combustion.

4 Given the following data:

$$C_2H_5OH(l) + 3O_2(g) \rightarrow 2CO_2(g) + 3H_2O(l) \qquad \Delta H^{\ominus}_1 = -1367 \text{ kJ mol}^{-1}$$

$$CH_3COOH(l) + 2O_2(g) \rightarrow 2CO_2(g) + 2H_2O(l) \qquad \Delta H^{\ominus}_2 = -874 \text{ kJ mol}^{-1}$$

$$CH_3COOC_2H_5(l) + 5O_2(g) \rightarrow 4CO_2(g) + 4H_2O(l) \qquad \Delta H^{\ominus}_3 = -2238 \text{ kJ mol}^{-1}$$

calculate the enthalpy change for the reaction by manipulating the equations:

$$C_2H_5OH(l) + CH_3COOH(l) \rightarrow CH_3COOC_2H_5(l) + H_2O(l)$$

Exercise 13.4 Standard enthalpy change of formation

In this exercise, you will begin by checking that you understand the **standard enthalpy change of formation** of a substance and how to write equations for this. You will then see how the following mathematical equation is derived:

$$\Delta H^{\ominus} = \Sigma\Delta H^{\ominus}_f(\text{products}) - \Sigma\Delta H^{\ominus}_f(\text{reactants})$$

Finally, you will practise questions for the different methods.

1 Give the balanced chemical equation for the standard enthalpy change of formation of the following substances:

a $C_3H_7OH(l)$

b $MgCO_3(s)$

c $HI(g)$

d $H_2O(l)$

2   Given the data in Table **13.4**:

a   Draw a Hess cycle and calculate the enthalpy change for the following reaction:

$CH_3CH{=}CH_2(g) + HCl(g) \rightarrow CH_3CHClCH_3(g)$

Substance	$\Delta H^\ominus_f$/kJ mol⁻¹
$CH_3CH{=}CH_2(g)$	+20
$HCl(g)$	−92
$CH_3CHClCH_3(g)$	−145

Table 13.4: Standard enthalpy changes of formation.

b   Use the Hess cycle you drew in part **a** to derive a mathematical equation for calculating the enthalpy change of a reaction from standard enthalpy change of formation data.

3   Using the mathematical equation derived in question 2b and data from Table **13.5**, calculate the enthalpy change for the combustion of benzene, $C_6H_6(l)$.

Substance	$\Delta H^\ominus_f$/kJ mol⁻¹
$C_6H_6(l)$	+49
$CO_2(g)$	−394
$H_2O(l)$	−286

Table 13.5: Enthalpy data

4   By manipulating the equations for the enthalpy changes of formation given, calculate the enthalpy change for the following reaction:

$C_2H_5OH(l) + CH_3COOH(l) \rightarrow CH_3COOC_2H_5(l) + H_2O(l)$

Given that

$2C(s) + 3H_2(g) + \frac{1}{2}O_2(g) \rightarrow C_2H_5OH(l)$ $\Delta H^\ominus_1 = -278$ kJ mol⁻¹

$2C(s) + 2H_2(g) + O_2(g) \rightarrow CH_3COOH(l)$ $\Delta H^\ominus_2 = -484$ kJ mol⁻¹

$4C(s) + 4H_2(g) + O_2(g) \rightarrow CH_3COOC_2H_5(l)$ $\Delta H^\ominus_3 = -479$ kJ mol⁻¹

$H_2(g) + \frac{1}{2}O_2(g) \rightarrow H_2O(l)$ $\Delta H^\ominus_4 = -286$ kJ mol⁻¹

TIP

Data given are formation data. Formation is the reaction in which a substance is formed from its elements. In these reactions, the reactants will be the elements in their standard states, so these are the substances that should be written in the third corner/ bottom line of the Hess cycle.

TIP

The mathematical equation used in question 3 is specifically mentioned in the IB subject guide, so you are expected to know this.

TIP

The reaction in question 4 is the same as in Exercise 13.3 question 4. It has been chosen deliberately, as it shows that the enthalpy change of a reaction is the same regardless of the route taken.

5 Using a method of your choice, calculate the enthalpy of formation of $SOCl_2(g)$ using the following data:

$$C_2H_5OH(l) + SOCl_2(g) \rightarrow C_2H_5Cl(g) + SO_2(g) + HCl(g) \qquad \Delta H^\ominus = -2 \text{ kJ mol}^{-1}$$

$$2C(s) + 3H_2(g) + \frac{1}{2}O_2(g) \rightarrow C_2H_5OH(l) \qquad \Delta H^\ominus_1 = -278 \text{ kJ mol}^{-1}$$

$$2C(s) + 2\frac{1}{2}H_2(g) + \frac{1}{2}Cl_2(g) \rightarrow C_2H_5Cl(l) \qquad \Delta H^\ominus_2 = -137 \text{ kJ mol}^{-1}$$

$$\frac{1}{2}H_2(g) + \frac{1}{2}Cl_2(g) \rightarrow HCl(g) \qquad \Delta H^\ominus_3 = -92 \text{ kJ mol}^{-1}$$

$$S(s) + O_2(g) \rightarrow SO_2(g) \qquad \Delta H^\ominus_4 = -297 \text{ kJ mol}^{-1}$$

Exercise 13.5 Energy cycles for ionic compounds

Born–Haber cycles are energy level diagrams used to show the energy changes in the formation of an ionic compound. They are an application of Hess's law. You will only encounter these for simple compounds made of just two elements (binary compounds). Born–Haber cycles include a number of different energy changes, so, in the exercises, you will start by checking that you can write the equations for these energy changes.

1 Write the chemical equation that represents the following standard enthalpy changes:

    a first ionisation energy of calcium

    b second ionisation energy of manganese

    c standard enthalpy change of formation of lithium fluoride

    d **first electron affinity** of oxygen

    e **second electron affinity** of sulfur

    f lattice enthalpy of calcium chloride

    g **standard enthalpy change of atomisation** of bromine

    h standard enthalpy change of atomisation of sodium

    i enthalpy of sublimation of magnesium

    j bond enthalpy of chlorine.

2 For each of the following enthalpy changes, suggest whether it is always exothermic, always endothermic, or if it could be either:

    a first ionisation energy

    b second ionisation energy

    c first electron affinity

    d second electron affinity

    e enthalpy of formation

TIP
Although it can seem like there is a long list of enthalpy change definitions to learn, it is important to do so. Remember that there is a pattern to these definitions in that they all refer to one mole of a substance and their names describe what each reaction is.

f   lattice enthalpy

g   bond energy

h   enthalpy of sublimation

i   enthalpy of atomisation.

3   Figure **13.4** shows the Born–Haber cycle for calcium oxide.

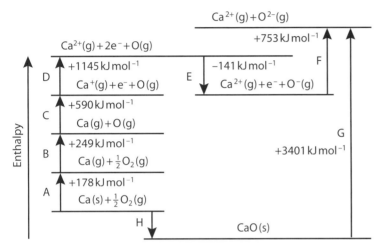

Figure 13.4: Born–Haber cycle for calcium oxide.

a   Identify the enthalpy changes A–H.

b   Using data given in Figure **13.4**, calculate the enthalpy of formation of calcium oxide.

c   The lattice enthalpy of MgO is 3791 kJ mol⁻¹. What does this suggest about the strength of the electrostatic force of attraction between the ions in MgO compared to those in CaO? Suggest a reason for this.

EXAM-STYLE QUESTIONS

1   Which statement is correct?

A   Bond forming is exothermic and $\Delta H < 0$.

B   Bond breaking is exothermic and $\Delta H < 0$.

C   Bond forming is endothermic and $\Delta H < 0$.

D   Bond breaking is endothermic and $\Delta H < 0$.

2   Which equation represents the average bond enthalpy of a C—H bond?

A $CH_4(g) \rightarrow C(s) + 2H_2(g)$

B $CH_4(g) \rightarrow C(g) + 4H(g)$

C $\frac{1}{4}CH_4(g) \rightarrow \frac{1}{4}C(g) + H(g)$

D $\frac{1}{4}CH_4(g) \rightarrow \frac{1}{4}C(s) + \frac{1}{2}H_2(g)$

CONTINUED

3 Which statement shows the correct order of increasing bond strength?

A H—H < H—O < O=O < O—O

B C—Cl < C—C < C=C < C≡C

C Cl—Cl < Br—Br < I—I

D C≡C < C=C < C—C

4 Which equation would give the correct value for the energy change, ΔH_r?

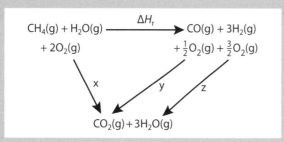

A $\Delta H_r = x + y + z$

B $\Delta H_r = y - x$

C $\Delta H_r = x - y - 3z$

D $\Delta H_r = x - y - z$

5 Given the following bond enthalpies:

H—H, 436 kJ mol^{-1}

C≡C, 839 kJ mol^{-1}

C=C, 614 kJ mol^{-1}

C—H, 414 kJ mol^{-1}

calculate the enthalpy change for the following reaction:

$C_2H_2(g) + H_2(g) \rightarrow C_2H_4(g)$

A −603 kJ mol^{-1}

B −212 kJ mol^{-1}

C −392 kJ mol^{-1}

D −167 kJ mol^{-1}

6 Given the following enthalpy changes:

$CaO(s) + 2HCl(aq) \rightarrow CaCl_2(aq) + H_2O(l)$　　　　　　$\Delta H = -220$ kJ mol^{-1}

$CaCO_3(s) + 2HCl(aq) \rightarrow CaCl_2(aq) + H_2O(l) + CO_2(g)$　　$\Delta H = -180$ kJ mol^{-1}

calculate the enthalpy change for the following reaction:

$CaCO_3(s) \rightarrow CaO(s) + CO_2(g)$

A +40 kJ mol^{-1}

B +400 kJ mol^{-1}

C −400 kJ mol^{-1}

D −40 kJ mol^{-1}

CONTINUED

7   Which equation represents the standard enthalpy change of formation of ammonia, NH_3?

   A $N(g) + 3H(g) \rightarrow NH_3(g)$

   B $N_2(s) + 3H_2(g) \rightarrow 2NH_3(g)$

   C $\frac{1}{2}N_2(g) + \frac{3}{2}H_2(g) \rightarrow NH_3(g)$

   D $NH_3(g) \rightarrow 3N\!-\!H(g)$

8   Given the following data:

   $\Delta H_c(CH_4) = -891 \text{ kJ mol}^{-1}$

   $\Delta H_c(C) = -394 \text{ kJ mol}^{-1}$

   $\Delta H_c(H_2) = -286 \text{ kJ mol}^{-1}$

   which mathematical expression could be used to calculate the enthalpy of formation of $CH_4(g)$?

   A $\Delta H^{\ominus} = \Sigma \Delta H^{\ominus}{}_c(\text{reactants}) - \Sigma \Delta H^{\ominus}{}_c(\text{products})$

   B $\Delta H^{\ominus} = \Sigma \Delta H^{\ominus}{}_c(\text{products}) - \Sigma \Delta H^{\ominus}{}_c(\text{reactants})$

   C $\Delta H^{\ominus} = \Sigma \Delta H^{\ominus}{}_f(\text{products}) - \Sigma \Delta H^{\ominus}{}_f(\text{reactants})$

   D $\Delta H^{\ominus} = \Sigma \Delta H^{\ominus}{}_f(\text{reactants}) - \Sigma \Delta H^{\ominus}{}_f(\text{products})$

9   Which equation represents the second electron affinity of sulfur?

   A $S(s) \rightarrow S^-(g) + e^-$

   B $S(g) \rightarrow S^-(g) + e^-$

   C $S^-(g) + e^- \rightarrow S^{2-}(g)$

   D $S(g) + e^- \rightarrow S^{2-}(g)$

10   Figure **13.5** shows the Born–Haber cycle for the formation of lithium bromide.

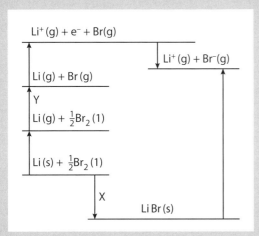

Figure 13.5: Born–Haber cycle for lithium bromide.

Which is the correct description for the steps X and Y?

	X	Y
A	Lattice enthalpy of LiBr	Enthalpy of atomisation of Br_2
B	Standard enthalpy of formation of LiBr	$\frac{1}{2}$ bond dissociation energy of Br_2
C	Lattice enthalpy of LiBr	Enthalpy of atomisation of Br_2 + $\frac{1}{2}$ bond dissociation energy of Br_2
D	Standard enthalpy of formation of LiBr	Enthalpy of atomisation of Br_2

11 The equation for the complete combustion of C_3H_6 can be written as shown in Figure **13.6**.

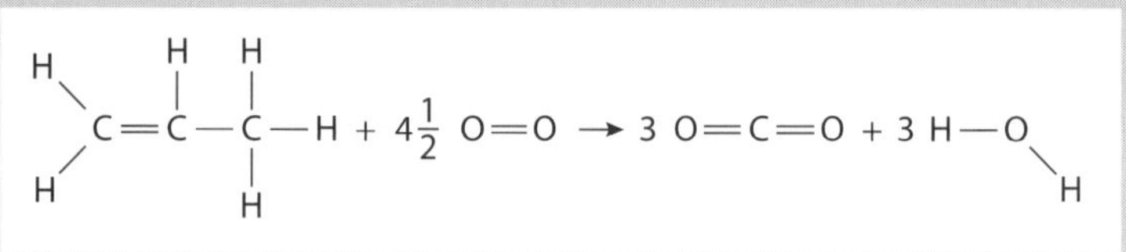

Figure 13.6: Combustion of C_3H_6.

a Given the following average bond enthalpy data, calculate the enthalpy change for this reaction. [3]

C—C 346 kJ mol^{-1}

C—H 414 kJ mol^{-1}

O=O 498 kJ mol^{-1}

O—H 463 kJ mol^{-1}

C=C 614 kJ mol^{-1}

C=O 804 kJ mol^{-1}

b Explain why the value given for the O=O bond can be described as its bond enthalpy, whereas data for the other bonds are described as average bond enthalpies. [1]

12 a State Hess's law. [1]

b Given the following data:

$K_2CO_3(aq) + 2HCl(aq) \rightarrow 2KCl(aq) + H_2O(l) + CO_2(g)$ $\Delta H = -125$ kJ mol^{-1}

$PbCO_3(s) + 2HCl(aq) \rightarrow PbCl_2(s) + H_2O(l) + CO_2(g)$ $\Delta H = -175$ kJ mol^{-1}

calculate the enthalpy change for the following reaction:

$2KCl(aq) + PbCO_3(aq) \rightarrow PbCl_2(s) + K_2CO_3(aq)$ [1]

13 a Give the equation for the enthalpy change of combustion of C_6H_5COOH. [3]

b Using the following data, calculate the value for this enthalpy change: [2]

$\Delta H^{\ominus}_f(C_6H_5COOH(s)) = -385$ kJ mol^{-1}

$\Delta H^{\ominus}_f(CO_2(g)) = -394$ kJ mol^{-1}

$\Delta H^{\ominus}_f(H_2O(l)) = -286$ kJ mol^{-1}

CONTINUED

14 Figure **13.7** shows a Hess cycle for the chlorination of benzene.

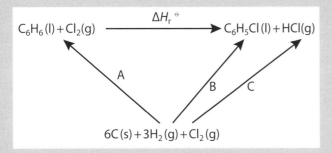

Figure 13.7: Hess cycle for chlorination of benzene.

a Label the Hess cycle to indicate the names of the enthalpy changes labelled A–C. [3]

b Given the following data, calculate the enthalpy change for this reaction: [2]
$\Delta H_f(C_6H_6(l)) = +49.0$ kJ mol^{-1}
$\Delta H_f(C_6H_5Cl(l)) = +11$ kJ mol^{-1}
$\Delta H_f(HCl(g)) = -92.3$ kJ mol^{-1}

15 a Construct a labelled Hess cycle to show how the enthalpy change for the following reaction can be calculated from the data provided. [3]

$3C(s) + 3H_2(g) \rightarrow C_3H_6(g)$
$\Delta H_c(C(s)) = -394$ kJ mol^{-1}
$\Delta H_c(H_2(g)) = -286$ kJ mol^{-1}
$\Delta H_c(C_3H_6(g)) = -2058$ kJ mol^{-1}

b Give the name of the enthalpy change calculated in part **a**. [1]

c Calculate the value for this enthalpy change. [2]

16 a Complete the Born–Haber cycle shown in Figure **13.8** for magnesium bromide by adding labels A–I. [4]

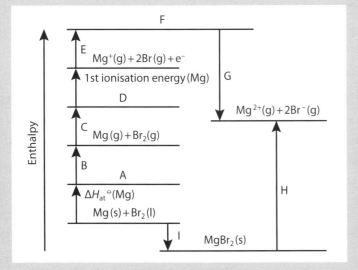

Figure 13.8: Born–Haber cycle for MgBr$_2$.

CONTINUED

b Given the following data, calculate the lattice enthalpy of $MgBr_2$: [3]

$\Delta H^{\ominus}_f(MgBr_2) = -524$ kJ mol^{-1}

enthalpy of atomisation of magnesium = 129 kJ mol^{-1}

first ionisation energy of magnesium = +738 kJ mol^{-1}

first electron affinity of bromine = –325 kJ mol^{-1}

enthalpy of vaporisation of Br_2 = 30 kJ mol^{-1}

second ionisation energy of magnesium = 1450 kJ mol^{-1}

bond enthalpy Br—Br = +193 kJ mol^{-1}

c Describe the effect of the charge and size of the ions on the magnitude of the lattice enthalpy of a compound. [2]

> Chapter 14

Energy from fuels

CHAPTER OUTLINE

In this chapter you will:

- understand that reactive metals, non-metals and organic compounds undergo combustion reactions

- discuss combustion reactions in terms of oxidation and reduction

- deduce equations for incomplete combustion of organic compounds

- discuss the advantages and disadvantages of fossil fuels

- calculate the carbon dioxide formed when fossil fuels burn

- understand what biofuels are

- explain the difference between renewable and non-renewable energy sources

- explain how fuel cells work

- deduce half-equations for the reactions occurring in fuel cells.

KEY TERMS

Make sure you understand the following key terms before you do the exercises.

combustion: burning, an exothermic reaction that occurs when a substance reacts with oxygen. Usually these reactions produce a flame and continue once the initial heat source is removed

oxidising agent (oxidant): oxidises other species and, in the process, is itself reduced; an oxidising agent takes electrons away from another species

reducing agent (reductant): reduces other species and, in the process, is itself oxidised; a reducing agent gives electrons to another species

complete combustion: the burning of a substance in a plentiful supply of oxygen

incomplete combustion: the burning of a substance in a limited supply of oxygen

fuel: something that is burnt to produce energy

renewable energy sources: sources of energy that are naturally replenished – they will not run out, e.g. solar energy or wind power

> ## CONTINUED
>
> **non-renewable energy sources:** sources of energy that are finite – they will eventually run out, e.g. coal
>
> **fuel cell:** a type of electrochemical cell that uses the reaction between a fuel (such as hydrogen or methanol) and an oxidising agent (e.g. oxygen) to produce electrical energy directly; it uses a continuous supply of reactants from an external source
>
> **climate change:** the change in the Earth's climate due to man-made factors, such as the increase in atmospheric carbon dioxide due to the increased burning of fossil fuels

Exercise 14.1 Combustion reactions

A **combustion** reaction is an exothermic reaction that occurs when a substance reacts with oxygen. Combustion can be described as complete or incomplete. **Complete combustion** occurs when there is a plentiful supply of oxygen, and **incomplete combustion** when the oxygen supply is more limited. The reaction of a substance with oxygen is called oxidation, but, in this exercise, you will look at some other ways of recognising an oxidation reaction and learn that oxidation reactions never happen without a corresponding reduction reaction too.

1   Give four definitions of oxidation.

2   Give four definitions of reduction.

3   Why should we not refer to a reaction as just an oxidation reaction or just a reduction reaction?

4   Identify which substance in the following equations has been oxidised and which substance has been reduced.

   a $4Na(s) + O_2(g) \rightarrow 2Na_2O(s)$

   b $2Li(s) + 2H_2O(l) \rightarrow 2LiOH(aq) + H_2(g)$

   c $Fe_2O_3(s) + 3CO(g) \rightarrow 2Fe(s) + 3CO_2(g)$

   d $C_2H_4(g) + H_2(g) \rightarrow C_2H_6(g)$

   e $2NaBr(aq) + Cl_2(aq) \rightarrow 2\ NaCl(aq) + Br_2(aq)$

   f $Cu(s) + 2Ag^+(aq) \rightarrow Cu^{2+}(aq) + 2Ag(s)$

5   Identify the **oxidising agent** in the following equations:

   a $Mg(s) + H_2SO_4(aq) \rightarrow MgSO_4(aq) + H_2(g)$

   b $2Fe^{3+}(aq) + Sn^{2+}(aq) \rightarrow 2Fe^{2+}(aq) + Sn^{4+}(aq)$

   c $4CuO(s) + CH_4(g) \rightarrow 4Cu(s) + 2H_2O(g) + CO_2(g)$

> **TIP**
>
> In question 4, note that both the substance oxidised and the substance reduced will be on the left/reactant side of the equation. Give the name of the substance rather than the name of a particular element.

> **TIP**
>
> An *agent* is something or someone that brings about a change. For example, a travel agent enables another person to travel, and an oxidising agent enables another substance to be oxidised.

6   Identify the **reducing agent** in the following reactions:

a $Zn(s) + 2HCl(aq) \rightarrow ZnCl_2(aq) + H_2(g)$

b $2Al(s) + Fe_2O_3(s) \rightarrow 2Fe(s) + Al_2O_3(s)$

c $Cu(s) + 4HNO_3(aq) \rightarrow Cu(NO_3)_2(aq) + 2NO_2(g) + 2H_2O(l)$

7   Write a balanced equation for the complete combustion of each of the following substances:

a C_4H_8

b $C_{10}H_{22}$

c C_3H_7OH

8   What products are formed during incomplete combustion of a hydrocarbon?

9   Write the balanced equation for the incomplete combustion of C_6H_{14} in which carbon monoxide is formed.

10   Write the balanced equation for the incomplete combustion of $C_5H_{11}OH$ in which carbon is formed.

11   Describe any differences in the appearance of a flame produced during incomplete combustion compared to complete combustion.

Exercise 14.2   Fuels

Fuels include substances such as coal, wood, straw, peat, charcoal and methane. The choice of fuel used in different parts of the world is most often dependent on availability. Many are renewable fuels but some are non-renewable fuels. In this exercise, you will consider the advantages and disadvantages of different fuels, but many of these will depend on your global viewpoint.

1   What is meant by the term *fossil fuel*?

2   Give three examples of fossil fuels.

3   Two disadvantages of all fossil fuels are that they all produce carbon dioxide during combustion and that they are non-renewable. Describe why these are disadvantages.

4   When comparing fossils fuels, a number of factors should be considered. Compare the following factors for coal, crude oil and natural gas:

a   ease of storage

b   ease of transport

c   how cleanly it burns

d   potential environmental issues

e   energy released per unit mass.

> **TIP**
>
> Be careful to distinguish between a fossil fuel and a fuel that is made from a fossil fuel. Gasoline (petrol) is not a fossil fuel, but it is made from one.

5   a   Write balanced equations for the complete combustion of the following substances:

   i   carbon

   ii   methane

   iii   octane

   iv   ethanol

   v   hydrogen.

   b   Calculate the mass of carbon dioxide that is produced when 1.00 g of each substance in part **a** is burnt.

   c   Given the data in **Table 14.1**, calculate the amount of carbon dioxide released per kJ of energy released per mol for each of the substances in part **a**.

Substance	Energy released / kJ mol⁻¹
i carbon	394
ii methane	891
iii octane	5470
iv ethanol	1367
v hydrogen	286

Table 14.1: Energy released by different fuels.

   d   Outline why coal can be regarded as the most environmentally damaging fossil fuel.

Exercise 14.3 Renewable and non-renewable energy sources and Exercise 14.4 Fuel cells

Energy sources can be categorised in many ways. One useful way is to distinguish between those energy sources for which there is a finite supply, known as **non-renewable energy sources**, and those that are naturally replenished, known as **renewable energy sources**. In this exercise, you will look at some of these renewable energy sources.

1   a   Biofuels are a source of renewable energy; describe what is meant by a *biofuel*.

   b   Name three other sources of renewable energy.

   c   List three advantages and three disadvantages of biofuels compared to using petrol in cars.

2 In an alkaline hydrogen–oxygen **fuel cell**, hydrogen and oxygen are continuously supplied to the cell and undergo redox reactions.

   a Give an equation for the reaction at the anode.

   b Give an equation for the reaction at the cathode.

   c Give the overall equation for the reaction.

3 Figure **14.1** represents a hydrogen–oxygen fuel cell with an acidic electrolyte.

> **TIP**
>
> - Oxidation always occurs at the anode.
> - As this is an alkaline fuel cell, H⁺ will not appear in any of these equations.
> - Hydrogen and oxygen both have an oxidation state of zero. Which will be oxidised and which reduced?

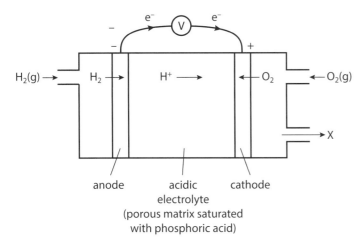

Figure 14.1: Hydrogen–oxygen fuel cell with an acidic electrolyte.

   a What is produced at the point marked X on the diagram?

   b Give an equation for the reaction occurring at the anode.

   c Give an equation for the reaction occurring at the cathode.

   d Give the overall equation for the cell.

> **TIP**
>
> As this is an acidic fuel cell, H⁺ will appear in the equations.

4 **a** Hydrogen for use in fuel cells can be produced by the reforming of natural gas according to the following two sequential equations:

$$CH_4(g) + H_2O(g) \rightarrow CO(g) + 3H_2(g)$$

$$CO(g) + H_2O(g) \rightarrow CO_2(g) + H_2(g)$$

     Calculate the mass of hydrogen that could be produced per tonne of methane.

> **TIP**
>
> 1 tonne = 1000 kg

   b Given that the enthalpy of combustion of hydrogen is −286 kJ mol⁻¹, calculate the amount of energy released per tonne of methane used in the reforming process.

5 Methanol can also be used in fuel cells.

   a Give an advantage of methanol as a fuel compared to hydrogen.

   b The overall equation for a methanol fuel cell is given below

$$CH_3OH(l) + \frac{3}{2} O_2(g) \rightarrow CO_2(g) + 2H_2O(l)$$

     Write the half equations for the reactions at the anode and cathode.

> **TIP**
>
> A methanol fuel cell works in a similar way to an acidic hydrogen–oxygen fuel cell.

EXAM-STYLE QUESTIONS

1 Which of the following is correct?

A Reduction can be defined as the loss of electrons or the loss of oxygen.

B Oxidation is defined as the gain of oxygen or the gain of electrons.

C Oxidising agents are reduced during a reaction.

D Reducing agents gain electrons during a reaction.

2 Which of the following reactions is **not** a combustion reaction?

A $C(s) + O_2(g) \rightarrow CO_2(g)$

B $2Mg(s) + O_2(g) \rightarrow 2MgO(s)$

C $2C(s) + O_2(g) \rightarrow 2CO(g)$

D $4Fe(s) + 3O_2(g) \rightarrow 2Fe_2O_3(s)$

3 In which of the following equations does the oxidation state of nitrogen decrease?

A $NH_3(g) + HCl(g) \rightarrow NH_4Cl(s)$

B $N_2H_4(g) + O_2(g) \rightarrow N_2(g) + 2H_2O(g)$

C $Cu(s) + 2HNO_3(aq) + 2H^+(aq) \rightarrow Cu^{2+} + 2NO_2(g) + 2H_2O(l)$

D $2NO_2(g) \rightarrow N_2O_4(g)$

4 Which of the following is **not** a renewable energy source?

A methanol

B ethane

C hydrogen

D ethanol

5 Which is the correct half-equation for the anode reaction in an alkaline hydrogen fuel cell?

A $H_2(g) + 2OH^-(aq) \rightarrow 2H_2O(l) + 2e^-$

B $O_2(g) + 2H_2O(l) + 2e^- \rightarrow 4OH^-(aq)$

C $H_2(g) \rightarrow 2H^+(aq) + 2e^-$

D $H_2(g) + \frac{1}{2}O_2(g) \rightarrow H_2O(l)$

6 The main fossil fuels are coal, oil and gas. They were formed from things that lived millions of years ago. Coal was mostly formed from trees and plants, whereas oil and gas were formed from aquatic organisms.

a Coal is mostly composed of carbon. What other elements are most likely to be present? [1]

b Rank coal, oil and gas in order of

   i cost of production [1]

   ii tendency to undergo incomplete combustion [1]

   iii likely world reserves/availability. [1]

c Apart from the factors in part **b**, state one other advantage of oil as a fuel compared to coal. [1]

d Apart from the factors in part **b**, state one advantage of gas as a fuel compared to oil. [1]

e Give a major disadvantage associated with all fossil fuels. [2]

CONTINUED

7 Figure **14.2** shows the variation in global temperatures and in carbon dioxide levels over the last 800 000 years.

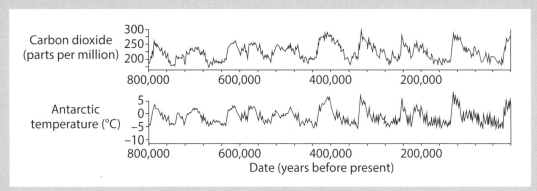

Figure **14.2:** Global temperatures and CO_2 levels.

a Outline how these data provide evidence in support of global warming. [1]

b Atmospheric carbon dioxide levels have increased rapidly in the last 100 years and are currently higher than they have ever thought to have been in over 500 000 years. Suggest why carbon dioxide levels have increased so rapidly in recent times. [1]

c State three consequences which have been observed as a result of climate change. [3]

> Chapter 15

Entropy and spontaneity

CHAPTER OUTLINE

In this chapter you will:

- understand the term *entropy*

- predict whether a chemical/physical reaction involves an increase or decrease in entropy

- calculate standard entropy changes

- understand the term *change in Gibbs energy*

- calculate the change in Gibbs energy

- relate the change in Gibbs energy to the spontaneity of a reaction

- explain the changes in Gibbs energy as a system reaches equilibrium

- calculate Gibbs energy changes for systems approaching equilibrium and at equilibrium.

KEY TERMS

Make sure you understand the following key terms before you do the exercises.

entropy (*S*): a measure of the disorder of a system (how the matter is dispersed/distributed) or how the available energy is distributed among the particles. Standard entropy ($S^\ominus$) is the entropy of a substance at 100 kPa and 298 K; units are J K^{-1} mol^{-1}. $\Delta S^\ominus$ is the entropy change under standard conditions – a positive value indicates an increase in entropy, i.e. the system becomes more disordered/the energy becomes more spread out (less concentrated)

Gibbs energy change (ΔG) or free energy change: ΔG is related to the entropy change of the universe and can be defined using the equation $\Delta G = \Delta H - T\Delta S$. For a reaction to be spontaneous, ΔG for the reaction must be negative. $\Delta G^\ominus$ is the standard energy change

KEY EQUATIONS

$\Delta G^\ominus = \Delta H^\ominus - T\Delta S^\ominus$

where

$\Delta G^\ominus$ is the standard Gibbs energy change, kJ mol^{-1}

$\Delta H^\ominus$ is the standard enthalpy change, kJ mol^{-1}

T is the temperature, K

$\Delta S^\ominus$ is the standard entropy change, kJ K^{-1} mol^{-1} (note the units here are kJ K^{-1} mol^{-1} rather than J K^{-1} mol^{-1})

$\Delta S^\ominus = \Sigma S^\ominus_{products} - \Sigma S^\ominus_{reactants}$

where

$\Delta S^\ominus$ is the standard entropy change of the reaction, J K^{-1} mol^{-1}

$\Sigma S^\ominus_{products}$ is the sum of the standard entropies of the products

$\Sigma S^\ominus_{reactants}$ is the sum of the standard entropies of the reactants

$\Delta G = \Delta G^\ominus + RT\ln Q$

where

ΔG is the Gibbs energy change for a reaction that is in progress; it allows us to calculate the value of ΔG for any mixture of reactants and products at a given temperature, J mol^{-1} (not kJ mol^{-1})

$\Delta G^\ominus$ is the standard Gibbs energy change, kJ mol^{-1}

R is the universal gas constant, 8.31 J K^{-1} mol^{-1}

T is the temperature, K

Q is the reaction quotient (see Chapter 18); this can be considered as a measure of the extent of the reaction, the higher the value, the higher the ratio of products to reactants

Exercise 15.1 Entropy

A spontaneous reaction is one that happens by itself – energy does not need to be supplied. This might lead you to think that all exothermic reactions are spontaneous or maybe that only exothermic reactions are spontaneous. Neither is true; endothermic reactions can happen spontaneously and some exothermic reactions do not. In this exercise, you will explore **entropy** and entropy change, which are used to explain why some reactions occur spontaneously and some do not.

1   Identify which of the substances in each pair has the higher entropy:

a $H_2O(l)$ or $H_2O(g)$

b   NaCl(s) at 25 °C or at 100 °C

c   nitrogen gas at a pressure of 200 kPa or at a pressure of 100 kPa

d   0.100 mol of NaCl(s) and 100 g of water separately or a solution made by dissolving 0.100 mol of NaCl in 100 g of water.

TIP

Entropy is most easily considered as a measure of the disorder of a system. For each pair, try to imagine in which substance the particles are arranged more randomly.

2 Predict the sign of the entropy change for the following reactions:

a $2NaNO_3(s) \rightarrow 2NaNO_2(s) + O_2(g)$

b $C_2H_4(g) + H_2O(g) \rightarrow C_2H_5OH(g)$

c $2CuSO_4(aq) + 4KI(aq) \rightarrow 2CuI(s) + 2K_2SO_4(aq) + I_2(aq)$

3 Using data from Table **15.1**, calculate the entropy change for the following reactions at 298 K:

a $C(diamond) \rightarrow C(graphite)$

b $CH_4(g) + 2O_2(g) \rightarrow CO_2(g) + 2H_2O(l)$

c $2Al(s) + Fe_2O_3(s) \rightarrow Al_2O_3(s) + 2Fe(s)$

Substance	Entropy / J K^{-1} mol^{-1}
C(graphite)	5.7
C(diamond)	2.4
$CH_4(g)$	186
$O_2(g)$	205
$CO_2(g)$	214
$H_2O(l)$	70
$Al_2O_3(s)$	51
Fe(s)	27
Al(s)	28
$Fe_2O_3(s)$	87

Table 15.1: Entropy data.

> **TIP**
>
> ΔS is positive if the entropy increases (becomes more disordered), and ΔS is negative if there is a decrease in entropy (the system becomes less disordered).

> **TIP**
>
> Remember to use the coefficients from the balanced equations in your calculation.

Exercise 15.2 Spontaneous reactions

In the previous exercise, you met the idea of entropy and entropy change but not its connection to spontaneity. In this exercise, you will meet the **Gibbs energy change (ΔG)** (or free energy change), which is calculated using the enthalpy change, entropy change and temperature of a reaction. It is this change in Gibbs energy that is used to determine if a reaction is spontaneous.

1 Give the mathematical expression used to calculate $\Delta G^\ominus$ from the enthalpy and entropy change of a reaction.

2 What information does $\Delta G^\ominus$ give about the rate of a reaction?

3 For what values of $\Delta G^\ominus$ is a reaction spontaneous?

4 Using the data provided, calculate the value of the free energy change for the following reactions at 298 K and state whether or not the reactions are spontaneous at this temperature.

a $2H_2O_2(l) \rightarrow 2H_2O(l) + O_2(g)$

$\Delta H^\ominus = -196$ kJ mol^{-1} and $\Delta S^\ominus = +125$ J K^{-1} mol^{-1}

b $C_2H_5OH(l) + 3O_2(g) \rightarrow 2CO_2(g) + 3H_2O(l)$

$\Delta H^\ominus_c = -1367$ kJ mol^{-1}

$S^\ominus(C_2H_5OH(l)) = 161$ J K^{-1} mol^{-1}

$S^\ominus(CO_2(g)) = 214$ J K^{-1} mol^{-1}

$S^\ominus(H_2O(l)) = 70$ J K^{-1} mol^{-1}

$S^\ominus(O_2(g)) = 206$ J K^{-1} mol^{-1}

c $2NaHCO_3(s) \rightarrow Na_2CO_3(s) + H_2O(g) + CO_2(g)$

Substance	$\Delta H^\ominus_f$ / kJ mol^{-1}	$S^\ominus$ / J mol^{-1}
$NaHCO_3(s)$	−951	102
$Na_2CO_3(s)$	−1131	135
$H_2O(g)$	−242	189
$CO_2(g)$	−394	214

TIP

The two most common errors in these calculations are using the incorrect units for temperature (it must be in kelvin) and using the incorrect value for $\Delta H^\ominus$ and $\Delta S^\ominus$ (these must both be J or both be kJ).

5 Complete Table **15.2** to indicate the relationship between $\Delta H^\ominus$, $\Delta S^\ominus$, $\Delta G^\ominus$ and temperature.

$\Delta H^\ominus$	$\Delta S^\ominus$	$\Delta G^\ominus$		Spontaneous?
positive				only at high temperatures
	negative	positive at all temperatures		
	positive	negative at all temperatures		always spontaneous
	negative	negative at low temperatures		

Table **15.2**: Relationship between $\Delta H^\ominus$, $\Delta S^\ominus$, $\Delta G^\ominus$ and temperature.

TIP

Rather than trying to memorise the information needed to complete Table **15.2**, it is much easier to think about the following expression:

$\Delta G^\ominus = \Delta H^\ominus - T\Delta S^\ominus$

Consider what values of $\Delta H^\ominus$ and $\Delta S^\ominus$ are most favourable for a spontaneous reaction; very exothermic reactions ($\Delta H^\ominus < 0$) where there is an increase in the entropy ($\Delta S^\ominus > 0$). Even if the reaction is endothermic ($\Delta H^\ominus > 0$), as long as the entropy change is favourable, that is, it is positive, and the temperature is high enough, then $\Delta G^\ominus < 0$.

6 Using data provided, calculate the temperature range for the reaction to be spontaneous.

a $Al_2O_3(s) + 3C(s) \rightarrow 4Al(s) + 3CO_2(g)$

$\Delta H^\ominus = 488.5$ kJ mol^{-1} $\Delta S^\ominus = 687$ J K^{-1} mol^{-1}

b $HCl(g) + NH_3(g) \rightarrow NH_4Cl(s)$

$\Delta H^\ominus = -176.5$ kJ mol^{-1} $\Delta S^\ominus = -285.4$ J K^{-1} mol^{-1}

c $4CuO(s) + CH_4(g) \rightarrow 4Cu(s) + 2H_2O(g) + CO_2(g)$

$\Delta H^\ominus = -184$ kJ mol^{-1} $\Delta S^\ominus = 365.2$ J K^{-1} mol^{-1}

Exercise 15.3 Gibbs energy and equilibrium

The value of $\Delta G^\ominus$ calculated using the expression $\Delta G^\ominus = \Delta H^\ominus - T\Delta S^\ominus$ is the value for the molar amounts of reactants in a given equation reacting to become the molar amounts of product: a reaction that goes to completion. The value of $\Delta G^\ominus$ for the reverse reaction is the same but has the opposite sign. The point at which $\Delta G^\ominus = 0$ is the point at which neither the forward nor backward reactions are spontaneous: the point of equilibrium. This exercise uses the expression $\Delta G = \Delta G^\ominus + RT\ln Q$, where Q is the reaction quotient. This gives a value for the relative amounts of products and reactants in a reaction mixture.

1 For the reaction $X \rightleftharpoons Y$, a mixture of X and Y was found to contain a much higher proportion of products than reactants. Will the value of Q be greater or less than one?

2 The reaction quotient for the following reaction:

$N_2O_4(g) \rightleftharpoons 2NO_2(g)$ $\Delta G^\ominus = -15$ kJ mol^{-1}

can be found using the following expression:

$Q = \dfrac{[NO_2]^2}{[N_2O_4]}$

a Calculate ΔG when $[N_2O_4] = 2.5$ mol dm^{-3} and $[NO_2] = 1.0$ mol dm^{-3} at $T = 450$ K.

b Suggest in which direction the equilibrium will spontaneously shift.

3 The reaction quotient for the following reaction:

$2NH_3(g) \rightleftharpoons N_2(g) + 3H_2(g)$ $\Delta G^\ominus = +33.2$ kJ mol^{-1}

can be found using the following expression:

$Q = \dfrac{[N_2][H_2]^3}{[NH_3]^2}$

a Calculate ΔG when $[NH_3] = 2.0$ mol dm^{-3}, $[H_2] = 1.5$ mol dm^{-3} and $[N_2] = 2.0$ mol dm^{-3} at $T = 350$ K.

b Suggest in which direction the equilibrium will spontaneously shift.

TIP

A quick way of checking if the temperature should be above or below the temperature calculated is to calculate the value of $\Delta G^\ominus$ using a value of temperature a few kelvin higher than the value given in the question. If $\Delta G^\ominus < 0$ at this higher temperature, then you know that the temperature calculated is the minimum required for a spontaneous reaction to occur.

Temperature *range* does not have to be a temperature *between* x *and* y, it can also mean temperature *above* x or *below* y.

TIP

The unit for R is J K^{-1} mol^{-1}, but ΔG is commonly given in kJ mol^{-1}. A common error is not changing this to J mol^{-1}.

4 At equilibrium, $\Delta G = 0$.

TIP

Watch the units of T and of $\Delta G^{\ominus}$.

 a Calculate the value of $\Delta G^{\ominus}$ if the value of the reaction quotient at 298 K for the following reaction is 4:

$$C_2H_5OH(l) + CH_3COOH(l) \rightleftharpoons CH_3COOC_2H_5(l) + H_2O(l)$$

 b What name is given to the reaction quotient at equilibrium?

5 Calculate the value of the reaction quotient for the following values of $\Delta G^{\ominus}$ if the reactions are at equilibrium:

 a $\Delta G^{\ominus} = 7.5$ kJ mol^{-1} at a temperature of 500 K.

 b $\Delta G^{\ominus} = -20.0$ kJ mol^{-1} at a temperature of 25 °C.

EXAM-STYLE QUESTIONS

1 Which of the following reactions will have the largest increase in entropy?

 A $C_2H_5OH(l) \rightarrow C_2H_4(g) + H_2O(l)$

 B $C(s) \rightarrow C(g)$

 C $H_2O(l) \rightarrow H_2O(g)$

 D $C_2H_5OH(l) + 3O_2(g) \rightarrow 2CO_2(g) + 3H_2O(l)$

2 Which statement about entropy is **true**?

 A The entropy of a substance depends on the temperature.

 B The entropy of an element is zero.

 C $\Delta S^{\ominus} > 0$ for exothermic reactions.

 D $\Delta S^{\ominus} < 0$ for exothermic reactions.

3 In which of the following physical changes does the entropy increase?

 I crystallisation

 II evaporation

 III melting

 A I only

 B II only

 C I and III

 D II and III

4 Which statement is **true** for the following endothermic reaction?

$$CaCO_3(s) \rightarrow CaO(s) + CO_2(g)$$

 A The reaction is spontaneous at high temperatures.

 B The reaction can never be spontaneous.

 C The reaction is spontaneous at low temperatures.

 D It is not possible to deduce whether the reaction is spontaneous or not from the information provided.

5 Given the data in Table **15.3**, calculate the entropy change at 298 K for the following reaction:

$CH_4(g) + H_2O(g) \rightarrow CO(g) + 3H_2(g)$

Substance	$S^{\ominus}$ / J mol^{-1}
$CH_4(g)$	+186
$H_2(g)$	+131
$H_2O(g)$	+190
$CO(g)$	+197

Table 15.3: Entropy data.

A +324

B +214

C −48

D +70

6 Calculate $\Delta G^{\ominus}$ for the following reaction at 400 K:

$C(g) + O_2(g) \rightarrow CO_2(g)$

$\Delta H^{\ominus} = -395$ kJ mol^{-1}

$\Delta S^{\ominus} = +5$ J K^{-1} mol^{-1}

A $\Delta G^{\ominus} = -2395$ kJ mol^{-1}

B $\Delta G^{\ominus} = -400$ kJ mol^{-1}

C $\Delta G^{\ominus} = -393$ kJ mol^{-1}

D $\Delta G^{\ominus} = -397$ kJ mol^{-1}

7 The graph in Figure **15.1** shows the entropy of a substance at different temperatures.

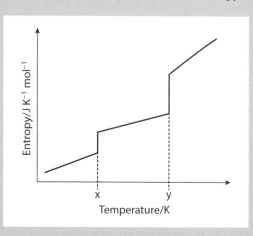

Figure 15.1: Graph of entropy against temperature.

a Suggest what changes are happening to the substance at the points labelled x and y on the graph. [2]

b Explain what is meant by the term *entropy*. [1]

CONTINUED

    c Describe how the entropy of a system changes when an ionic substance is dissolved in water. [1]

    d Given that the enthalpy change of solution of potassium chloride is $+20 \text{ kJ mol}^{-1}$ and the Gibbs energy change, $\Delta G^{\ominus}$, is -5.5 kJ mol^{-1}, calculate the entropy change when 1 mol of potassium chloride is dissolved in water at 298 K. [2]

8 Copper carbonate decomposes on heating to form copper oxide and carbon dioxide.

    a Write an equation for the reaction. [1]

    b Given that $\Delta H^{\ominus} = +46.0 \text{ kJ mol}^{-1}$ and $\Delta S^{\ominus} = +153.5 \text{ J K}^{-1} \text{ mol}^{-1}$, calculate at what range of temperature the reaction is feasible. [2]

9 The reaction quotient for the following reversible reaction:

$$H_2(g) + I_2(g) \rightleftharpoons 2HI(g)$$

can be calculated using the following expression:

$$Q = \frac{[HI]^2}{[H_2][I_2]}$$

1.0 mol of hydrogen, 1.5 mol of iodine and 2.5 mol of hydrogen iodide were mixed in a flask with a volume of 2.0 dm³ at a temperature of 500 K.

    a Calculate the concentration of each of the three substances in the flask immediately after they were mixed. [3]

    b Calculate the reaction quotient, Q, for the mixture. [1]

    c Given that $\Delta G^{\ominus}$ for the reaction is $-23.2 \text{ kJ mol}^{-1}$, calculate the value of ΔG of the mixture at this temperature. [2]

    d The mixture was left to stand until it had reached equilibrium. Use the value of ΔG calculated in part **c** to suggest how the composition of the mixture changes. [2]

How much, how fast, how far?

> Chapter 16

How much?
The amount of
chemical change

CHAPTER OUTLINE

In this chapter you will:

- understand how to write chemical equations

- use the mole ratio from a chemical equation in calculations

- understand how to work out which are the limiting reactants

- understand how to calculate theoretical and percentage yield

- understand the term *atom economy*.

KEY TERMS

Make sure you understand the following key terms before you do the exercises.

chemical equation: this tells us the mole ratio in which reactants combine and the relationship to the number of moles of products formed

mole ratio: the relationship between the number of moles of the various substances in a reaction

limiting reactant: the reactant that is used up first in a chemical reaction; when the amount in moles of each species is divided by their coefficient in the stoichiometric equation, the limiting reactant is the one with the lowest number; all other reactants are in excess

ionic equation: an equation that leaves out the formulas of substances which are not changed during a reaction

spectator ion: a substance that is not changed during a chemical reaction

yield: the amount of the desired product obtained from a chemical reaction

theoretical yield: the maximum possible amount of the desired product formed in a reaction

experimental (or actual) yield: the amount of desired product actually formed in a reaction

CONTINUED

percentage yield: the percentage yield compares the actual experimental yield and the theoretical maximum yield:

$$\% \text{ yield} = \frac{\text{experimental yield}}{\text{theoretical yield}} \times 100$$

atom economy: a measure of how efficient a particular reaction is in converting as much of the starting materials as possible into useful products

$$\text{atom economy} = \frac{\text{molar mass of desired product}}{\text{total molar mass of all reactants}} \times 100\%$$

The higher the atom economy, the greener the process, because more of the starting materials end up in the desired product

titration: a technique that involves adding measured volumes of a solution (from a burette) to another solution to determine the amounts that react exactly with each other

KEY EQUATION

$$\text{atom economy} = \frac{\text{molar mass of desired product}}{\text{total molar mass of all reactants}} \times 100$$

Exercise 16.1 The meaning of chemical equations

A balanced equation shows the simplest whole number **mole ratio** of the number of each type of particle in a chemical reaction. Being able to balance **chemical equations** is an important skill. In this exercise, you will start by looking at the basic principles of what a balanced equation represents. Later in the exercise, you will practise calculations from equations and working out the **limiting reactant**.

1   Given the following equation for the combustion of butanol, answer the questions below:

$C_4H_9OH(l) + 6O_2(g) \rightarrow 4CO_2(g) + 5H_2O(l)$

a   Determine how many moles of butanol would be required to produce 40 moles of carbon dioxide.

b   What number of oxygen molecules would be needed to react with 100 butanol molecules?

c   State how the total number of moles of substance changes during this reaction.

d   State how the total mass of all the atoms changes during this reaction.

TIP

Remember that only *big* numbers can be used in front of a formula. *Small* numbers are part of the formula of a substance and must not be changed, as this would change the identity of the substance.

2 Balance the following equations:

a $Na + Cl_2 \rightarrow NaCl$

b $N_2 + O_2 \rightarrow NO_2$

c $Li(s) + H_2O(l) \rightarrow LiOH(aq) + H_2(g)$

d $C_2H_6 + O_2 \rightarrow CO_2 + H_2O$

e $Fe_2O_3 + CO \rightarrow Fe + CO_2$

f $Cu + HNO_3 \rightarrow Cu(NO_3)_2 + NO_2 + H_2O$

3 **Ionic equations** only include the substances that change during a chemical reaction. Follow the sequence of steps **a–e** to deduce the ionic equation for the reaction between magnesium and hydrochloric acid. The equation for the reaction is as follows:

$Mg(s) + 2HCl(aq) \rightarrow MgCl_2(aq) + H_2(g)$

a Identify the ionic substances in the equation that are solutions.

b Re-write the equation using the formulas of the aqueous ions instead of the formulas of the substances identified in part **a**.

c Identify which ions are identical on both sides of the equation.

d Re-write the equation leaving out these ions.

e What name is given to ions that are left out of an ionic equation?

4 Re-write the following equations as ionic equations:

a $Cu(s) + 2AgNO_3(aq) \rightarrow Cu(NO_3)_2(aq) + 2Ag(s)$

b $H_2SO_4(aq) + 2NaOH(aq) \rightarrow Na_2SO_4(aq) + 2H_2O(l)$

c $CuSO_4(aq) + Na_2CO_3(aq) \rightarrow CuCO_3(s) + Na_2SO_4(aq)$

d $FeSO_4(aq) + BaCl_2(aq) \rightarrow FeCl_2(aq) + BaSO_4(s)$

5 Balance the following ionic equations:

a $H^+(aq) + CO_3^{2-} \rightarrow H_2O(l) + CO_2(g)$

b $Sn^{4+}(aq) + Cr^{2+}(aq) \rightarrow Sn^{2+}(aq) + Cr^{3+}(aq)$

c $Fe^{3+}(aq) + C_2O_4^{2-}(aq) \rightarrow Fe^{2+}(aq) + CO_2(g)$

d $BrO_3^-(aq) + H^+(aq) + Br^-(aq) \rightarrow Br_2(aq) + H_2O(l)$

6 Calculate the following:

a the number of moles of sodium atoms in 10.0 g of sodium

b the mass of 0.300 mol of $Cu(NO_3)_2$

c the relative formula mass if 0.250 mol of the substance has a mass of 54.0 g

d the number of moles in 250 cm^3 of methane at STP

TIP

If an element occurs in several different substances, as oxygen does in questions 2c and d, then it is often best to tackle this element last.

TIP

State symbols are essential in this question, as the ions are only free to move in ionic liquids (you will not encounter these very much) and ionic solutions. In solids, the ions are locked in position by the strong electrostatic forces of attraction, and so, the ions are not free to move.

TIP

In question 5, the **spectator ions** have already been removed, but the equations are not balanced. As well as the number of each type of atom balancing, the total charge on the left of the equation must be equal to the total charge on the right.

e the volume of 0.25 mol of CO_2 at STP

f the concentration of 300 cm^3 of solution containing 0.20 mol of solute

g the number of moles of NaCl in 75 cm^3 of solution with a concentration of 0.15 mol dm^{-3}

h the concentration of 150 cm^3 of solution that contains 2.50 g of $FeSO_4$.

7 Copper(II) oxide reacts with methane to produce copper, steam and carbon dioxide according to the following equation:

$$4CuO + CH_4 \rightarrow 4Cu + 2H_2O + CO_2$$

In an experiment, 1.25 g of copper(II) oxide were used.

a Calculate the number of moles of copper(II) oxide used.

b Use the ratio in the balanced equation to calculate the number of moles of carbon dioxide produced.

c Calculate the mass of carbon dioxide produced.

> **TIP**
>
> In question 7, you will need to choose which of the following three expressions can be used to calculate the amount of substance to use:
>
> $n = \dfrac{m}{M}$
>
> $n = V \times C$
>
> $n = \dfrac{V}{\text{molar volume}}$

> **TIP**
>
> Calculations from equations can be broken down into three main stages:
>
> - Calculate the number of moles of the substance/substances for which you have some other information, such as the mass.
>
> - Use the ratio in the balanced equation to find the number of moles of the substance that you are being asked about.
>
> - Convert this number of moles into the units that the question demands (e.g. mass, volume or concentration).

8 What mass of magnesium can be burnt in 2.50 g of carbon dioxide?

$$2Mg + CO_2 \rightarrow 2MgO + C$$

9 What mass of aluminium oxide is required to produce 1000 kg of aluminium?

$$2Al_2O_3 \rightarrow 4Al + 3O_2$$

Give the answer to four significant figures.

10 What volume of carbon dioxide would be produced for each kilogram of iron formed in the reaction between iron(III) oxide and carbon monoxide at STP?

$$Fe_2O_3 + 3CO \rightarrow 2Fe + 3CO_2$$

11 What volume of a solution of hydrochloric acid with a concentration of 0.250 mol dm^{-3} would be required to react with 0.25 g of calcium carbonate?

$$CaCO_3(s) + 2HCl(aq) \rightarrow CaCl_2(aq) + H_2O(l) + CO_2(g)$$

12 2.50 g of sulfur was heated with 2.50 g of iron to form iron(II) sulfide.

$Fe(s) + S(s) \rightarrow FeS(s)$

  a Calculate the number of moles of iron used.

  b Calculate the number of moles of sulfur used.

  c Identify which is the limiting reactant.

  d Using the number of moles of the limiting reagent, calculate the mass of iron(II) sulfide that can be formed.

13 Aluminium reacts with iodine according to the following equation:

$2Al(s) + 3I_2(s) \rightarrow 2AlI_3(s)$

In an experiment, 1.0 g of aluminium powder was mixed with 2.0 g of iodine. Identify the limiting reactant and calculate the mass of aluminium iodide that was formed.

14 1.00 g of copper was added to 150 cm³ of nitric acid with a concentration of 5.00 mol dm⁻³. The equation for the reaction can be written as follows:

$Cu(s) + 4HNO_3(aq) \rightarrow Cu(NO_3)_2(aq) + 2NO_2(g) + 2H_2O(l)$

Calculate the volume of nitrogen dioxide formed at STP.

TIP
In question 12c, you need to consider the ratio of the substances in the balanced equation. The limiting reactant is not always simply the reactant present in the lowest quantity, as can be seen in question 13.

Exercise 16.2 Yield and atom economy of chemical reactions

Not all reactions produce the quantity of product that is theoretically possible. The amount produced is often quoted as a percentage of the theoretical maximum that could have been obtained. In this exercise, you must first calculate the **theoretical yield** and then calculate the actual experimental **yield** to find the **percentage yield**. The first question takes you through this step by step.

You will also calculate atom economy using the following formula:

$$\text{atom economy} = \frac{\text{molar mass of desired product}}{\text{total molar mass of all reactants}} \times 100$$

Atom economy can be used as a measure of the efficiency of a reaction. Reactions with only one product always have an atom economy of 100%. Atom economy is calculated from the balanced chemical equation and is not the same as experimental yield.

1 Calcium oxide is made by the thermal decomposition of calcium carbonate, which is found in limestone. In an experiment it was found that 3.0 g of calcium carbonate produced 1.5 g of calcium oxide.

$CaCO_3 \rightarrow CaO + CO_2$

  a Calculate the number of moles of calcium carbonate used in the experiment.

  b Calculate the theoretical yield of calcium oxide that could be made from the number of moles of calcium carbonate calculated in part **a**.

  c Calculate the percentage of this theoretical yield that was actually formed.

2 Ethanol, C_2H_5OH, can be made from ethene, C_2H_4, using the following reaction:

$$C_2H_4(g) + H_2O(g) \rightarrow C_2H_5OH(g)$$

It was found that 10.0 g of ethene produced 14.6 g of ethanol. Calculate the percentage yield.

3 In an experiment to prepare chrome yellow pigment (lead(II) chromate), 25.0 cm³ of lead(II) nitrate with a concentration of 0.400 mol dm⁻³ was mixed with 75.0 cm³ of potassium chromate solution with a concentration of 0.250 mol dm⁻³.

$$Pb(NO_3)_2(aq) + K_2CrO_4(aq) \rightarrow PbCrO_4(s) + 2KNO_3(aq)$$

The precipitate of lead chromate was separated from the mixture by filtration, washed and dried. The mass of precipitate formed was found to be 1.80 g.

a Calculate the percentage yield.

b In a similar experiment, another student calculated the percentage yield to be over 100%. Assuming their calculation was correct, suggest a reason why the mass of the product was larger than is theoretically possible.

4 Calculate the atom economy of the following processes:

a the manufacture of cyclohexene from cyclohexanol

$$C_6H_{11}OH \rightarrow C_6H_{10} + H_2O$$

b the production of iron from iron(III) oxide

$$Fe_2O_3 + 3CO \rightarrow 2Fe + 3CO_2$$

c the preparation of ethyne from calcium carbide.

$$CaC_2 + 2H_2O \rightarrow C_2H_2 + Ca(OH)_2$$

5 Give a reason why a reaction with a high atom economy is good for the environment.

6 Suggest two other environmental factors that should be considered when choosing how to make a product and outline their importance.

Exercise 16.3 Titrations

Titration is a technique used for reactions that involve solutions. It uses apparatus that allows the volumes of the solutions to be measured accurately. One solution is added to another, and some sort of visual observation is used to detect when the two solutions are in the molar ratio that matches the chemical equation. This could be observing an indicator change colour or the point at which one of the reactants no longer changes colour on addition of the other reactant. In this exercise, you will start by undertaking some basic mole calculations, and then move on to titration calculations.

1 Calculate the concentrations of the following solutions in mol dm⁻³:

a 100 cm³ of sodium chloride solution containing 0.10 mol of NaCl.

b a solution of volume 250 cm³ containing 4.50 g of hydrated sodium carbonate ($Na_2CO_3 \cdot 10H_2O$).

> **TIP**
>
> In this calculation, you will first need to work out which reactant was the limiting reactant.

> **TIP**
>
> A formula with '•xH₂O' means that the solid is hydrated and contains water of crystallisation.
> The molar mass for the solid includes these water molecules.

2 How many moles of solute are there in the following solutions?

    a 25.00 cm^3 of 0.100 mol dm^{-3} NaOH(aq)

    b 50.0 cm^3 of 0.025 mol dm^{-3} K$_2$Cr$_2$O$_7$(aq)

3 What volume of calcium nitrate solution (Ca(NO$_3$)$_2$) with a concentration of 0.45 mol dm^{-3} will contain 0.025 mol of the solute?

4 A titration experiment was performed to find the concentration of a solution of sodium hydroxide. It was found that an average titre of 20.45 cm^3 of sulfuric acid with a concentration of 0.200 mol dm^{-3} was required to neutralise 25.00 cm^3 of the sodium hydroxide solution.

    a Calculate the number of moles of sulfuric acid used per titre.

    b Give the equation for the reaction.

    c Use the balanced equation to find the number of moles of sodium hydroxide per titre.

    d Calculate the concentration of the sodium hydroxide solution.

> **TIP**
>
> Question 4 has been structured. Follow the steps used to answer the following questions.

5 What volume of 0.200 mol dm^{-3} hydrochloric acid will neutralise 25.0 cm^3 of 0.150 mol dm^{-3} sodium carbonate solution?

The equation for the reaction is:

Na$_2$CO$_3$ + 2HCl → 2NaCl + H$_2$O + CO$_2$

6 Three moles of sodium hydroxide will neutralise one mole of citric acid. What volume of 0.250 mol dm^{-3} sodium hydroxide would react with 50.0 cm^3 of 0.200 mol dm^{-3} citric acid?

7 1.25 g of hydrated oxalic acid crystals, H$_2$C$_2$O$_4$•xH$_2$O, were dissolved in water and made up to a volume of 250.0 cm^3. 25.00 cm^3 portions of this solution were then titrated against dilute sodium hydroxide of concentration 0.100 mol dm^{-3}. The average titre was found to be 19.85 cm^3.

    a Calculate the number of moles of sodium hydroxide used per titre.

    b The balanced equation for the reaction is:

        H$_2$C$_2$O$_4$(aq) + 2NaOH(aq) → C$_2$O$_4$Na$_2$(aq) + 2H$_2$O(l)

    Deduce the number of moles of oxalic acid in 25.00 cm^3 of solution.

    c Calculate the number of moles of oxalic acid, H$_2$C$_2$O$_4$, in the original crystals.

    d Calculate the mass of oxalic acid, H$_2$C$_2$O$_4$, present in the crystals.

    e Calculate the mass of the water of crystallisation.

    f Calculate the number of moles of water of crystallisation.

    g Calculate the ratio of the number of moles of water to the number of moles of oxalic acid and, hence, determine the value for x in the formula of the hydrated oxalic acid.

> **TIP**
>
> The mass (and hence, the molar mass) of oxalic acid excludes the water of crystallisation, as this water is released when the solid is dissolved.

8 Succinic acid has a molar mass of 118.1 g mol^{-1}. In an experiment to find the number of hydrogen ions per succinic acid molecule, 1.01 g of succinic acid crystals were dissolved in water to make a solution of volume 250 cm^3. This solution was then titrated against 25.00 cm^3 portions of 0.100 mol dm^{-3} sodium hydroxide until concordant results were obtained. It was found that an average titre of 24.40 cm^3 was required. Determine the ratio for the reaction between succinic acid and sodium hydroxide.

When reactions are linked, the product of one reaction becomes the reactant in a second reaction. This means that calculations can involve several steps. In the next two questions you will practise this type of calculation. The first question is structured to take you through the process one step at a time.

9 In an experiment to find the purity of a sample of magnesium iodide, MgI$_2$, 1.50 g of the impure solid was dissolved in water and made up to a volume of 250 cm^3. A 25.00 cm^3 portion of the solution was transferred into a beaker and an excess of potassium iodate(V) solution was added, which liberated iodine. The equation for the reaction is as follows:

$$KIO_3(aq) + 5I^-(aq) + 6H^+ \rightarrow 3I_2(aq) + 3H_2O(l)$$

The amount of iodine liberated was determined by titrating the mixture with 0.050 mol dm^{-3} sodium thiosulfate solution. The average titre was 23.40 cm^3.

The equation for the reaction of iodine with thiosulfate ions is as follows:

$$2S_2O_3^{2-}(aq) + I_2(aq) \rightarrow S_4O_6^{2-}(aq) + 2I^-(aq)$$

Calculate the purity of the magnesium iodide by following steps **a–g**.

a Calculate the number of moles of thiosulfate used in the titration.

b Use the balanced equation for the titration reaction to calculate the number of moles of liberated iodine that must have reacted with the number of moles of thiosulfate calculated in part **a**.

c Use the balanced equation for the reaction of KIO$_3$ with iodide ions, and the number of moles of iodine liberated calculated in part **b** to find the number of moles of iodide ions in the beaker.

d Use the answer to part **c** to calculate the number of moles of iodide ions in the 250 cm^3 of original solution.

e Use the answer to part **d** to calculate the number of moles of magnesium iodide in the 250 cm^3 of solution.

f Use the answer to part **e** to calculate the mass of magnesium iodide dissolved in the 250 cm^3 of solution.

g Calculate the percentage purity.

TIP

This question has not been structured, so, at first sight, it appears difficult. Start, as always, by calculating the number of moles of what you know. Set your work out clearly, showing each step.

TIP

Note that, in most titration experiments, the titration is the last stage. Processing these data is often the first stage in the calculation. You essentially work backwards through the procedure.

10 The active ingredient in household bleach is NaOCl. To find the concentration of NaOCl in a sample of bleach, a 25.00 cm³ sample of bleach was mixed with an excess of iodide ions.

The equation for the reaction is as follows:

$OCl^-(aq) + 2I^-(aq) + 2H^+(aq) \rightarrow I_2(aq) + Cl^-(aq) + H_2O(l)$

The liberated iodine was titrated with $Na_2S_2O_3$ solution. The titration required 18.60 cm³ of 0.040 mol dm³ of $Na_2S_2O_3$ solution.

The equation for the reaction of iodine with thiosulfate ions is as follows:

$2S_2O_3^{2-}(aq) + I_2(aq) \rightarrow S_4O_6^{2-}(aq) + 2I^-(aq)$

Calculate the concentration of NaOCl in the bleach.

> **TIP**
>
> Follow a similar sequence of steps as those in question 9.

EXAM-STYLE QUESTIONS

1 Calculate the sum of the coefficients when the following equation is balanced with the smallest possible whole numbers:

$H_2O_2 + KI + H_2SO_4 \rightarrow I_2 + K_2SO_4 + H_2O$

A 6

B 7

C 8

D 9

2 Calculate which of the following contains the largest number of moles at STP (molar gas volume at STP = 22.7 dm³):

A 2.00 g of magnesium

B 230 cm³ of oxygen

C 100 cm³ of HCl with a concentration of 1 mol dm⁻³

D 9 g of water.

3 Molten iron can be produced by the reaction of iron(III) oxide with aluminium powder according to the following equation:

$Fe_2O_3 + 2Al \rightarrow 2Fe + Al_2O_3$

Calculate how many moles of iron would be produced when 120 mol of iron(III) oxide is completely reacted with aluminium.

A 60 mol

B 120 mol

C 180 mol

D 240 mol

CONTINUED

4 What is the maximum mass of carbon dioxide that is made when 10.0 g of calcium carbonate is reacted with an excess of hydrochloric acid?

A 10.0 g

B 44.0 g

C 0.10 g

D 4.4 g

5 Barium hydroxide reacts with potassium chromate, forming a precipitate of barium chromate:

$Ba(OH)_2(aq) + K_2CrO_4(aq) \rightarrow BaCrO_4(s) + 2KOH(aq)$

In an experiment, 100 cm^3 of barium hydroxide with a concentration of 0.100 mol dm^{-3} was mixed with 50 cm^3 of potassium chromate solution with a concentration of 0.250 mol dm^{-3}. Which statement is correct?

A Barium hydroxide is the limiting reactant and 0.0100 mol of barium chromate will be produced.

B Barium hydroxide is the limiting reactant and 0.0125 mol of barium chromate will be produced.

C Potassium chromate is the limiting reactant and 0.0125 mol of barium chromate will be produced.

D Potassium chromate is the limiting reactant and 0.0100 mol of barium chromate will be produced.

6 In an experiment to produce iron(III) chloride, 5.6 g of iron wool was heated in a stream of chlorine gas. 8.13 g of iron(III) chloride, $FeCl_3$, were produced.

$2Fe(s) + 3Cl_2(g) \rightarrow 2FeCl_3(s)$ $A_r(Fe) = 55.85, M(FeCl_3) = 162.20$

What is the percentage yield?

A $= \dfrac{162.20 \times 55.85 \times 100}{5.6 \times 8.13}$

B $= \dfrac{5.6 \times 8.13 \times 100}{55.85 \times 2 \times 162.20}$

C $= \dfrac{8.13 \times 55.85 \times 100}{5.6 \times 162.20}$

D $= \dfrac{5.6 \times 100}{8.13}$

7 Which of the following reactions has the highest atom economy assuming that the organic compound is the only useful product formed?

A $C_2H_5Br + NaOH \rightarrow C_2H_5OH + NaBr$

B $C_2H_4 + H_2O \rightarrow C_2H_5OH$

C $C_2H_5OH \rightarrow C_2H_4 + H_2O$

D $C_2H_5OH + HCOOH \rightarrow C_2H_5OOCH + H_2O$

8 Aluminium reacts with iodine to form aluminium iodide according to the following equation:

$2Al + 3I_2 \rightarrow 2AlI_3$

In an experiment using 0.27 g of aluminium and an excess of iodine, 2.04 g of aluminium iodide were produced. Which statement is correct?

A The percentage yield is 50% and the atom economy is 100%.

B The percentage yield is 100% and the atom economy is 100%.

C The percentage yield is 50% and the atom economy is 50%.

D The percentage yield is 100% and the atom economy is 50%.

9 During a titration experiment, hydrochloric acid with a concentration of 0.100 mol dm^{-3} was added slowly to 25 cm^3 of sodium hydroxide with a concentration of 0.150 mol dm^{-3} until the indicator used changed colour and identified the equivalence point for the reaction.
Calculate what volume of hydrochloric acid was added.

A 18.75 cm^3

B 25.00 cm^3

C 37.50 cm^3

D 50.00 cm^3

10 Calculate the concentration of sulfuric acid if 25 cm^3 of the solution are neutralised by 20 cm^3 of calcium hydroxide with a concentration of 0.0250 mol dm^{-3}.

A 0.0150 mol dm^{-3}

B 0.0200 mol dm^{-3}

C 0.0250 mol dm^{-3}

D 0.0300 mol dm^{-3}

11 In an experiment to find the identity of a Group 2 element, M, 50.0 cm^3 of 0.100 mol dm^{-3} of sodium carbonate solution were mixed with 50.0 cm^3 of a solution of $M(NO_3)_2$, with a concentration of 0.200 mol dm^{-3}. The two solutions reacted together to form a precipitate according to the following equation:

$Na_2CO_3(aq) + M(NO_3)_2(aq) \rightarrow MCO_3(s) + 2NaNO_3(aq)$

The precipitate was filtered, washed, dried carefully and found to have a mass of 0.74 g.

a Deduce which reagent was in excess.   [1]

b Calculate the number of moles of the Group 2 carbonate precipitate formed.   [1]

c Determine the molar mass of the carbonate and, hence, suggest the identity of the Group 2 element.   [3]

12 Silicon dioxide occurs as an impurity in the ores that are used to make iron.
It is removed by reacting it with calcium oxide:

$CaO + SiO_2 \rightarrow CaSiO_3$

Calcium oxide is formed by the thermal decomposition of limestone:

$CaCO_3 \rightarrow CaO + CO_2$

a Calculate the mass of calcium oxide required to remove each tonne of silicon dioxide.
1 tonne = 1000 kg   [2]

b If limestone containing an average of 95% calcium carbonate was used, then what mass of limestone would be required per tonne of silicon dioxide?   [2]

13 In an experiment to deduce the formula of $MgSO_4 \cdot xH_2O$, a sample of the solid was heated to constant mass in a crucible to remove the water of crystallisation. The following data were obtained.

mass of empty crucible = 18.27 g

mass of crucible and hydrated magnesium sulfate (before heating) = 21.19 g

mass of crucible and anhydrous magnesium sulfate (after heating) = 19.70 g

a Describe what is meant by 'constant mass' and why this is necessary in order to achieve accurate data.   [2]

b Use the data to find the value of x in the formula.   [4]

c The balance used had an uncertainty of ±0.01 g. Calculate the percentage uncertainties in the masses of both the hydrated and anhydrous magnesium sulfate.   [2]

Chapter 17

How fast? The rate of chemical change

KEY TERMS

Make sure you understand the following key terms before you do the exercises.

rate of reaction: the speed at which reactants are used up or products are formed or, more precisely, the change in concentration of reactants or products per unit time:

$$\text{average rate} = \frac{\text{change in concentration}}{\text{time}}$$

It could also be defined in terms of change in mass or volume etc. over time

collision theory: a method that is used to explain the variation of rate of reaction. A reaction can occur only when two particles collide in the correct orientation and with $E \geq E_a$

activation energy (E_a): the minimum energy that colliding particles must have before collision results in a chemical reaction

CONTINUED

catalyst: a substance that increases the rate of a chemical reaction without itself being used up in the reaction. A catalyst acts by allowing the reaction to proceed by an alternative pathway of lower activation energy

rate equation (rate expression/rate law): an experimentally determined equation that relates the rate of a reaction to the concentrations of the substances in the reaction mixture, e.g. rate = $k[A]^m[B]^n$

mechanism: a series of elementary steps that make up a more complex reaction. Each step involves the collision of two particles

rate constant (k): a constant of proportionality relating the concentrations in the experimentally determined rate expression to the rate of a chemical reaction; the rate constant is only a constant for a particular reaction at a particular temperature

order of a reaction: the power of the concentration of a particular reactant in the experimentally determined rate equation, e.g. in the rate equation:

rate = $k[A]^m[B]^n$, the order with respect to A is m and the order with respect to B is n

half-life: the time taken for the concentration of a reactant or number of radioactive nuclei in a sample to fall to half of its original value

rate-determining step: the slowest step in a reaction mechanism. It is the step with the highest activation energy

reaction intermediate: a substance that is produced in one step of a reaction and then goes on to be used in a subsequent step

molecularity: the number of reactant 'molecules' that take part in a particular elementary step in a reaction mechanism

overall order of reaction: the sum of the powers of the concentration terms in the experimentally determined rate equation, e.g. in the rate equation:

rate = $k[A]^m[B]^n$, the overall order is $m + n$

transition state (activated complex): a maximum on the potential energy profile/the highest energy species on the reaction pathway between reactants/intermediates and intermediates/products

Arrhenius factor (A) (pre-exponential factor): a constant that takes into account the frequency of collisions with the correct orientation

KEY EQUATIONS

Arrhenius equation (given in the IB data book)

$$k = Ae^{\frac{-E_a}{RT}}$$

or

$$\ln k = -\frac{E_a}{RT} + \ln A$$

CONTINUED

where

k = rate constant (units depend on the rate equation for the reaction)

E_a = activation energy for the reaction, J mol⁻¹

R = gas constant (8.31 J K⁻¹ mol⁻¹)

T = temperature, K

A = pre-exponential factor (units are the same as the rate constant)

Exercise 17.1 What is 'rate' of reaction? and Exercise 17.2 Experiments to measure the rate of reaction

To determine the rate of a chemical reaction, we need to be able to measure how the amount of a reactant decreases with time or how the amount of a product increases with time. The way that this is measured depends on the reaction and what is most easily observed. In this exercise, you will start by considering data collected from simple chemical reactions and how these data can be analysed.

1   In an experiment to measure the **rate of reaction** between magnesium carbonate and hydrochloric acid, the volume of carbon dioxide gas produced was measured every 15 s for a period of 4 min. Data collected are given in Table **17.1**.

Time / s	Volume of gas / cm³
0	0.0
15	32.0
30	44.0
45	49.0
60	52.0
75	54.0
90	56.0
105	57.5
120	59.0
135	60.0
150	61.0
165	62.0
180	62.5
195	63.0
210	63.0
225	63.0
240	63.0

Table 17.1: Volume of gas collected against time.

a   Draw a graph of volume of carbon dioxide against time, and calculate the rate of reaction in $cm^3 s^{-1}$ at the following times:

i   initial rate

ii   rate at 1 min

iii   rate at 2 min

iv   rate at 4 min.

b   Calculate the average rate over the first two minutes of the reaction.

c   How can you tell from the graph when the reaction has finished?

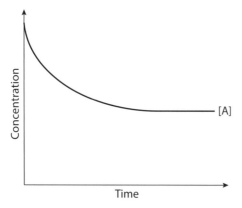

TIP

The rate of reaction at a given time can be found by finding the gradient of the tangent at that point on the graph.

2   The rate of reaction for the reaction between iodine, I_2, and thiosulfate ions, $S_2O_3^{2-}$, was measured, and it was found that the average change in concentration of the thiosulfate ions over the first two minutes was 0.0250 mol dm^{-3} s^{-1}.

The equation for the reaction is as follows:

$$2S_2O_3^{2-}(aq) + I_2(aq) \rightarrow S_4O_6^{2-}(aq) + 2I^-(aq)$$

a   Calculate the average change in concentration of iodine over the same time period.

b   Calculate the average rate of production of iodide ions over the first two minutes.

c   Calculate the average rate of production of $S_4O_6^{2-}$ ions over the first two minutes.

TIP

Do not overcomplicate these calculations. Look at the coefficients in the balanced equation. $S_2O_3^{2-}$ and I_2 react in the ratio 2 : 1.

3   Figure **17.1** is a sketch showing the change in the concentration of A against time for the reaction $A + 2B \rightarrow C$

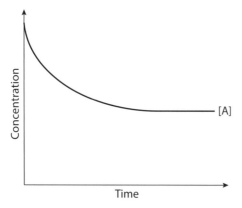

Figure 17.1: Concentration–time graph for $A + 2B \rightarrow C$

a   Assuming that the concentration of B initially was the same as the concentration of A, draw a line to show how the concentration of B changes over time.

b   Draw a line to show the change in concentration of C.

4 Calcium hydroxide reacts with hydrochloric acid according to the following equation:

$$Ca(OH)_2(s) + 2HCl(aq) \rightarrow CaCl_2(aq) + 2H_2O(l)$$

In a reaction, 10 g of $Ca(OH)_2$ which is an excess, was reacted with 100 cm³ of HCl, which had a concentration of 1.0 mol dm⁻³.

Figure **17.2** shows the change in concentration of $CaCl_2$ over time.

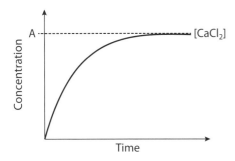

Figure 17.2: Concentration–time graph for the $Ca(OH)_2$/HCl reaction.

TIP

Note that calcium hydroxide is in excess, so the amount of calcium chloride is dependent on the amount of hydrochloric acid present.

a What is the final concentration of $CaCl_2$, labelled A in Figure **17.2**?

b The experiment was repeated again using a fresh 10 g sample of $Ca(OH)_2$ with only 50 cm³ of 1.0 mol dm⁻³ HCl. Draw a line on the graph to show the change in the concentration of $CaCl_2$ with time for this experiment.

Exercise 17.3 Collision theory

Collision theory describes how a chemical reaction happens. In this short exercise, you will check that you understand collision theory and how reactions can be represented using **potential energy profile diagrams**.

1 Give two reasons why not all collisions between reactants result in a chemical reaction.

2 Explain the term **activation energy**.

3 Sketch the energy profile diagram of an endothermic reaction, clearly showing the activation energy for the reaction.

Exercise 17.4 Factors affecting reaction rate

Collision theory can be used to explain the factors that affect the rate of chemical reactions. In this exercise, you will explore these factors.

1 List the main factors that affect the rate of a chemical reaction.

2 Complete the boxes in Table **17.2** by describing how the frequency of collisions, the proportion of successful collisions and the activation energy are affected by each of the changes in the first column.

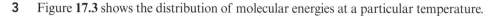

Factor	Effect on the frequency of collisions	Effect on the proportion of successful collisions	Effect on the activation energy
changing the concentration of a reactant			
changing the pressure of a gas			
changing the surface area of a solid			
using a **catalyst**			
changing the temperature			

Table 17.2: Factors that affect the rate of a reaction.

3   Figure **17.3** shows the distribution of molecular energies at a particular temperature.

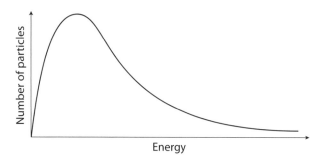

Figure 17.3: Distribution of molecular energy.

a   Add a line to the graph to represent the distribution at a higher temperature and use this to explain why the rate of a reaction increases at higher temperatures.

b   What does the total area under the curve represent?

4   Sketch a graph of the distribution of molecular energies, and use this to explain why the addition of a catalyst increases the rate of a chemical reaction.

5   Explain why the rate of reaction increases when the following changes are made:

a   the concentration of a reactant is increased

b   the temperature is increased

c   the pressure of a reaction involving gases is increased

d   the size of the particles in a reaction involving a solid is reduced

e   a catalyst is used.

6   Catalysts increase the rate of a reaction without being used up. Draw an energy profile diagram for an exothermic reaction including the following labels:

a   reactants

b   products

TIP

Details to consider include the following: Should the curve start at (0,0)? Should the curve touch the *x*-axis at high energies? Should the maximum of the new curve be higher or lower than the first curve? Where should the position of the maximum of the new curve be along the *x*-axis relative to the first curve? Should the right-hand side of the new curve finish above, below or with the first curve?

TIP

Any question about how a factor affects the rate of a reaction should be answered in terms of the effect on the *frequency* of collisions and on the *proportion of successful collisions*. An alternative to 'frequency' would be to describe the change in the number of collisions per unit time. The 'per unit time' is essential; 'more collisions' on its own is incorrect.

c   activation energy for the catalysed reaction

d   activation energy for the uncatalysed reaction

e   the reaction pathway for the catalysed reaction

f   reaction pathway for the uncatalysed pathway

g ΔH for the reaction.

Exercise 17.5 The rate equation

In this exercise, you will first explore mathematical relationships between the rate of a reaction and the concentrations of the different reactants. These relationships are expressed in the **rate equation** for the reaction. You will then go on to look at how the rate equation for a reaction can be used to determine the **mechanism** of the reaction.

1   In a single word, how is the rate expression deduced?

2   The rate equation for a reaction between reactants A and B was found to be
rate = $k[A]^a[B]^b$

a   What name is given to k in the expression above and what does it represent?

b   What name is given to terms such as a and b in this rate equation?

c   For the rate equation, what name is given to the sum of a and b?

d   What is the effect of temperature on the values of a, b and k in a rate equation, such as that given here?

3   Deduce the units of the **rate constant** for each of the following rate equations:

a   rate = $k[A]$

b   rate = $k[A][B]$

c   rate = $k[A]^2$

d   rate = $k[A][B]^2$

4   For each of the following examples, deduce the rate equation, calculate the value of k and give the units of k.

a   for the reaction A + B → C (Table **17.3**)

Experiment	[A] / mol dm⁻³	[B] / mol dm⁻³	Initial rate / mol dm⁻³ s⁻¹
1	1	1	2
2	1	2	4
3	2	2	4

Table 17.3: Experimental rate data.

> **TIP**
> In question 3, the units of rate are mol dm⁻³ s⁻¹.

> **TIP**
> For question 4, choose a pair of experiments in which one of the reactant concentrations does not change. This will enable you to determine the **order of a reaction** with respect to the substance that does change. Deduce the factor by which the concentration and the rate have both changed. If this change is the same, then the reaction is first order. If the change in the rate is the square of the change in the concentration, then the reaction is second order.

b for the reaction A + 2B → C + D (Table **17.4**)

Experiment	[A] / mol dm⁻³	[B] / mol dm⁻³	Initial rate / mol dm⁻³ s⁻¹
1	0.1	0.5	1.6
2	0.1	0.25	0.4
3	0.3	0.5	4.8

Table 17.4: Experimental rate data.

c for the reaction F + G → 2H (Table **17.5**)

Experiment	[F] / mol dm⁻³	[G] / mol dm⁻³	[J] / mol dm⁻³	Initial rate / × 10⁻² mol dm⁻³ s⁻¹
1	0.2	0.5	0.10	3.0
2	0.1	0.5	0.10	1.5
3	0.6	0.5	0.20	18
4	0.3	0.25	0.40	4.5

Table 17.5: Experimental rate data.

d In part **c**, substance J does not appear in the balanced equation. What name is given to a substance that appears in the rate equation but is not in the chemical equation?

5 Sketch the shapes of the following graphs:

a concentration of reactant against time for a zero-order reaction

b concentration of reactant against time for a first-order reaction

c concentration of reactant against time for a second-order reaction

d rate against concentration of reactant for a zero-order reaction

e rate against concentration of reactant for a first-order reaction

f rate against concentration of reactant for a second-order reaction.

> **TIP**
>
> Deduce the order with respect to F first, and then use this information when deducing the order with respect to the other substances.

> **TIP**
>
> When calculating *k* in part **c**, look closely at the column header for the actual values of the initial rate.

> **TIP**
>
> Try to work out the shapes of the graphs from the relationships, rather than just memorising them.

Exercise 17.6 Mechanisms of reactions

1   The reaction between bromine and methanoic acid is catalysed by hydrogen ions.
The equation for the reaction is as follows:

$$Br_2(aq) + HCOOH(aq) \rightarrow 2Br^-(aq) + 2H^+ (aq) + CO_2(g)$$

In an experiment to find the order of the reaction with respect to bromine,
an excess of methanoic acid was mixed with a solution of bromine, and the
concentration of bromine was measured using a colorimeter.
The results are given in Table **17.6**.

Time / s	$[Br_2]$ / mol dm^{-3}
0	0.0100
30	0.0090
60	0.0081
90	0.0073
120	0.0066
180	0.0053
240	0.0044
300	0.0036
360	0.0029
480	0.0020
600	0.0013

Table 17.6: Concentration of bromine against time.

a   Why was an excess of methanoic acid used in the experiment?

b   Plot a graph of concentration of bromine against time.

In parts **c** and **d** of this question, you will process data from this graph in two
different ways to find the order of the reaction with respect to bromine.

c   i   Draw construction lines on the graph you drew for part **b** to find the time
taken for the concentration of bromine to fall to half of its original value.

   ii   What name is given to the time it takes for the concentration of a
substance to fall to half of its original value?

   iii   Draw a further construction line to find the time taken for the
concentration of bromine to fall by half again, that is, to fall from
half its original value to one-quarter of its original value.

   iv   Draw a further construction line to find the time taken for the
concentration of bromine to fall by half again, that is to fall from
one-quarter of its original value to one eighth of its original value.

   v   From the values calculated in parts **i**, **iii** and **iv**, deduce the order of
reaction with respect to bromine.

d **i** Using the graph plotted in part b, find the rate of reaction at time = 0, $t = 90$, $t = 180$, $t = 360$ and $t = 480$ s by drawing tangents at these points on the graph of concentration against time, and finding their gradients.

ii Plot a graph of rate (gradient) against concentration of bromine and deduce the order of reaction with respect to bromine.

2 Figure **17.4** is a graph of concentration of a reactant against time for a second-order reaction.

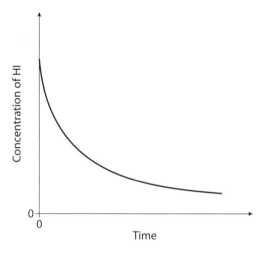

Figure 17.4: Concentration–time graph for a second-order reaction.

a Draw construction lines on the graph to show the first three **half-lives**.

b Describe the trend in these values.

c Suggest the trend in the half-lives for a reaction that has an order of less than one.

3 The following two different two-step mechanisms were proposed for the reaction $A + 2B \rightarrow C$

Mechanism 1

step 1: $2B \rightarrow D$ (slower step)

step 2: $D + A \rightarrow C$

Mechanism 2

step 1: $A + B \rightarrow D$ (slower step)

step 2: $D + B \rightarrow C$

The rate equation for the reaction was found to be the following:
rate = $k[B]^2$

a Which mechanism agrees with this rate equation?

b What name is given to a substance that is produced in one step and then used up in a subsequent step?

> **TIP**
>
> The rate equation includes all the reactants in the **rate-determining step**.

4   The proposed mechanism for a reaction is given as follows:

step 1: $NO_2 + Br_2 \rightarrow NOOBr + Br$

step 2: $NO_2 + Br \rightarrow NOOBr$

   a   Deduce the overall equation for the reaction.

   b   Give the rate equation if step 1 is the rate-determining step.

   c   Give the rate equation if step 2 is the rate-determining step.

TIP

The rate equation can only include substances that are found in the original reaction mixture.

If any of these substances are products of an earlier step, that is, they are **reaction intermediates**, then their concentration depends on the concentrations of the reactants in the equation by which they have been made.

For example, if the rate equation for the rate-determining step includes substance X, and X is an intermediate made by the reaction of A and B, then [X] can be substituted by [A][B].

---

5   The mechanism for a reaction is as follows:

step 1: $OCl^-(aq) + H_2O(l) \rightarrow HOCl(aq) + OH^-(aq)$

step 2: $I^-(aq) + HOCl(aq) \rightarrow IOH(aq) + Cl^-(aq)$

step 3: $IOH(aq) + OH^-(aq) \rightarrow IO^-(aq) + H_2O(l)$

   a   Give the overall equation for the reaction.

   b   Given that the rate equation for this reaction was found to be the following:
       rate = $k[I^-][OCl^-]$

       which is the rate-determining step in this mechanism?

   c   Which substances in the mechanism act as intermediates?

   d   Why does the concentration of water not appear in the rate equation?

6   What is meant by the term *elementary step*?

7   A proposed mechanism for the breakdown of ozone in the atmosphere is as follows:

step 1: $O_3 + Cl \rightarrow ClO + O_2$ (fast)

step 2: $ClO + O \rightarrow O_2 + Cl$ (slow)

   a   What is the **molecularity** of each step?

   b   Give the overall equation for the reaction.

c Deduce the overall rate equation for this reaction.

d What is the **overall order of the reaction**?

e What term is used to describe ClO in this reaction?

f What name is used to describe the role of Cl in this reaction?

g Given that both step 1 and step 2 are exothermic, sketch the energy profile diagram for the reaction.

TIP

The energy profile diagram should have as many humps/peaks as there are steps in the mechanism. Note that you are told that both steps are exothermic, so your sketch should show this. You also know that the second step is the slow step; think carefully about how this can be shown on the graph. Remember to include labels for the axes and to show the position of the reactants, **transition states**, intermediates, and products.

---

8 Figure **17.5** shows the energy profile diagram for a reaction.

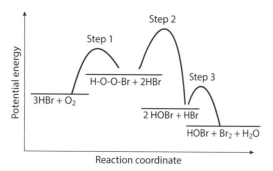

Figure 17.5: Energy profile diagram for the reaction between HBr and O_2.

a What is the overall equation for the reaction?

b Which step in the reaction is endothermic?

c Identify the rate-determining step.

d Give equations for the three steps.

e Deduce the rate equation for the reaction.

TIP

Note that the labels on each line of the energy profile diagram all contain the same number of each type of atom, three H, three Br and two O; they form balanced equations. To deduce the mechanism for the reaction, look at each step/pair of labels in turn and simplify the equations to cancel out substances that appear on both sides.

Exercise 17.7 Variation of the rate constant with temperature

Given that rate increases with temperature, and the rate depends on the rate constant for a reaction, there must be a relationship between the rate constant and temperature. This relationship is described by the Arrhenius equation. The Arrhenius equation can be written in two different forms, and these are given in the IB data book:

$$k = Ae^{\frac{-E_a}{RT}} \text{ and } \ln k = -\frac{E_a}{RT} + \ln A$$

In this exercise, you will first look at the terms in these equations and then go on to use them in some practice calculations.

1   What do the terms $\ln$, k, A, T, E_a and R represent in the Arrhenius equation?

2   Given that the activation energy of a reaction is 35 kJ mol^{-1} and the exponential factor has a value of 12.5 dm^3 mol^{-1} s^{-1}, calculate the rate constant at 25 °C.

3   Explain how the expression $\ln k = -\dfrac{E_a}{RT} + \ln A$ can be used graphically to find the activation energy of a reaction.

4   Explain why it is appropriate to consider the Arrhenius equation as describing the relationship between *rate* and temperature even though *rate* does not appear in the Arrhenius equation.

5   To find the activation energy of a reaction, a series of identical experiments were completed to measure the rate of reaction at different temperatures. The rate constant, k, at different temperatures was then calculated. Figure **17.6** is a graph of $\ln k$ against $\frac{1}{T}$.

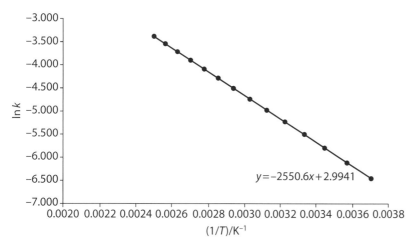

Figure 17.6: Graph of $\ln k$ against $\frac{1}{T}$.

TIP

Generally, $k = Ae^{\frac{-E_a}{RT}}$ is used for calculations and

$\ln k = -\dfrac{E_a}{RT} + \ln A$

is used for questions involving graphs.

TIP

The form of the expression given in question 3 is similar to that of a straight line, $y = mx + c$, so consider what you would plot and what the gradient of the straight line would be equal to.

TIP

In question 4, you should think about the relationship between rate and k.

TIP

The ideas in question 5b and c are not specifically mentioned in the syllabus, but it is useful to point them out here. Thinking that the Arrhenius factor can be found from the intercept of a graph of $\ln$ rate against $\frac{1}{T}$ graph is a common misconception.

a Use the graph in Figure **17.6** to deduce the **Arrhenius factor** and the activation energy for the reaction.

b Suggest what the magnitude of the value of A indicates about the likelihood that the particles collide with the correct orientation.

c In a similar experiment, rather than calculating the rate constant at each temperature, the value of the rate of the reaction was used in the place of k.

   i Explain why it is still possible to find the value of the activation energy by finding the gradient of a graph of ln rate against $1/T$.

   ii Explain why the value of the intercept of a graph of ln rate against $1/T$ is not equal to ln A.

EXAM-STYLE QUESTIONS

1 Which of the methods, **A–D**, could **not** be used to follow the rate of the following reaction?

$$CuCO_3(s) + 2HCl(aq) \rightarrow CuCl_2(aq) + H_2O(l) + CO_2(g)$$

A measuring the mass of the reaction mixture with time

B measuring the volume of water produced with time

C measuring the pH of the reaction mixture with time

D measuring the volume of gas produced with time

2 For the reaction $X + Y \rightarrow 3W + 2Z$

which graph (**A**, **B**, **C** or **D**) shows the change in the concentration of the products with time when equal amounts of X and Y are mixed together?

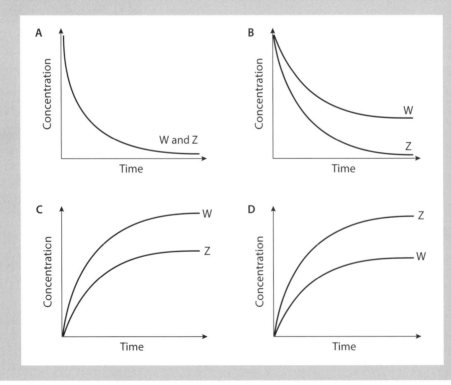

CONTINUED

3   Which row in the table gives the correct values for the initial rate and the average rate of the reaction shown in the graph?

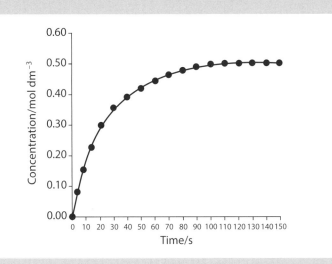

	Initial rate / mol dm^{-3} s^{-1}	Average rate / mol dm^{-3} s^{-1}
A	0.015	0.00500
B	0.300	0.00333
C	0.000	0.5000
D	0.005	0.00500

4   Which statements can be used to explain why increasing the temperature increases the rate of a reaction?

I   The particles collide more frequently.

II   The proportion of collisions that are successful increases.

III The activation energy is lower.

A I and II

B I and III

C II and III

D I, II and III

5   Which change is likely to have the greatest effect on the rate of reaction between a single lump of zinc of mass 1 g and 50 cm^3 of 0.200 mol cm^3 sulfuric acid at 25 °C?

A using 50 cm^3 of 0.200 mol dm^3 sulfuric acid at 25 °C with powdered zinc

B using 100 cm^3 of 0.200 mol dm^3 sulfuric acid at 25 °C with a single lump of zinc

C using 50 cm^3 of 0.200 mol dm^3 sulfuric acid at 10 °C with powdered zinc

D using 50 cm^3 of 0.250 mol dm^3 sulfuric acid at 40 °C with powdered zinc

CONTINUED

6 The rate expression for the reaction A + B → C is rate = $k[A][B]^2$

What effect will doubling the concentrations of both A and B have on the overall rate?

A overall rate will increase by a factor of 2

B overall rate will increase by a factor of 4

C overall rate will increase by a factor of 6

D overall rate will increase by a factor of 8

7 Using data from the table, deduce the rate expression for the following reaction:

$Na_2S_2O_3(aq) + 2HCl(aq) → 2NaCl(aq) + S(s) + SO_2(aq) + H_2O(l)$

$[Na_2S_2O_3(aq)]$ / mol dm^{-3}	[HCl(aq)] / mol dm^{-3}	Rate / mol dm^{-3} s^{-1}
0.10	0.10	0.040
0.20	0.10	0.080
0.40	0.20	0.160

A rate = $k[Na_2S_2O_3(aq)][HCl(aq)]$

B rate = $k[Na_2S_2O_3(aq)]$

C rate = $k[Na_2S_2O_3(aq)]^2$

D rate = $k[Na_2S_2O_3(aq)][HCl(aq)]^2$

8 The equation for the reaction of CH_3COCH_3 and I_2 is as follows:
$CH_3COCH_3(aq) + I_2(aq) → CH_3COCH_2I(aq) + H^+(aq) + I^-(aq)$

A series of experiments were conducted and the rate equation was found to be
rate = $k[CH_3COCH_3][H^+]$

Which statement is **not** correct?

A The overall order of the reaction is second order.

B If the concentration of both reactants is doubled, then the rate will also double.

C Hydrogen ions act as a catalyst.

D The reaction can be followed colorimetrically.

CONTINUED

9 Which graph (**A**, **B**, **C** or **D**) represents a first-order reaction?

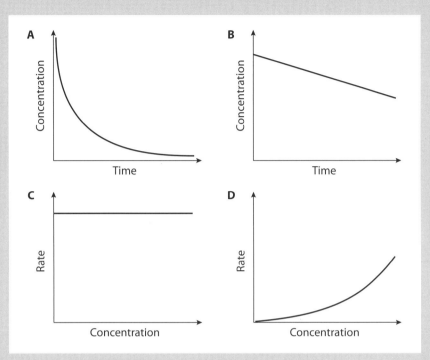

10 A series of experiments were conducted to measure the rate of a reaction at different temperatures. Which of the following statements is correct?

  A The gradient of a graph of rate against temperature in kelvin would equal the activation energy.

  B The gradient of a graph of ln rate against temperature in kelvin would equal the activation energy.

  C The gradient of a graph of ln rate against $1/T$ (in kelvin) would equal the activation energy.

  D The gradient of a graph of ln rate against $1/T$ (in kelvin) would equal $\dfrac{-E_a}{R}$.

11 Collision theory is used to explain the factors that affect the rate of a chemical reaction.

  a State what is meant by *collision theory*. [3]

  b State the effect of the following changes on the rate of a reaction:

    i increasing the temperature [1]

    ii increasing the concentration of a reactant [1]

    iii decreasing the surface area of a reactant [1]

    iv decreasing the pressure of a gaseous reactant [1]

    v adding a catalyst. [1]

12 Figure **17.7** shows the results of an experiment following the decomposition of hydrogen peroxide with a concentration of 0.100 mol dm^{-3} in the presence of granules of manganese(IV) catalyst.

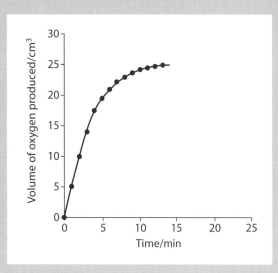

Figure 17.7: Decomposition of hydrogen peroxide.

The equation for the reaction is as follows:

$$2H_2O_2(aq) \rightarrow 2H_2O(l) + O_2(g)$$

The progress of the reaction was followed by measuring the volume of oxygen produced.

a Calculate the following:

  i the initial rate of reaction in cm^3 of O$_2$ per minute   [1]

  ii the rate of reaction at 5 min in cm^3 of O$_2$ per minute   [1]

  iii the average rate of reaction in cm^3 of O$_2$ per minute.   [1]

b Add lines to the graph in Figure **17.7** to show how the volume of oxygen produced against time would differ if the following changes were made:

  i the catalyst was ground to a finer powder, but nothing else was changed from the original experiment   [2]

  ii the same volume of 0.050 mol dm^{-3} hydrogen peroxide was used, but nothing else was changed from the original experiment.   [2]

13 The rate of a chemical reaction can be increased by the use of a suitable catalyst.

a Define the term *catalyst*.   [3]

b In terms of collision theory, explain how a catalyst increases the rate of a reaction.   [3]

c Draw a fully labelled sketch of a potential energy profile for an endothermic reaction with and without a catalyst.   [3]

CONTINUED

14 Figure **17.8** shows the graph obtained during an experiment to determine the kinetics of the reaction between bromide ions and bromate ions, which react according to the following equation:

$$5Br^-(aq) + BrO_3^-(aq) + 6H^+(aq) \rightarrow 3Br_2(aq) + 3H_2O(l)$$

The concentration of bromide ions was calculated by determining the concentration of bromine produced at timed intervals.

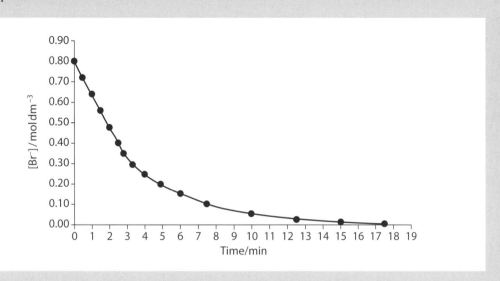

Figure 17.8: Kinetics of bromate/bromide reaction.

a Use the graph to determine the order of reaction with respect to bromide ions. [3]

A series of further experiments were conducted and produced the results shown in Table **17.7**.

Experiment	[Br⁻] / mol dm⁻³	[BrO₃⁻] / mol dm⁻³	[H⁺] / mol dm⁻³	Rate of reaction / × 10⁻⁵ mol dm⁻³ s⁻¹
1	0.025	0.020	0.010	4.6
2	0.025	0.020	0.020	18.4
3	0.025	0.030	0.020	27.6
4	0.050	0.040	0.020	73.6
5	0.050	0.010	0.020	18.4

Table 17.7: Concentration and rate data for a series of experiments between bromide and bromate(V) ions.

CONTINUED

    b Deduce the order of reaction with respect to bromate and to hydrogen ions.   **[2]**

    c Give the overall rate equation for the reaction and the overall order of the reaction.   **[2]**

    d Calculate the value of the rate constant for the reaction and its units.   **[3]**

    e State the effect of decreasing the temperature on the rate of the reaction and on the value of the rate constant.   **[2]**

    f Suggest what data could be used to determine the activation energy for this reaction.   **[2]**

15 The equation for the reaction between hydrogen and iodine monochloride is as follows:

$$H_2(g) + 2ICl(g) \rightarrow I_2(g) + 2HCl(g) \qquad \Delta H^{\ominus} = -155 \text{ k mol}^{-1}$$

The mechanism for the reaction was found to have the following rate equation:

rate $= k[H_2][ICl]$

    a State the overall order of the reaction.   **[1]**

    b Sketch a graph of rate against concentration for the reaction.   **[1]**

    c Suggest a two-step mechanism for the reaction and identify the rate-determining step.   **[3]**

    d Sketch the energy profile diagram for your proposed mechanism.   **[4]**

Chapter 18

How far? The extent of chemical change

KEY TERMS

Make sure you understand the following key terms before you do the exercises.

reversible reaction: a reaction that can go either way, so the reactants become the products, but the products of the reaction can also react to re-form the reactants. The symbol ⇌ shows that a reaction is reversible. A reversible reaction will eventually reach a state of equilibrium

Le Chatelier's principle: if a system at equilibrium is subjected to some change, the position of equilibrium will shift in order to minimise the effect of the change

dynamic equilibrium: macroscopic properties (all concentrations of reactants and products) are constant and the rate of the forward reaction is equal to the rate of the reverse reaction

CONTINUED

reaction quotient (Q): the ratio of the concentrations of the reactants and products (raised to the appropriate powers) at any point in time. An expression for Q is exactly the same as that for the equilibrium constant – except that the concentrations are not equilibrium concentrations.

So, for the reaction: $H_2(g) + I_2(g) \rightleftharpoons 2HI(g)$

$$Q = \frac{[HI(g)]^2}{[H_2(g)][I_2(g)]}$$

KEY EQUATIONS

For a reaction $aA + bB \rightleftharpoons cC + dD$, the reaction quotient is $Q = \dfrac{[C]^c[D]^d}{[A]^a[B]^b}$

At equilibrium, $Q = K$

where

K = equilibrium constant

$\Delta G^\ominus = -RT\ln K$

where

$\Delta G^\ominus$ is the change in Gibbs free energy, J mol^{-1}

R = gas constant, 8.31 J K^{-1} mol^{-1}

T = absolute temperature, K

$\ln K$ = natural logarithm of the equilibrium constant

Exercise 18.1 Reversible reactions and equilibrium

Not all reactions are reversible. Many reactions go to completion, as all of the reactants turn into products. In this exercise, you will explore what happens when a **reversible reaction** occurs in a closed system and some of the basic ideas that underpin the topic.

1 Describe what is meant by the term *closed system*.

2 Describe what is meant by the term *dynamic equilibrium*.

3 The term *equilibrium* implies that something is 'equal', but what property is equal at equilibrium?

4 What term can be used to describe the concentrations of all the reactants and products present at equilibrium?

TIP

If a term has two words, then you should generally explain the meaning of both words separately: what is meant by *dynamic* and what is meant by *equilibrium*?

Exercise 18.2 The position of equilibrium

In this exercise, you will explore how the rates of the forward and backward reactions change as an equilibrium is established, the characteristics of an equilibrium and **Le Chatelier's principle**.

1   Figure **18.1** is a graph of concentration against time when a mixture of equal amounts of N_2O_4 and NO_2 are put into a sealed vessel at a constant temperature and pressure.

The equation for the reaction is as follows:

$N_2O_4(g) \rightleftharpoons 2NO_2(g)$

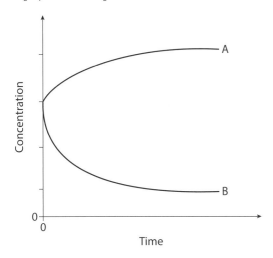

Figure 18.1: Concentration–time graph for a reversible reaction.

a   Identify which line on the graph represents the change in the concentration of N_2O_4.

b   Indicate on the graph the time when equilibrium is reached.

c   Sketch a graph of rate against time for this reaction to show how the rates of the forward and backward reactions change as equilibrium is reached. Label the point at which equilibrium is reached.

2   List the characteristics of a chemical equilibrium.

3   The term *position of equilibrium* is used to describe the relative amounts of products and reactants present at equilibrium.

a   A system at equilibrium contains relatively more reactants than products. How might the position of this equilibrium be described?

b   A system at equilibrium contains relatively more products than reactants. How might the position of this equilibrium be described?

> **TIP**
>
> For part **a**, look at how much each concentration has changed. Think about the ratio of N_2O_4 and NO_2 in the balanced equation.

4   List three factors that affect the position of an equilibrium.

5   State Le Chatelier's principle.

6   State the effect of the following changes made to a system in dynamic equilibrium. In each case, give a reason for your answer.

a   increasing the temperature for a reaction if the forward direction is exothermic

b   increasing the temperature for a reaction if the forward reaction is endothermic

c   increasing the concentration of a reactant

d   removing some product from the equilibrium mixture

e   adding a catalyst

f   increasing the pressure of a reaction that involves gases.

7   State the effect of increasing the pressure of the following systems in dynamic equilibrium and give a reason for your answers:

a $PCl_3(g) + Cl_2(g) \rightleftharpoons PCl_5(g)$

b $2NH_3(g) \rightleftharpoons N_2(g) + 3H_2(g)$

c $H_2(g) + I_2(g) \rightleftharpoons 2HI(g)$

d $CaCO_3(s) \rightleftharpoons CaO(s) + CO_2(g)$

e $H_2O(l) \rightleftharpoons H_2O(g)$

8   State the effect of decreasing the concentration of the species **in bold** on the position of the following systems in dynamic equilibrium. Give a reason for your answer.

a $CH_3OH(l) + CH_3COOH(l) \rightleftharpoons \mathbf{CH_3COOCH_3}(l) + H_2O(l)$

b $Cu^{2+}(aq) + \mathbf{4Cl^-}(aq) \rightleftharpoons CuCl_4^{2+}(aq)$

c $Fe^{3+}(aq) + \mathbf{SCN^-}(aq) \rightleftharpoons [FeSCN]^{2+}(aq)$

9   The following equilibrium mixture was a yellow–orange colour, as it contained a mixture of orange $Cr_2O_7^{2-}$ ions and yellow CrO_4^{2-} ions.

$Cr_2O_7^{2-}(aq) + H_2O(l) \rightleftharpoons 2CrO_4^{2-}(aq) + 2H^+(aq)$

What effect will adding alkali have on the colour of the mixture? Give a reason for your answer.

Exercise 18.3 Equilibrium constants

Equilibrium constants describe the mathematical relationship between the concentrations of the substances present at equilibrium. In this exercise, you will practise deriving these equilibrium constants from a chemical equation. Higher Level students will go on to complete calculations using these types of mathematical expressions in Exercise 18.4.

1   Deduce the equilibrium law expression for the following reactions:

   a $2H_2(g) + CO(g) \rightleftharpoons CH_3OH(g)$

   b $H_2(g) + I_2(g) \rightleftharpoons 2HI(g)$

   c $[Co(H_2O)_6]^{2+}(aq) + 4Cl^-(aq) \rightleftharpoons [CoCl_4]^{2-}(aq) + 6H_2O(l)$

2   The equilibrium expression for a reaction is as follows:

$$K = \frac{[CO][H_2]^3}{[CH_4][H_2O]}$$

   Deduce the balanced chemical equation for this reaction.

3   Give equilibrium expressions for the following reactions and determine the relationships between their values:

   Equation 1: $CO(g) + 2H_2(g) \rightleftharpoons CH_3OH(g)$

   Equation 2: $CH_3OH(g) \rightleftharpoons CO(g) + 2H_2(g)$

4   The equilibrium constant for the following reaction has a value of 25 at a temperature of 298 K:

   $2NO + Cl_2 \rightleftharpoons 2NOCl$

   Calculate the value of the equilibrium constant for the following reaction:

   $2NOCl \rightleftharpoons 2NO + Cl_2$

5   The equilibrium constant for the reaction $N_2 + 3H_2 \rightleftharpoons 2NH_3$ has a value of 7.76×10^{-5} at 700 K. What does this value suggest about the position of the equilibrium at this temperature?

6   Which of the following changes affect the value of an equilibrium constant?

   a   increasing the pressure

   b   increasing the temperature

   c   increasing the concentrations of reactants

   d   increasing the concentrations of products

   e   adding a catalyst

7   The equilibrium constant for the following reaction

   $C_2H_4(g) + H_2O(g) \rightleftharpoons C_2H_5OH(g)$ $\Delta H = -45$ kJ mol^{-1}

   is $K = \dfrac{[C_2H_5OH]}{[C_2H_4][H_2O]}$

   In terms of the effect of the equilibrium constant, describe the effect of the following changes on the position of equilibrium:

   a   removing ethanol, C_2H_5OH, from the mixture as it is formed

   b   increasing the temperature

> **TIP**
>
> The answers for question 7 here differ from those for Exercise 18.2 question 6 as, this time, the reason for the change in the position of equilibrium focuses on the equilibrium constant.

> **TIP**
>
> A useful way of phrasing the answers for question 7 would be to refer to the top and bottom of the K expression, such as by saying, "K is/ is not affected by…, so if the value of … on the top/bottom of the K expression increases/decreases, then the equilibrium position must move to the left/right in order to increase/ decrease the values on the bottom/top of the expression."

c   increasing the pressure of the system

d   using a catalyst.

Exercise 18.4 Calculations involving equilibrium constants

K calculations involve the concentrations of different species present at equilibrium. Although concentration is not a term commonly associated with gaseous reactions, it is frequently used for these types of calculations. In this exercise, you will practise equilibrium calculations.

1   An equilibrium mixture at 298 K was found to have a concentration of 0.250 mol dm^{-3} aqueous ammonia, 2.11×10^{-3} mol dm^{-3} hydroxide ions and 2.11×10^{-3} mol dm^{-3} ammonium ions.

$NH_3(aq) + H_2O(l) \rightleftharpoons NH_4^+(aq) + OH^-(aq)$

   a   Write an expression for the equilibrium constant for this reaction.

   b   Calculate the value of the equilibrium constant at this temperature for the reaction.

2   A sealed flask of volume 3 dm^3 at temperature T at equilibrium was found to contain 1 mol of PCl_3, 2 mol of PCl_5 and 1.5 mol of Cl_2.

The equation for the reaction is as follows:

$PCl_3(g) + Cl_2(g) \rightleftharpoons PCl_5(g)$

   a   Write an expression for the equilibrium constant for this reaction.

   b   Calculate the concentrations of the three gases at equilibrium in mol dm^{-3}.

   c   Calculate the equilibrium constant at this temperature.

3   1 mol of nitrogen was mixed with 4 mol of hydrogen in a sealed vessel of volume 2 dm^3 at a fixed temperature and allowed to reach equilibrium.

The equation for the reaction is as follows:

$N_2(g) + 3H_2(g) \rightleftharpoons 2NH_3(g)$

Once established, it was found that the mixture contained only 2.2 mol of hydrogen.

   a   Write an expression for the equilibrium constant for this reaction.

   b   Deduce the amount of hydrogen that has been used in this reaction.

   c   Deduce the amount of nitrogen used, and hence, the amount of nitrogen remaining at equilibrium.

   d   Deduce the amount of ammonia formed.

> **TIP**
>
> Question 4 is very similar to question 3 but has not been structured. Follow a similar sequence of steps to determine the value of the equilibrium constant.

e   Deduce the equilibrium concentrations of nitrogen, hydrogen and ammonia in mol dm^{-3}.

f   Use the answers for part **e** to calculate the value of the equilibrium constant.

4   A solution containing 0.050 mol of Fe^{3+} was added to an equal volume of a solution containing 0.030 mol of SCN^- ions. On mixing, a blood-red solution of $[FeSCN]^{2+}$ was formed according to the following equation:

$$Fe^{3+}(aq) + SCN^-(aq) \rightleftharpoons [FeSCN]^{2+}(aq)$$

At equilibrium, the mixture contained 0.020 mol of $[FeSCN]^{2+}$ ions. The total volume of the mixture was 0.50 dm^3. Calculate the equilibrium constant for the reaction.

5   A mixture of 0.01 mol of ester and 0.01 mol of water was allowed to reach equilibrium at room temperature according to the following equation:

$$ester(l) + water(l) \rightleftharpoons carboxylic\ acid(l) + alcohol(l)$$

Given that the equilibrium constant for this reaction is 0.25 at room temperature, deduce the composition of the equilibrium mixture.

6   A mixture of phosphorus(III) chloride, phosphorus(V) chloride and chlorine in a sealed flask with a total volume of 2 dm^3 was analysed and found to contain 1.2 mol of PCl_3, 2.5 mol of PCl_5 and 0.2 mol of Cl_2.

The equation for the reaction is as follows:

$$PCl_3(g) + Cl_2(g) \rightleftharpoons PCl_5(g)$$

a   Calculate the **reaction quotient** for this mixture.

b   Given that K for the reaction at 298 K is 5.5×10^6, how will the composition of the mixture change if it is left to stand at the same temperature?

7   A reversible reaction has a reaction quotient of 0.258 at a given temperature. The mixture was allowed to reach equilibrium, and it was found that the equilibrium constant was 0.123. Predict the difference in the composition of the mixture before and after the equilibrium position was established.

Exercise 18.5 Relationship between equilibrium constants and Gibbs energy

In this exercise, you will examine the relationship between the spontaneity of a reaction, ΔG (met in Chapter 15) and the equilibrium constant. In question **1** you will explore the value of G during a reaction. Although this is not specifically mentioned in the syllabus, an appreciation of this can be helpful. In questions **2** and **3** you will practise applying this understanding.

> **TIP**
>
> Remember to find the equilibrium amounts and then calculate the equilibrium concentrations. Do not use equilibrium amounts in the K expression.

> **TIP**
>
> Question 5 is very similar to question 4 but is much more challenging. Imagine the amount of ester reacting is x, so the amount remaining at equilibrium is $0.01 - x$. Then follow a similar sequence of steps to question 4.

1   Figure **18.2** shows how the value of the Gibbs energy varies as the composition of an equilibrium mixture varies.

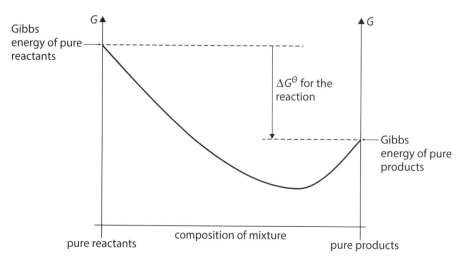

Figure 18.2: Variation in the Gibbs energy for a reaction.

a   Mark on the *x*-axis of the graph the point where the reaction is at equilibrium.

b   What is the sign of ΔG for the reaction when the composition changes from pure reactants to that of the equilibrium mixture?

c   What is the sign of ΔG for the reaction when the composition changes from pure products to that of the equilibrium mixture?

d   What do the signs of ΔG in the answers to parts **c** and **d** tell us about the spontaneity of both the forward and backward reactions?

2   Calculate $\Delta G^{\ominus}$ given the following values of K and comment on the position of equilibrium in each case.

a $K = 4.56$ at a temperature of 298 K.

b $K = 1.25 \times 10^{-4}$ at a temperature of 100 °C.

3   Calculate the equilibrium constant for the following values of $\Delta G^{\ominus}$ and comment on the position of equilibrium in each case.

a $\Delta G^{\ominus} = 7.5$ kJ mol^{-1} at a temperature of 500 K.

b $\Delta G^{\ominus} = -20.0$ kJ mol^{-1} at a temperature of 25 °C.

> TIP
>
> As the unit of *R* is J K^{-1} mol^{-1}, the unit of $\Delta G^{\ominus}$ will be J mol^{-1} and not kJ mol^{-1}.

EXAM-STYLE QUESTIONS

1 Which of the following statements about dynamic equilibrium is **true**?

A The forward and backward reactions have both stopped.

B The rate of both the forward and backward reactions is zero.

C The rate of both the forward and backward reactions is the same.

D The concentrations of the reactants and of the products are always the same.

2 Which of the following systems can reach a state of dynamic equilibrium?

A an open container of water

B a closed container of water

C an open container of a saturated solution of sodium chloride

D a closed container of sodium chloride crystals

3 Consider the endothermic reaction $2HI(g) \rightleftharpoons H_2(g) + I_2(g)$

Which option (**A, B, C** or **D**) in Table **18.1** describes the effect of increasing the temperature on the amount of hydrogen iodide, the position of equilibrium and on the value of the equilibrium constant?

	Amount of HI(g)	Position of equilibrium	Equilibrium constant
A	increases	shifts to the left	decreases
B	decreases	shifts to the right	stays the same
C	increases	stays the same	increases
D	decreases	shifts to the right	increases

Table 18.1

4 Which is the correct equilibrium expression for the following reaction:

$4NH_3(g) + 5O_2(g) \rightleftharpoons 4NO(g) + 6H_2O(g)$

A $\dfrac{[NO]^4 \times [H_2O]^6}{[NH_3]^4 \times [O_2]^5}$

B $\dfrac{[NO]^4 \times [H_2O]^6}{[NH_3]^4 \times [O_2]^5}$

C $\dfrac{4[NO] \times 6[H_2O]}{4[NH_3] \times 5[O_2]}$

D $\dfrac{[NH_3]^4 \times [O_2]^5}{[NO]^4 \times [H_2O]^6}$

CONTINUED

5 The value of the equilibrium constant for the following reaction is 4.00 at 100 °C:

$2A(aq) + B(aq) \rightleftharpoons 2C(aq) + 2D(aq)$

Deduce the value of the equilibrium constant for the following reaction at the same temperature:

$2C(aq) + 2D(aq) \rightleftharpoons 2A(aq) + B(aq)$

A 2.00

B 16.00

C 0.25

D 0.50

6 Consider the reaction $SO_3(g) + NO(g) \rightleftharpoons SO_2(g) + NO_2(g)$.

Which of the following mixtures would not reach a state of dynamic equilibrium?

A a mixture of 1 mol of SO_3 with 1 mol of $NO(g)$

B a mixture of 1 mol of SO_3 with 1 mol of $NO_2(g)$

C a mixture of 1 mol of SO_3 with 2 mol of $NO(g)$ and 1 mol of $NO_2(g)$

D a mixture of 1 mol of SO_2 with 1 mol of $NO_2(g)$

7 A mixture was found to contain 2.00 mol dm^{-3} of substance A, 1.00 mol dm^{-3} of substance B and 2.00 mol dm^{-3} of substance C at a temperature of 50 °C. If the equation for the reaction is $2A + B \rightleftharpoons C$, and its equilibrium constant is 2.0, then which statement is **true**?

A The reaction is at equilibrium.

B The reaction is not at equilibrium and will proceed to the left.

C The reaction is not at equilibrium and will proceed to the right.

D The reaction cannot reach equilibrium.

8 100 cm^3 of a solution in a state of dynamic equilibrium were found to contain a mixture of 5 mol of A, 2 mol of B and 5 mol of C.

The equation for the reaction is $A(aq) + 2B(aq) \rightleftharpoons 3C(aq)$. Calculate the equilibrium constant for the reaction.

A 6.25

B 31.25

C 12.5

D 1.25

9 The equilibrium constant at a fixed temperature for the following reaction is 1.25:

$NO(g) + NO_2(g) \rightleftharpoons N_2O_3(g)$

Which statement correctly describes a mixture with a composition of 1 mol dm^{-3} of NO, 1.5 mol dm^3 NO_2 and 2 mol dm^{-3} of N_2O_3?

A $Q = 0.8$ and the system is not at equilibrium.

B $Q = 1.33$ and the system is at equilibrium.

C $Q = 0.75$ and the system is at equilibrium.

D $Q = 1.33$ and the system is not at equilibrium.

CONTINUED

10 The reaction between carbon monoxide and hydrogen to produce methanol has a free energy change of +8.82 kJ mol^{-1} at 298 K. The equation for the reaction is as follows:

$CO(g) + 2H_2(g) \rightleftharpoons CH_3OH(g)$

What information can be deduced from this free energy value?

A K must be negative as ΔG is positive.

B K must be positive because ΔG is positive.

C $K > 1$ and the position of equilibrium lies to the right.

D $K < 1$ and the position of equilibrium lies to the left.

11 Chlorine reacts with water to form a mixture of hydrochloric and chloric(I) acids according to the following equation:

$Cl_2(aq) + H_2O(l) \rightleftharpoons HCl(aq) + HClO(aq)$

a Deduce an expression for the equilibrium constant for this reaction. [1]

b Determine the effect on both the position of the equilibrium and on the value of the equilibrium constant if additional chlorine gas was dissolved in the mixture. [2]

c Explain the effect of adding alkali to the mixture. [3]

12 A sealed flask containing a volatile liquid and its vapour are in a state of dynamic equilibrium. The temperature of the flask is increased by a few degrees. Describe the change to the composition of the flask at the new temperature and explain your answer. [3]

13 The production of sulfur(VI) oxide is one stage in the industrial manufacture of sulfuric acid by the Contact process. The reaction is catalysed by vanadium(V) oxide. The equation for the reaction is as follows:

$2SO_2(g) + O_2(g) \rightleftharpoons 2SO_3(g)$

a Deduce an expression for the equilibrium constant, K, for this reaction. [1]

b Describe the effect of the catalyst on the position of the equilibrium and on the value of K. [2]

c State the effect of increasing the temperature and increasing the pressure on the position of this equilibrium and on the value of the equilibrium constant. [4]

14 A mixture of 3.5 mol of TiCl$_4$ and 2.5 mol of TiCl$_2$ was allowed to react in a vessel of volume 2 dm^3. At equilibrium, it was found that the mixture contained 1.4 mol of TiCl$_3$.

The equation for the reaction is as follows:

$TiCl_2(g) + TiCl_4(g) \rightleftharpoons 2TiCl_3(s)$

Calculate the equilibrium constant for this reaction. [5]

Unit 6

Mechanisms of chemical change

> Chapter 19

Proton transfer reactions

CHAPTER OUTLINE

In this chapter you will:

- understand that acids react with bases in neutralisation reactions
- understand the Brønsted–Lowry definition of acids and bases
- understand what pH is and calculate pH and [H$^+$(aq)]
- understand that water dissociates and relate [H$^+$(aq)] and [OH$^-$(aq)] to acidity and basicity
- distinguish between strong and weak acids and bases
- understand the shape of a pH curve for a strong acid–strong base titration.

> understand what pOH is and use it in calculations

> understand the connection between the values of K_a, K_b, pK_a and pK_b and the strengths of acids and bases

> solve problems using K_a, K_b, pK_a and pK_b

> understand the connection between K_a and K_b for a conjugate acid–base pair

> predict the pH of a salt solution

> sketch and explain pH curves

> understand how acid–base indicators work and predict a suitable indicator for a titration

> understand what a buffer solution is and explain how they work

> solve problems involving buffer solutions.

KEY TERMS

Make sure you understand the following key terms before you do the exercises.

neutralisation reaction: a chemical reaction in which an acid reacts with a base/alkali to form a salt plus water. Neutralisation reactions are exothermic

salt: a compound formed when the hydrogen ion (H$^+$) in an acid is replaced by a metal ion (or ammonium ion)

CONTINUED

Brønsted–Lowry acid: a proton (H⁺) donor

Brønsted–Lowry base: a proton (H⁺) acceptor

conjugate acid–base pair: two species that differ by one proton (H⁺); when an acid donates a proton, it forms the conjugate base (CH_3COO^- is the conjugate base of CH_3COOH); when a base gains a proton, it forms the conjugate acid (H_3O^+ is the conjugate acid of H_2O)

amphiprotic: a substance that can donate a proton (acting as a Brønsted–Lowry acid) and accept a proton (acting as a Brønsted–Lowry base), e.g. HCO_3^-

pH: a measure of the concentration of H⁺ ions in an aqueous solution; it can be defined as the negative logarithm to base ten of the hydrogen ion concentration in aqueous solution

$$pH = -\log_{10}[H^+(aq)]$$

strong acid: an acid, such as HCl, H_2SO_4, HNO_3, that dissociates completely in aqueous solution

$$HCl(aq) \rightarrow H^+(aq) + Cl^-(aq)$$

strong base: a base that ionises completely in aqueous solution; strong bases are the Group 1 hydroxides (LiOH, NaOH, etc.) and $Ba(OH)_2$

weak acid: an acid, such as a carboxylic acid (ethanoic acid, propanoic acid, etc.) or carbonic acid (H_2CO_3), that dissociates only partially in aqueous solution

$$CH_3COOH(aq) \rightleftharpoons H^+(aq) + CH_3COO^-(aq)$$

weak base: a base that ionises only partially in aqueous solution, e.g. ammonia and amines

$$NH_3(aq) + H_2O(l) \rightleftharpoons NH_4^+(aq) + OH^-(aq)$$

pOH: a measure of the concentration of hydroxide ions in an aqueous solution

acid dissociation constant (K_a): equilibrium constant for the dissociation of a weak acid. In general, for the dissociation of acid HA, $HA(aq) \rightleftharpoons H^+(aq) + A^-(aq)$, the expression for the acid dissociation constant is

$$K_a = \frac{[A^-(aq)][H^+(aq)]}{[HA(aq)]}$$

the higher the value of K_a, the stronger the acid

base ionisation constant (K_b): equilibrium constant for the ionisation of a weak base, B, which ionises according to the equation:

$$B(aq) + H_2O(l) \rightleftharpoons BH^+(aq) + OH^-(aq)$$

$$K_b = \frac{[BH^+(aq)][OH^-(aq)]}{[B(aq)]}$$

the higher the value of K_b, the stronger the base

CONTINUED

salt hydrolysis: the reaction of the conjugate base of a weak acid or the conjugate acid of a weak base with water

pH range of an indicator: the pH range over which intermediate colours for an indicator can be seen because comparable amounts of the un-ionised and ionised forms are present

buffer solution: a solution that resists changes in pH when small amounts of acid or alkali are added

ion product constant for water (K_w): an equilibrium constant for the dissociation of water:

$K_w = [H^+(aq)][OH^-(aq)]$

K_w has a value of 1.0×10^{-14} at 25 °C. The ion product constant is also known as the ionic product constant

KEY EQUATIONS

$pH = -\log_{10}[H^+]$
$K_w = [H^+][OH^-]$
$pOH = -\log_{10}[OH^-]$
$K_a \times K_b = K_w$
$pK_a + pK_b = K_w$
Acid dissociation constant (K_a)
For a weak acid, HA, dissociating according to the equation:
$HA(aq) \rightleftharpoons H^+(aq) + A^-(aq)$
$K_a = \dfrac{[H^+][A^-]}{[HA]}$
$pK_a = -\log_{10}K_a$
Base ionisation constant (K_b)
For a base, B, which ionises according to the equation:
$B(aq) + H_2O(l) \rightleftharpoons BH^+(aq) + OH^-(aq)$
then $K_b = \dfrac{[BH^+][OH^-]}{[B]}$
and $pK_b = -\log_{10}K_b$
Henderson–Hasselbalch equation
$pH = pK_a + \log_{10}\dfrac{[salt]}{[acid]}$

Exercise 19.1 Acids, bases and salts, and Exercise 19.2 Reactions of acids

Substances have been classified as acids or **bases** from long before their chemistry was understood. In this exercise, you will look at some examples of both acids and bases and the equations for their reactions with each other, known as **neutralisation reactions**.

TIP

Try to learn the formulas of the most commonly met acids and bases.
The **strong acids** that you need to know are HCl, HNO_3 and H_2SO_4.
The **strong bases** are the Group 1 hydroxides.
Weak acids include all organic acids.
The **weak bases** are ammonia, simple amines, soluble carbonates and hydrogencarbonates, which are those of the Group 1 elements and ammonium carbonate/ hydrogencarbonate.

1   Complete Table **19.1** for the following common laboratory chemicals and identify whether they are acids or bases.

Name	Formula	Acid or base?
hydrochloric acid		
barium hydroxide		
	K_2CO_3	
ammonia		
ethylamine		
	H_2SO_4	
	HNO_3	
magnesium oxide		
	CH_3COOH	
carbonic acid		
potassium hydrogencarbonate		

Table 19.1: Common laboratory acids and bases.

2   All alkalis are bases, but not all bases are alkalis. What is the difference between a base and an alkali?

3   Table **19.2** shows the names of some acids and their **salts**. Complete the table.

Name of acid	Formula of acid	Name of salt	Formula of the anion in the salt
nitric acid			NO_3^-
phosphoric acid			PO_4^{3-}
	C_6H_5COOH		
		sulfate	SO_4^{2-}
hydrochloric acid			

Table 19.2: Acids and their salts.

4 What is the name of the salt formed by the reaction of the following bases with hydrochloric acid?

    a ammonia

    b propylamine

    c phenylamine

5 Write balanced equations for the following neutralisation reactions and name the salts formed:

    a magnesium hydroxide and nitric acid

    b copper(II) carbonate and sulfuric acid

    c sodium hydrogencarbonate and ethanoic acid.

6 Identify the parent acid and base that could be used to prepare the following salts:

    a calcium sulfate

    b ammonium chloride

    c barium propanoate.

TIP

Remember the following general equations:

acid + base or alkali → salt + water

acid + carbonate/hydrogen carbonate → salt + water + carbon dioxide

---

7 Give the ionic equation for a neutralisation reaction.

8 Acids also react with some metals to form a salt.

    a What is the other product formed during the reaction between an acid and a metal?

    b What type of reaction is this?

TIP

It is not a neutralisation reaction.

Exercise 19.3 Brønsted–Lowry acids and bases

The Brønsted–Lowry acid–base reactions involve the transfer of a hydrogen ion between species. In this exercise, you will begin by practising identifying **conjugate acid–base pairs**.

1 Deduce the conjugate acid–base pairs for the species in Table **19.3**.

	Conjugate acid	Conjugate base
a	$HClO_4$	
b	H_2SO_4	
c	HCl	
d	HNO_3	
e		NO_2^-
f	H_2S	
g		SO_3^{2-}
h		HPO_4^{2-}
i	HCN	
j		NH_3
k	H_2CO_3	
l	HCO_3^-	
m		PO_4^{3-}
n		OH^-
o	NH_3	

Table 19.3: Conjugate acid–base pairs.

2 Identify the acid–base conjugate pairs in the following equations:

a $H_2SO_4(aq) + HNO_3(aq) \rightarrow H_2NO_3^+(aq) + HSO_4^-(aq)$

b $NH_3(aq) + H_2O(l) \rightarrow NH_4^+(aq) + OH^-(aq)$

c $HSO_4^-(aq) + H_2O(l) \rightarrow H_3O^+(aq) + SO_4^{2-}(aq)$

d $H_2PO_4^-(aq) + HCO_3^-(aq) \rightarrow HPO_4^{2-}(aq) + H_2CO_3(aq)$

3 Table **19.3** includes several **amphiprotic** species, such as the HSO_4^- ion.

a Write an equation to show this ion acting as an acid.

b Write an equation to show this ion acting as a base.

Exercise 19.4 pH

The 'p' in **pH** is a mathematical term meaning $-\log_{10}$; the 'H' refers to hydrogen ions. In this exercise, you will practise using your calculator correctly to calculate pH. Make sure that you practise with the same calculator that you will use in the final exams.

1 A solution of hydrochloric acid is diluted by a factor of 100. Determine the change in its pH.

> **TIP**
>
> The pairs are always made up of substances from different sides of the equation.

> **TIP**
>
> pH is a log (base 10) scale. This means that one pH unit represents a ten-fold change in the hydrogen ion concentration.

2 Calculate the pH of the following solutions:

a $[H^+] = 0.25$ mol dm^{-3}

b $[H^+] = 0.025$ mol dm^{-3}

c $[H^+] = 1.56 \times 10^{-2}$ mol dm^{-3}

d $[H^+] = 2.0$ mol dm^{-3}

3 What is the hydrogen ion concentration of solutions with the following pH?

a pH = 2.0

b pH = 4.5

c pH = 7.0

d pH = 10.2

> **TIP**
>
> Always give pH values to two decimal places.

> **TIP**
>
> You need to be able to get this conversion from pH to $[H^+]$ the correct way around. $[H^+] = 10^{-pH}$.

Exercise 19.5 Strong and weak acids and bases

The pH scale is not a measure of the strength of an acid. pH is a measure of the concentration of hydrogen ions in a solution. In this exercise, you will look at the meaning of strong and weak acids and bases.

1 Give an equation to show that nitric acid is a strong acid.

2 Give an equation to show that ethanoic acid is a weak acid.

3 Give an equation to show how ammonia acts as a weak base.

4 Explain why a weak acid has a higher pH than a strong acid of the same concentration.

5 If the pH of a strong base and a weak base are equal, what can be deduced about the concentrations of the two solutions?

6 Describe the differences in the observations for a strong and a weak acid of the same concentration in the following experiments:

a A short length of magnesium ribbon is added to a small volume of each acid in separate test tubes.

b The pH of each acid was tested with universal indicator solution.

c The conductivity of a sample of each acid is determined using a conductivity meter.

7 Benzoic acid is a weak monoprotic acid with the formula C_6H_5COOH. The equation for its dissociation is as follows:

$$C_6H_5COOH \rightleftharpoons C_6H_5COO^- + H^+$$

> **TIP**
>
> A weak base is a proton acceptor.

> **TIP**
>
> The key word is 'observations': what would you see?

a Suggest whether the position of this equilibrium lies to the left or to the right.

b Write an equation to show the conjugate base of benzoic acid acting as a base, and suggest whether the position of the equilibrium lies to the left or to the right.

c Describe the relationship between the relative strength of an acid–base conjugate pair.

Exercise 19.6 The dissociation of water

The **Brønsted–Lowry definition of acids and bases** applies in aqueous solutions. In this exercise, you will look at the dissociation of water into H^+ ions and OH^- ions and how pH value can be used to calculate the concentration of OH^- ions.

1 Give an equation to show the dissociation of water.

2 The pH of water at 25 °C is 7. Calculate the concentration of hydrogen ions in water at this temperature.

3 Given that K_w for water at 25 °C is 1.0×10^{-14}, and that $K_w = [H^+][OH^-]$, calculate $[OH^-]$ for the following solutions:

a a solution of NaOH with a concentration of 0.10 mol dm^{-3}

b a solution with $[H^+] = 4.65 \times 10^{-4}$ mol dm^{-3}

c a solution with a pH of 2.52

d a solution with a pH of 8.67.

4 K_w is dependent on temperature. At 85 °C, $K_w = 31.3 \times 10^{-14}$.

a Does this value for K_w suggest that water is more or less dissociated into its ions at higher temperatures?

b Calculate the pH of water at this temperature.

c Explain whether or not water is neutral at this temperature.

Exercise 19.7 Calculating pH values

In this exercise, you will practise pH calculations, including the pH of acids and bases that are not monoprotic.

1 Calculate the pH of the following strong acids:

a 0.15 mol dm^{-3} HCl

b 0.025 mol dm^{-3} H_2SO_4

c 0.075 mol dm^{-3} HNO_3

2 Calculate the concentration of the following strong acids:

a HNO_3 with a pH of 3.40

b HCl with a pH of 2.50

c H_2SO_4 with a pH of 1.50

3 Calculate the pH of the following strong bases:

    a   0.033 mol dm^{-3} NaOH

    b   0.125 mol dm^{-3} Ba(OH)$_2$

    c   1.54 × 10^{-2} mol dm^{-3} KOH

4 Calculate the concentration of the following strong bases:

    a   LiOH with a pH of 10.50

    b   NaOH with a pH of 13.10

    c   Ba(OH)$_2$ with a pH of 9.80

Exercise 19.8 Acid–base titrations

Titration works well as an analytical technique because there is a sharp change in pH at the end point rather than a gradual change as the acid and alkali react with each other. In this exercise, you will look at the shape of pH titration curves in more detail and how to calculate the pH at different points of a curve.

1 What is meant by the term *equivalence point*?

2 Sketch the shape of the curve that would be obtained if 50 cm^3 of 0.20 mol dm^{-3} HCl was added to 25 cm^3 of 0.10 mol dm^{-3} NaOH.

3 Calculate the pH when 25.0 cm^3 of 0.10 mol dm^{-3} of HNO$_3$ is added to 10.0 cm^3 of 0.20 mol dm^{-3} KOH by following this sequence of steps:

    a   Calculate the number of moles of H$^+$ used.

    b   Calculate the number of moles of OH$^-$ used.

    c   Identify whether H$^+$ or OH$^-$ is in excess and calculate the amount of excess remaining.

    d   Calculate the concentration of excess H$^+$ or OH$^-$ in the solution.

    e   Calculate the pH of the solution.

4 For each of the following, calculate the pH of the solution formed:

    a   15.0 cm^3 of 0.10 mol dm^{-3} KOH is added to 10.0 cm^3 of 0.25 mol dm^{-3} HNO$_3$

    b   10.0 cm^3 of 0.50 mol dm^{-3} NaOH is added to 25.0 cm^3 of 0.25 mol dm^{-3} HCl

    c   20.0 cm^3 of 0.10 mol dm^{-3} H$_2$SO$_4$ is added to 25.0 cm^3 of 0.25 mol dm^{-3} KOH

    d   10.0 cm^3 of 0.10 mol dm^{-3} Ba(OH)$_2$ (a strong base) is added to 15.0 cm^3 of 0.10 mol dm^{-3} HCl.

TIP

For question 2, you should consider:

- the initial pH (this can be calculated)

- the volume at equivalence (this can be calculated)

- the pH at the equivalence point (pH = 7 for strong acid/strong base titrations)

- the shape of the curve

- the final pH (this can be estimated as tending towards a calculated value).

TIP

In question 4a, note that the total volume of the solution is 35.0 cm^3.

TIP

In each case, follow the same sequence of steps as in question **3**. Note that H$_2$SO$_4$ is diprotic in part **c** and Ba(OH)$_2$ in part **d** is dibasic.

Exercise 19.9 pOH

The 'p' in pH means $-\log_{10}$. This mathematical notation can be used for other values as well as for the concentration of hydrogen ions. This exercise is about **pOH**, which is simply $-\log_{10}[OH^-]$, and pK_w, which is $\log_{10}K_w$. For all the questions in this exercise, assume the temperature is 25 °C.

1   Calculate the pOH and pH for the following solutions:

   a $[OH^-] = 0.010$ mol dm^{-3}

   b $[OH^-] = 0.42$ mol dm^{-3}

   c $[OH^-] = 1.40$ mol dm^{-3}

   d $[OH^-] = 3.2 \times 10^{-6}$ mol dm^{-3}

2   Calculate $[OH^-]$ and $[H^+]$ for the following solutions:

   a   pOH = 4.5

   b   pOH = 10.2

   c   pOH = 0.75

   d   pOH = 2.30

3   Calculate the pOH and pH of the following solutions:

   a   0.25 mol dm^{-3} Ba(OH)$_2$ (a strong base)

   b   0.45 mol dm^{-3} H$_2$SO$_4$

> **TIP**
>
> Remember that $K_w = 1 \times 10^{-14}$ at 25 °C. This value is given in the IB data book.

Exercise 19.10 Ionisation constants for acids and bases

Weak acids are only slightly dissociated in water. The **acid dissociation constant** for a weak acid, K_a, can be used as a measure of its relative strength, as it indicates the degree of dissociation. In this exercise, you will calculate pH for weak acids using their equilibrium constants. For all questions, assume the temperature is 25 °C.

1   Write the expression for K_a for the following weak acids:

   a   ethanoic acid, CH$_3$COOH

   b   benzoic acid, C$_6$H$_5$COOH

   c   propanoic acid, CH$_3$CH$_2$COOH.

2   The K_a value for ethanoic acid is 8.57×10^{-3} and for benzoic acid is 0.015. Which acid is the weaker?

3 Calculate the pK_a values for the following weak acids:

a $K_a = 8.57 \times 10^{-3}$

b $K_a = 3.78 \times 10^{-5}$

c $K_a = 1.75 \times 10^{-4}$

4 Calculate K_a for the following weak acids:

a $pK_a = 5.30$

b $pK_a = 4.98$

c $pK_a = 2.83$

5 The pK_a value for phenylethanoic acid is 4.31; butanoic acid has pK_a of 4.83. Which acid is stronger?

6 Calculate the pH of the following weak acids:

a 0.50 mol dm^{-3} phenol ($K_a = 4.59 \times 10^{-5}$)

b 0.010 mol dm^{-3} fluoroethanoic acid ($pK_a = 2.59$)

c 0.25 mol dm^{-3} nitric(III) acid, HNO_2, ($pK_a = 3.16$)

> **TIP**
>
> For a weak acid HA,
> $[H^+] = [A^-]$
>
> Therefore, $K_a = \dfrac{[H^+]^2}{[HA]}$

Exercise 19.11 The base ionisation constant, K_b

Like weak acids, weak bases are only slightly dissociated in water. The **base ionisation constant** (K_b) can be used as a measure of the relative strength of a base, as it indicates the degree of dissociation. In this exercise, you will calculate pH for weak bases using their equilibrium constants. For all questions, assume the temperature is 25 °C.

1 Write an equation to show the dissociation of the following weak bases and give the expressions for the base ionisation constant for each:

a NH_3

b $C_6H_5NH_2$

c CH_3NH_2

2 Calculate the following:

a pK_b if $K_b = 4.56 \times 10^{-5}$ mol dm^{-3}

b K_b if $pK_b = 6.3$

c pOH of a weak monobasic base with $[OH^-]$ of 0.0034 mol dm^{-3} and K_b of 3.50×10^{-3}

d pH of a weak monobasic base with $[OH^-]$ of 0.075 mol dm^{-3} and pK_b of 4.10.

> **TIP**
>
> For a weak base B,
> $[BH^+] = [OH^-]$
>
> Therefore, $K_a = \dfrac{[OH^-]^2}{[B]}$

3 Put the following weak bases in order of increasing strength:

ammonia, $K_b = 1.78 \times 10^{-5}$

phenylamine, $K_b = 7.41 \times 10^{-10}$

ethylamine, $pK_b = 3.35$

diethylamine, $pK_b = 3.16$

Exercise 19.12 The strength of an acid and its conjugate base

Conjugate acid–base pairs are related to each other by a hydrogen ion, H^+.
The value of the acid dissociation constant for a weak acid is, therefore, related to the base ionisation constant of its conjugate base.

1 At 25 °C, calculate the K_a of the following weak acids:

   a HCN if CN^- has a $K_b = 1.62 \times 10^{-5}$

   b $CH_3NH_3^+$ if the base ionisation constant of $CH_3NH_2 = 4.38 \times 10^{-4}$

   c benzoic acid if K_b of the benzoate ion = 1.58×10^{-10}

> **TIP**
>
> Remember:
> $K_a \times K_b = K_w$

2 At 25 °C, calculate the following:

   a pK_a of HOCl if pK_b of $OCl^- = 6.54$

   b pK_a of $HONH_3^+$ if pK_b of $HONH_2 = 7.96$

   c pK_a of HCO_3^- if pK_b of $CO_3^{2-} = 3.74$

> **TIP**
>
> Remember
> $pK_a + pK_b = 14$

3 Given that the K_b of $HPO_4^{2-} = 1.60 \times 10^{-7}$ at 25 °C, calculate the following:

   a the pK_a of its conjugate acid

   b the formula of its conjugate acid.

4 Given the following data:

HCOOH: $K_a = 1.8 \times 10^{-4}$

NH_4^+: $K_a = 5.6 \times 10^{-10}$

$HCOO^-$: $K_a = 4.79 \times 10^{-11}$

C_2H_5OH: $pK_a = 15.5$

$C_6H_5NH_3^+$: $pK_a = 4.87$

   a rank all the species given in order of their strength as acids

   b give the formula of their conjugate bases.

Exercise 19.13 The pH of salt solutions

When an acid and base react, the pH of the salt solution formed will mirror the stronger of its parent acid and base. The pH of these salts is due to the hydrolysis of the ion in the salt that comes from the weaker parent. This is known as **salt hydrolysis**. In this exercise, you will practise equations for these hydrolysis reactions and then predict the pH of the salts. The first two questions in this exercise are a reminder of the skills met at Standard Level.

1   Identify the names of the parent acid and parent base that could be used to make the following salts:

    a   lithium ethanoate

    b   ammonium chloride

    c   sodium sulfate.

2   Identify the following as strong or weak acids or bases:

    a HCl

    b HNO_3

    c $NaOH$

    d $Ba(OH)_2$

    e NH_4OH

    f H_2SO_4

    g CH_3COOH

    h CH_3NH_2

3   Give an equation for the reaction for the hydrolysis of each of the following ions:

    a CH_3COO^-

    b HCO_3^-

    c NH_3

    d CO_3^{2-}

4   In question **1**, you identified the parent acids and bases of the following salts. Suggest, with a reason, the pH of these salt solutions, listed again here:

    a   lithium ethanoate

    b   ammonium chloride

    c   sodium sulfate.

> **TIP**
>
> The best choice of parent base for ammonium salts and Group 1 and 2 salts are their hydroxides. Group 13 and transition metal salts are not included in this section of the syllabus.

> **TIP**
>
> Hydrolysis means the reaction with water.

5 The pH of a salt solution can be calculated from its concentration and the pK_a or pK_b value of its weak parent. Calculate the pH of the following solutions at 25 °C:

a 0.50 mol dm^{-3} CH_3CH_2COONa given that the pK_a of propanoic acid = 4.87

b 0.125 mol dm^{-3} $C_6H_5CH_2COOK$ given that the pK_a of $C_6H_5CH_2COOH$ = 4.31

c 0.050 mol dm^{-3} NH_4Cl given that the pK_b of ammonia = 4.75

d 0.040 mol dm^{-3} $CH_3NH_3NO_3$ given that the pK_b of methylamine = 3.34.

6 Using the $pK_{a/b}$ values given in Table **19.4**, suggest whether the pH of a 0.100 mol dm^{-3} solution of the following substances will be less than 7, around 7 or above 7:

a sodium nitrate(III)

b potassium chlorate(I)

c ammonium ethanoate

d phenylammonium ethanoate

e phenylammonium propanoate.

	pK_a	pK_b
chloric(I) acid	7.43	
nitrous acid (nitric(III) acid)	3.34	
ethanoic acid	4.76	
propanoic acid	4.87	
phenylamine		9.13
ammonia		4.75

Table 19.4: pK_a and pK_b values.

> **TIP**
>
> For salts of a weak acid, use $pK_a + pK_b = 14$ to find pK_b, then use $K_b = \dfrac{[OH^-]^2}{[B]}$ to find $[OH^-]$, and then use $pOH + pH = 14$ to find the pH. Similar steps can be used to find the pH of a weak base, starting by finding pK_a, then $[H^+]$, and finally pH.

Exercise 19.14 More pH curves

Exercise 19.8 looked at pH titration curves for the reaction of a strong acid with a strong base. In this exercise, you will investigate the pH titration curves of weak acids and bases. There will be differences in the start and end pH and the pH of the equivalence point, as well as in the shape of the curve for a weak acid/base compared to a strong acid/base of the same concentration.

1 The pH of the salt of a weak acid or base can be found from the pH at the equivalence point of a pH titration curve. Sketch the pH curve that would be produced during the following experiments:

a a total of 50 cm^3 of 0.100 mol dm^{-3} CH_3COOH added in small portions to 10 cm^3 of 0.200 mol dm^{-3} NaOH

b a total of 100 cm^3 of 0.250 mol dm^{-3} NH_3(aq) added in small portions to 50 cm^3 of 0.200 mol dm^{-3} HCl

> **TIP**
>
> When sketching pH curves, in addition to the general shape and the initial and final pH values, as met previously in Exercise 19.8 question **2**, you should also think about the length and the pH at the midpoint of the vertical section. Remember that this pH will mirror the strong parent. If the acid is stronger than the base, then the pH < 7 and vice versa.

c   a total of 75 cm³ of 0.100 mol dm⁻³ CH₃COOH are added in small portions to 25 cm³ of 0.200 mol dm⁻³ NH₃(aq).

2   Explain how the pK_a of a weak acid and the pK_b of a weak base can be deduced from a titration curve.

3   An indicator with a formula represented by HIn is red in acid solutions and yellow in alkaline solutions. Give an equation to show the dissociation of the indicator and clearly indicate which species is red and which is yellow.

4   Thymol blue is an acid–base indicator with a **pH range** of 8.0–9.6. It is yellow in acid solutions and blue in alkaline solutions. Suggest its pK_a value and explain whether or not it is suitable to use for a titration between HCl and NH₃.

TIP

Consider the expression

$$K_a = \frac{[H^+][A^-]}{[HA]}.$$

When $[A^-] = [HA]$, then pH = pK_a. This occurs when half of the HA has reacted to form A⁻ ions. This is known as the half-neutralisation point. Where will this be on a titration curve?

Exercise 19.15 Buffer solutions

Buffers are used in foods and cosmetics and occur naturally in many biological systems. **Buffer solutions** with pH < 7 are described as acidic buffers and those with pH > 7 as basic buffers. This exercise looks at what a buffer is and how it works.

1   Describe the composition of an acidic buffer solution.

2   Describe the composition of a basic buffer solution.

3   Suggest two alternative substances that could be added to a solution containing 0.100 mol of ethanoic acid in order to form a buffer solution.

4   Annotate the graphs in Figures **19.1** and **19.2** to show the 'buffer regions', justifying your choice.

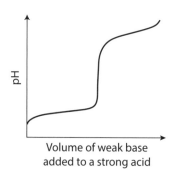

Figure 19.1: Buffer region for a strong acid/weak base titration.

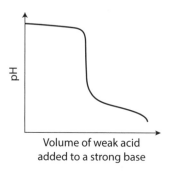

Figure 19.2: Buffer region of a weak acid/strong base titration.

5 Explain how an acidic buffer works.

TIP

Explain means to give a detailed account including reasons or causes. In some questions, there can be marks for describing as well as explaining, so it is always worth at least describing what happens even if you cannot explain it.

TIP

This question is quite common, so it is well worth practising how to explain how both acidic and basic buffers work during your revision. Remember to include an equation for the dissociation of the weak acid/base and that there are relatively large concentrations of both the weak acid and its conjugate base (or weak base and its conjugate acid).

6 Explain the effect of diluting a buffer on its effectiveness.

7 Calculate the pH of the following solutions:

a a buffer made from a mixture containing 0.125 mol dm^{-3} of CH_3COO^- and 0.252 mol dm^{-3} CH_3COOH ($pK_a = 4.76$)

b a buffer made when 0.350g of sodium ethanoate, $CH_3COO^-Na^+$, is dissolved in 100 cm^3 of 0.100 mol dm^{-3} CH_3COOH ($pK_a = 4.76$)

c a buffer made by mixing 100 cm^3 of 0.200 mol dm^{-3} CH_3COOH ($pK_a = 4.76$) with 30 cm^3 of 0.400 mol dm^{-3} NaOH.

TIP

You will first need to calculate the concentration of sodium ethanoate.

TIP

Ethanoic acid and sodium hydroxide react with each other.
You will need to do the following:

1 find the number of moles of each being used, and so, which is in excess

2 find the number of moles of excess in the mixture

3 find the number of moles of salt formed

4 using the results of steps 2 and 3, find the concentration of both the acid and the salt

5 finally, use the Henderson–Hasselbalch equation (given in the IB data book) to find the pH.

8 A buffer has a pH of 4.20 and was made by mixing 50 cm^3 of a weak acid with a pK_a of 3.98 and a concentration of 0.200 mol dm^{-3} with 50 cm^3 of its salt. Calculate the concentration of salt solution used.

9 A basic buffer was made by mixing 25 cm^3 of 0.100 mol dm^{-3} ammonia ($pK_b = 4.75$) with 40 cm^3 0.100 mol dm^{-3} ammonium chloride solution. Calculate the pH of the buffer solution at 25 °C.

TIP

[acid] $= 0.100$ mol dm^{-3} in the mixture, as it has been diluted to twice its original volume when it is mixed with the salt solution.

EXAM-STYLE QUESTIONS

1 Which of the following is the correct equation for the formation of magnesium ethanoate?

   A $Mg + CH_3COOH \rightarrow MgCH_3COOH + H_2$

   B $MgOH + CH_3COOH \rightarrow CH_3COOMg + H_2O$

   C $Mg(OH)_2 + C_2H_5OOH \rightarrow C_2H_5OOMg + H_2O$

   D $MgCO_3 + 2CH_3COOH \rightarrow (CH_3COO)_2Mg + H_2O + CO_2$

2 What is the name of the salt formed from the reaction of methylamine and hydrochloric acid?

   A methylammonium chlorate

   B methylammonium chloride

   C methylammonium hydrogenchloride

   D hydrochloric methylammonium salt

3 Which statement is **true** about BF_3?

   A It is a Lewis acid but not a Brønsted–Lowry acid.

   B It is both a Lewis acid and a Lewis base.

   C It is a Brønsted–Lowry acid and a Lewis acid.

   D It is a Brønsted–Lowry base and a Lewis base.

4 Identify the correct acid – base conjugate pairs in the following reaction:

$HCO_3^-(aq) + OH^-(aq) \rightleftharpoons CO_3^{2-}(aq) + H_2O(l)$

	Acid/its conjugate base	Base/its conjugate acid
A	CO_3^{2-}/OH^-	H_2O/HCO_3^-
B	HCO_3^-/CO_3^{2-}	OH^-/H_2O
C	H_2O/HCO_3^-	CO_3^{2-}/OH^-
D	OH^-/H_2O	HCO_3^-/CO_3^{2-}

5 Sufficient water was added to 25 cm^3 of a solution of hydrochloric acid with a pH of 1 to make a solution with a total volume of 2.50 dm^3. The solution was thoroughly mixed. What is the pH of the diluted solution?

   A 1.0

   B 2.0

   C 3.0

   D 4.0

6 Which of the following can be used to distinguish between a monoprotic strong acid and a monoprotic weak acid?

   I Measuring the conductivity of solutions of equal concentration.

   II Measuring the pH of solutions with equal concentration.

   III Measuring the volume of alkali required to neutralise equal amounts of acid.

   A I only

   B I and II only

   C II and III only

   D I, II and III

CONTINUED

7   The strengths of four bases are as follows:

ammonia: $K_b = 1.78 \times 10^{-5}$

aniline: $pK_b = 9.37$

pyridine: $pK_b = 8.71$

diethylamine: $K_b = 6.9 \times 10^{-4}$

Deduce the order of increasing base strength.

A   aniline < pyridine < diethylamine < ammonia

B   pyridine < ammonia < diethylamine < aniline

C   diethylamine < aniline < ammonia < pyridine

D   aniline < pyridine < ammonia < diethylamine

8   Which of the following mixtures would act as a buffer solution?

A   25 cm³ of 0.100 mol dm⁻³ NaOH and 25 cm³ of 0.200 mol dm⁻³ propanoic acid

B   25 cm³ of 0.100 mol dm⁻³ ammonia solution and 25 cm³ of 0.200 mol dm⁻³ propanoic acid

C   100 cm³ of 0.200 mol dm⁻³ sodium ethanoate with 50 cm³ of 0.200 mol dm⁻³ sodium hydroxide

D   50 cm³ of 1.00 mol dm⁻³ ammonia and 50 cm³ of 1.00 mol dm⁻³ hydrochloric acid

9   Which of the following procedures could have produced this curve?

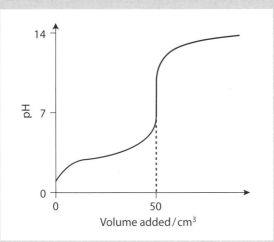

A   100 cm³ of 0.100 mol dm⁻³ NaOH added to 25 cm³ 0.100 mol dm⁻³ HCl

B   50 cm³ of 0.100 mol dm⁻³ HCl added to 25 cm³ 0.100 mol dm⁻³ NH₃ solution

C   100 cm³ of 0.100 mol dm⁻³ NaOH added to 25 cm³ 0.200 mol dm⁻³ CH₃COOH

D   50 cm³ of 0.100 mol dm⁻³ HNO₃ added to 25 cm³ 0.200 mol dm⁻³ CH₃CH₂COOH

10 Which of the following salts will dissolve in water to form a solution with a pH greater than seven?

A   KCl

B   NH₄NO₃

C   CH₃COONa

D   CH₃NH₃Cl

11 When chlorine 'dissolves' in water, it actually forms a mixture of hydrochloric acid and chloric(I) acid. The formula for chloric(I) acid is HClO.

   a Construct an equation for this reaction. [1]

   b Hydrochloric acid is a strong acid, whereas chloric(I) acid is a weak acid.

   i Explain what is meant by the terms *strong acid* and *weak acid*. [2]

   ii Describe three simple laboratory experiments that could be used to distinguish between solutions of equal concentration of a strong and a weak acid. Include the expected observations in your answer. [6]

   c Give equations to represent the dissociation of hydrochloric acid and chloric(I) acid into their ions, and identify the conjugate base of both acids. [3]

   d pH is a measure of the concentration of hydrogen ions in an aqueous solution. Explain why it would be incorrect to define it as describing the strength of an acid. [1]

12 Barium hydroxide is a strong base with the formula $Ba(OH)_2$.

   a Comment on how the pH of a 0.500 mol dm^{-3} solution of barium hydroxide would compare to that of a solution of 0.500 mol dm^{-3} potassium hydroxide. [2]

   b Calculate the pH of a 0.500 mol dm^{-3} solution of barium hydroxide at 25 °C given that K_w at this temperature = 1×10^{-14} [2]

   c Sketch the pH curve that would be produced if hydrochloric acid solution with a concentration of 0.100 mol dm^{-3} was added to 20 cm^3 of 0.050 mol dm^{-3} potassium hydroxide solution. [3]

13 Figure 19.3 shows how the ion product constant of water (K_w) varies with temperature.

Figure 19.3: Ion product constant of water at different temperatures.

   a Write an equation for the ionisation of water. [1]

   b Write an expression for K_w and use the graph to explain whether the ionisation of water is endothermic or exothermic. [2]

   c Use the graph to find the pH of water at 87 °C. [2]

   d The pH of water at 25 °C is 7. Explain whether water is only neutral at this temperature. [1]

CONTINUED

14 2-Methylpropanoic acid ($CH_3CH(CH_3)COOH$) is a weak acid with a pK_a value of 4.84.

   a Calculate the pH of a 0.200 mol dm^{-3} solution of 2-methylpropanoic acid. [3]

   b **i** 25.0 cm^3 of the 0.200 mol dm^{-3} 2-methylpropanoic acid solution is titrated with 0.150 mol dm^{-3} of sodium hydroxide solution. Identify a suitable indicator for the titration from the table of acid–base indicators in the IB data book and justify your choice. [2]

     ii At the equivalence point, the solution contains $CH_3CH(CH_3)COO^-$ with a concentration of 0.100 mol dm^{-3}. Calculate the pH of the salt solution. [3]

15 The strengths of two acids with formulas represented as HX and HY were compared by measuring the pH of solutions of concentration of 0.100 mol dm^{-3} at 25 °C. Acid HX was found to have a pH of 4.51 and acid HY had a pH of 5.78.

   a Calculate the value of K_a for the two acids. [3]

   b Write an equation for the dissociation of the stronger of the two acids and identify its conjugate base. [2]

   c Deduce the relative strength of the conjugate bases of both HX and HY. [1]

   d The sodium salt of acid HY has the formula NaY.

     i Give an equation for the reaction of Y^- ions with water and explain why Y^- ions are acting as a base. [2]

     ii Using the information given about HY above, calculate the pK_b for the Y^- ion. [2]

     iii Calculate the pH of a 0.050 mol dm^{-3} solution of NaY. [3]

16 Ethylamine is a weak base with the formula $C_2H_5NH_2$. It dissociates in water according to the following equation:

$$C_2H_5NH_2 + H_2O \rightleftharpoons C_2H_5NH_3^+ + OH^-$$

When mixed with its salt, for example, with ethylammonium chloride, a basic buffer solution is formed.

   a State what is meant by a buffer solution. [2]

   b Explain, with reference to the dissociation equation given, how a basic buffer solution works. [5]

Chapter 20

Electron transfer reactions

CHAPTER OUTLINE

In this chapter you will:

- understand redox reactions in terms of electron transfer and changes in oxidation state

- write half-equations for oxidation and reduction reactions

- construct equations for redox reactions

- understand the reactions that occur in a voltaic cell

- understand how rechargeable batteries work

- understand electrolysis of molten salts

- describe the oxidation of alcohols and aldehydes

- describe the reduction of aldehydes, ketones and carboxylic acids

- describe the reduction of unsaturated compounds.

> understand what a standard electrode potential is

> use standard electrode potentials to calculate cell potentials

> understand the connection between the standard Gibbs energy change and standard electrode potentials

> solve problems involving $\Delta G^{\ominus}$ and $E^{\ominus}$

> understand the reactions that occur when aqueous solutions are electrolysed

> understand how electroplating works.

KEY TERMS

Make sure you understand the following key terms before you do the exercises.

redox reaction: a reaction involving both oxidation and reduction; if one species is oxidised, another species must be reduced

half-equation: a balanced equation that shows only the oxidation half or the reduction half of a redox reaction

CONTINUED

activity series: a list of metals, carbon and hydrogen in order of how easily they are oxidised to form positive ions

electrochemical cell: a device that interconverts chemical energy and electrical energy

voltaic cell: an electrochemical cell that converts chemical energy into electrical energy

electrolytic cell: an electrochemical cell that converts electrical energy into chemical energy

salt bridge: completes the circuit in a voltaic cell by providing an electrical connection between two half-cells, allowing ions to flow into or out of the half-cells to balance out the charges in the half-cells. The salt bridge contains a concentrated solution of an ionic salt, such as KCl

electrolysis: the breaking down of a substance (in molten state or solution) by the passage of electricity through it

secondary cell: a cell (battery) that can be recharged using mains electricity and is often called a rechargeable battery. The chemical reactions in a rechargeable battery are reversible and can be reversed by connecting them to an electricity supply

standard electrode potential: the electromotive force (voltage) of a half-cell connected to a standard hydrogen electrode, measured under standard conditions; all solutions must be of concentration 1 mol dm^{-3} and pressure 100 kPa. A standard electrode potential is always quoted for the reduction reaction

standard hydrogen electrode: the standard half-cell relative to which standard electrode potentials are measured. Hydrogen gas at 100 kPa (1 bar) pressure is bubbled around a platinum electrode of very high surface area in a solution of H$^+$ ions of concentration 1 mol dm^{-3}

The reaction occurring in this half-cell is $2H^+(aq) + 2e^- \rightleftharpoons H_2(g)$

and this is assigned a standard electrode potential ($E^\ominus_{cell}$) of 0.00 V

standard cell potential: the electromotive force (voltage) produced when two half-cells are connected under standard conditions (all concentrations 1 mol dm^{-3} and pressure 100 kPa). This drives the movement of electrons through the external circuit from the negative electrode to the positive electrode

---

KEY EQUATIONS

$E^{\ominus}_{cell} = E^{\ominus}_{red} + E^{\ominus}_{ox}$

where

$E^{\ominus}_{cell}$ = standard cell potential

$E^{\ominus}_{red}$ and $E^{\ominus}_{ox}$ are the standard electrode potentials of the reduction and oxidation reactions.

$\Delta G^{\ominus} = -nFE^{\ominus}$ (given in the IB data book)

where

$\Delta G^{\ominus}$ = change in standard Gibbs free energy

$E^{\ominus}$ = standard cell potential

n = number of moles of electrons

F = Faraday's constant = 9.65×10^4 C mol^{-1} (given in the IB data book)

Exercise 20.1 Redox reactions

Oxidation numbers were first met in Chapter 10. In this exercise, you will begin by revisiting oxidation numbers. You will then use oxidation numbers to identify if a substance has been oxidised or reduced.

1 What is the oxidation number of each element in the following substances?

   a F_2

   b CO_2

   c   HCl

   d CH_4

   e KIO_3

   f C_2H_5OH

2 Complete **Table 20.1**.

   The first row has been filled in as an example.

Formula	Name
$CuSO_4$	copper(II) sulfate(VI)
	nitrogen(IV) oxide
VO_3^-	
	bromate(I) ion
CrO_4^{2-}	

Table 20.1: Names of common salts and ions.

> **TIP**
>
> Oxidation numbers are the charge on an element if it were imagined to be ionic. Oxidation numbers are always written as a charge (+/−) followed by a number.
> This is different from the charge on an ion, where the number is written first.

3　Determine the oxidation numbers of the substances in the following equations and use these to identify which substance has been oxidised and which has been reduced.

　a　$Zn(s) + 2H^+(aq) \rightarrow Zn^{2+}(aq) + H_2(g)$

　b　$Mg(s) + 2Fe^{3+}(aq) \rightarrow Mg^{2+}(aq) + 2Fe^{2+}(aq)$

　c　$C_2H_4 + H_2 \rightarrow C_2H_6$

　d　$Mg(s) + H_2O(g) \rightarrow MgO(s) + H_2(g)$

4　For the following reactions, identify the name of the element that has been oxidised and give the formula of the oxidising agent:

　a　$2Fe^{3+} + 2I^- \rightarrow 2Fe^{2+} + I_2$

　b　$2Mg + CO_2 \rightarrow 2MgO + C$

　c　$2Na + 2H_2O \rightarrow 2NaOH + H_2$

　d　$MnO_4^-(aq) + 8H^+(aq) + 5Fe^{2+}(aq) \rightarrow Mn^{2+}(aq) + 5Fe^{3+}(aq) + 4H_2O(l)$

Exercise 20.2　Redox equations

Half-equations, like all equations, must be balanced in terms of the number of each species and the overall charge. For species in solution, the IB syllabus only includes neutral or acidic conditions. In this exercise, you will practise writing half-equations and combining these.

1　Balance the following half-equations and identify whether each represents oxidation or reduction:

　a　$Ce^{4+} \rightarrow Ce^{2+}$

　b　$V \rightarrow V^{2+}$

　c　$H_2 \rightarrow H^+$

　d　$Cl_2 \rightarrow Cl^-$

2　Balance the half-equation $NO_3^- \rightarrow NO_2$ by following these steps:

　a　Deduce the oxidation numbers of the elements and identify which element is oxidised or reduced.

　b　Add the number of electrons to the equation that equals the change in oxidation state. For reduction, place these on the left. For oxidation, place these on the right.

　c　Calculate the total charge of all the substances on each side of the equation. Add as many H^+ ions to one side or the other, as needed, to make the charges on both sides the same.

　d　Add H_2O to the other side to balance the number of hydrogen atoms in the equation.

TIP

When asked to identify which substance has been oxidised or reduced, always give the full name or formula, rather than the name of the individual element. In question 3c, for example, you would say that C_2H_4 has been oxidised or reduced and not carbon or hydrogen.

TIP

Always read exam questions carefully. In question 4, you have been specifically asked to name the element rather than the substance that was oxidised.

TIP

Balance the number of each type of atom first and then balance the charges, by adding electrons to the appropriate side of the equation. Electrons should be added on the right for oxidation half-equations (oxidation is loss of electrons) and on the left in reduction half-equations (reduction is gain of electrons).

3 Balance the following half-equations:

a $SO_2 \rightarrow SO_4^{2-}$

b $MnO_4^- \rightarrow Mn^{2+}$

c $BrO_3^- \rightarrow Br_2$

d $Cr^{3+} \rightarrow Cr_2O_7^{2-}$

4 Combine the following half-equations to give the balanced overall equation:

a $Zn \rightarrow Zn^{2+} + 2e^-$ and $VO_2^+ + 2H^+ + e^- \rightarrow VO^{2+} + H_2O$

b $Cu^{2+} + e^- \rightarrow Cu^+$ and $2I^- \rightarrow I_2 + 2e^-$

c $IO_3^- + 6H^+ + 5e^- \rightarrow \frac{1}{2}I_2 + 3H_2O$ and $2I^- \rightarrow I_2 + 2e^-$

d $H_2O_2 \rightarrow O_2 + 2H^+ + 2e^-$ and $MnO_4^- + 5e^- + 8H^+ \rightarrow Mn^{2+} + 4H_2O$

5 Balance the following half-equations and then combine them to find an overall equation for each reaction:

a $Fe^{3+} \rightarrow Fe^{2+}$ and $Zn \rightarrow Zn^{2+}$

b $H^+ \rightarrow H_2$ and $Mg \rightarrow Mg^{2+}$

c $MnO_4^- \rightarrow Mn^{2+}$ and $Fe^{2+}(aq) \rightarrow Fe^{3+}$

d $S_2O_3^{2-} \rightarrow S_4O_6^{2-}$ and $I_2 \rightarrow I^-$

6 Balance the redox equation $Br_2 + SO_2 \rightarrow H_2SO_4 + HBr$ by following these steps:

a Work out the oxidation numbers of all the substances and identify what is oxidised and what is reduced.

b Write the balanced equation for the oxidation half-equation.

c Write the balanced equation for the reduction half-equation.

d Multiply the half-equations by whatever factor is necessary so that both the half-equations have the same number of electrons.

e Combine the two half-equations devised in part **d** back together and cancel out anything that appears on both sides of the equation.

7 Balance the following redox equations using the same sequence of steps as in question **6**:

a $H_2SO_4 + I^- \rightarrow I_2 + H_2S$

b $C_2O_4^{2-} + Cr_2O_7^{2-} \rightarrow CO_2 + Cr^{3+}$

c $BrO_3^- + Br^- \rightarrow Br_2$

TIP

Firstly, balance all the atoms, except H and O, then follow the steps in question 2.

TIP

Balancing an overall equation by combining half-equations is most easily done by multiplying the half-equations by whatever factor is needed so that both half-equations have the same number of electrons. These will then cancel out when the two half-equations are combined.

TIP

In exam questions like this, it can be assumed that these reactions take place under neutral or acidic conditions as alkaline conditions are not on the syllabus.

Exercise 20.3 Arranging metals in order of reactivity

The IB data book lists the **activity series** of some common metals in order of how easily they are oxidised. This exercise makes use of this activity series, so make sure that you have the data book available. Towards the end of this exercise, you will use the relative position of the halogens in the periodic table to deduce their reactions.

1   Using the activity series, will the following reactions occur?

    a $Mg(s) + Zn^{2+}(aq) \rightarrow Mg^{2+}(aq) + Zn(s)$

    b $Bi(s) + 2H^+(aq) \rightarrow Bi^{2+}(aq) + H_2(g)$

    c $2Al(s) + Fe_2O_3(s) \rightarrow Al_2O_3(s) + 2Fe(s)$

    d $Sb_2S_3(s) + 2Sn(s) \rightarrow Sn_2S_3(s) + 2Sb(s)$

2   In an experiment to deduce the position of a metal in the activity series, the following observations were made:

    I   When a small piece of the metal was placed into dilute acid, bubbles of hydrogen gas were produced.

    II   When a small piece of metal was placed into a solution of nickel nitrate solution, the surface of the metal became coated with a grey substance.

    III   When a small piece of metal was placed into a solution of chromium nitrate solution, there was no apparent reaction.

    a   Use the activity series in the IB data book to suggest possible identities for the metal.

    b   Suggest suitable simple displacement reactions that could be used to deduce the identity of the metal.

3   Although there are some exceptions, the reactivity of a metal is linked to its position in the periodic table.

    a   Describe the expected trend in reactivity down the Group 1 and 2 metals.

    b   Using ideas about ionisation energy, explain this trend.

    c   Give an equation for the first ionisation energy of sodium.

    d   Define *first ionisation energy*.

> **TIP**
>
> Keep your description simple, include the likely observations and how this would enable you to make a deduction.

> **TIP**
>
> Learning definitions is very important because they aid understanding of the underlying concepts.

4 The relative ease of reduction of the halogens can be deduced from their position in the periodic table.

    a Which halogen is most easily reduced?

    b Identify which of the following displacement reactions would happen:

        i $Cl_2 + 2I^- \rightarrow 2Cl^- + I_2$

        ii $Br_2 + 2I^- \rightarrow 2Br^- + I_2$

        iii $Br_2 + 2Cl^- \rightarrow 2Br^- + Cl_2$

5 There are two broad classes of **electrochemical cells**: **voltaic cells** and **electrolytic cells**. Using the activity series, identify in which type of cell the following reactions would occur:

    a $Zn(s) + Cu^{2+}(aq) \rightarrow Zn^{2+}(aq) + Cu(s)$

    b $Mg(s) + Ni^{2+}(aq) \rightarrow Mg^{2+}(aq) + Ni(s)$

    c $2Ag(s) + Cu^{2+}(aq) \rightarrow 2Ag^+(aq) + Cu(s)$

    d $Fe(s) + Zn^{2+}(aq) \rightarrow Fe^{2+}(aq) + Zn(s)$

> **TIP**
>
> Voltaic cells generate electrical energy from a spontaneous chemical reaction. Think about the relative position of the elements in the activity series: would the reaction occur spontaneously? If not, then electrical energy in an electrolytic cell would be needed to make the reaction occur.

Exercise 20.4 Voltaic cells

Voltaic cells and electrolytic cells are often considered as opposites because voltaic cells use chemical energy to produce electrical energy and electrolytic cells convert electrical energy into chemical energy. A common error is to consider everything about these two types of electrochemical cells as being opposite, which is not true. The first question in this exercise compares voltaic and electrolytic cells. In the remainder of the exercise you will practise interpreting and writing cell notation as a shorthand way of representing a voltaic cell.

1 Complete Table **20.2**.

	Voltaic cell	Electrolytic cell
the name of the electrode where oxidation occurs		
the name of the electrode where reduction occurs		
the sign of the electrode where oxidation occurs		
the sign of the electrode where reduction occurs		

Table 20.2: Comparison of voltaic and electrolytic cells.

2 In a voltaic cell, the substance that is most easily oxidised will give up its electrons to the external circuit and is the anode of the cell.

a In a simple voltaic cell made from two metals and solutions of their ions, would the metal higher in the activity series form the anode or the cathode of the cell?

b In a voltaic cell, in which direction do the electrons flow in the external circuit?

3 In the voltaic cell in Figure **20.1**, Fe^{3+} ions are reduced to Fe^{2+} ions, and zinc atoms are oxidised to Zn^{2+} ions.

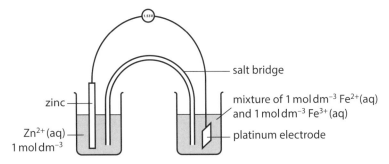

Figure 20.1: Voltaic cell; $Zn(s) \mid Zn^{2+}(aq) \parallel Fe^{2+}(aq), Fe^{3+}(aq) \mid Pt$

a What is the purpose of the **salt bridge**?

b Give equations for the reactions in each half-cell.

c What changes would be observed in each beaker?

d Label the diagram to show the following:

- the direction of electron flow through the external circuit
- the anode
- the cathode
- the positive electrode
- the negative electrode
- the direction of ion flow in the salt bridge.

4 Cell notation is used as shorthand to describe voltaic cells, for example:

$$Cu(s) \mid Cu^{2+}(aq) \parallel H^+(aq), Cr_2O_7^{2-}(aq), Cr^{3+}(aq) \mid Pt(s)$$

a What is the single vertical line used to represent?

b What is the double vertical line used to represent?

c What are the two electrodes made from in this cell?

d Give the half-equations occurring at each electrode.

e Give the overall equation for the cell.

TIP

The convention is that the anode (oxidation) is shown on the left and the cathode (Reduction) on the Right. Both half-equations can be read from left to right.

5   Give the cell diagram for the voltaic cell that has the following overall equations:

a $Ag^+(aq) + Cu(s) \rightarrow Ag(s) + Cu^{2+}(aq)$

b $Cu(s) + 2NO_3^-(aq) + 4H^+(aq) \rightarrow Cu^{2+}(aq) + 2NO_2(g) + 2H_2O(l)$

c $5IO_4^-(aq) + 2Mn^{2+}(aq) + 3H_2O(l) \rightarrow 5IO_3^-(aq) + 2MnO_4^-(aq) + 6H^+(aq)$

6   Use the activity series in the IB data book to put the following voltaic cells in increasing order of the voltage they produce. Assume that any differences in conditions, such as concentration and temperature, can be ignored.

A $Zn^{2+} + Mg \rightarrow Mg^{2+} + Zn$

B $2Cr^{3+} + 3Zn \rightarrow 2Cr + 3Zn^{2+}$

C $3Mg^{2+} + 2Cr \rightarrow 2Cr^{3+} + 3Mg$

7   For the voltaic cell $Cu^{2+} + Sn \rightarrow Sn^{2+} + Cu$

a   state which is the more reactive metal

b   state which metal is the negative electrode

c   state which metal is the cathode

d   state which direction the electrons flow in the external circuit.

Exercise 20.5 Rechargeable batteries

Voltaic cells that make use of spontaneous **redox reactions** are also known as primary cells. In this exercise, you will look at electrochemical cells that make use of reversible reactions, also called **secondary cells**. Secondary cells are used in rechargeable batteries. They act as voltaic cells when they are being used, but as electrolytic cells when they are being charged. In the last few questions of this exercise, you will look at the **electrolysis** of molten salts and electroplating.

1   Rechargeable batteries can be both *charged* and *discharged*. What do these two terms mean?

2   In a rechargeable battery, does oxidation occur at the anode or cathode when the cell is being discharged?

3   In a rechargeable battery, does oxidation occur at the anode or cathode when the cell is being charged?

4   When a rechargeable battery is being discharged, is the anode negative or positive?

> **TIP**
>
> Start on the left with the oxidation process. In part **a**, this is $Cu \rightarrow Cu^{2+}$. Then insert $\parallel$ to represent the salt bridge, followed by the reduction process, $Ag^+ \rightarrow Ag$. Always include state symbols and a single vertical line to represent a phase boundary. In parts **b** and **c**, commas should be used to separate the species that are in the same solution. Platinum is used to provide a surface for the electron movement between the solutions and the wires.

> **TIP**
>
> A battery is the correct term for a collection of electrochemical cells. In this syllabus, either term can be used, although *cell* is probably better.

5 When a rechargeable battery is being charged, is the anode negative or positive?

6 Electrons flow in the external part of an electrochemical cell. What type of particle moves through the electrolyte of a cell?

7 When the engine of a vehicle containing a lead–acid battery is running, the lead–acid battery is charged up by the following reactions:

anode: $PbSO_4(s) + 2H_2O(l) \rightarrow PbO_2(s) + 2e^- + 4H^+(aq) + SO_4^{2-}(aq)$

cathode: $PbSO_4(s) + 2e^- \rightarrow Pb(s) + SO_4^{2-}(aq)$

Lead(II) sulfate occurs as an insoluble coating on the surface of both metal electrodes.

a Give the equations when the lead–acid battery is being discharged.

b Using the equations, identify a suitable electrolyte in a lead–acid battery.

8 Most laptops and mobile phones use lithium-ion batteries. These can generate higher voltages than nickel–cadmium batteries. Figure **20.2** shows a lithium-ion battery.

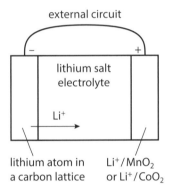

Figure 20.2: Lithium-ion battery.

a What happens to the lithium *atoms* at the anode while the battery is being used?

b At the cathode, lithium *ions* become inserted into the lattice of the manganese(IV) oxide or cobalt(IV) oxide, from which the electrode is made, causing the transition metal ion to be reduced to an oxidation state of +3. Give an equation for the reduction of Co^{4+} to Co^{3+}.

9 Describe the main advantages and disadvantages of fuel cells and of rechargeable batteries.

TIP

The negative electrode is the electrode that has electrons *pushed* onto it. During charging, the electrons are being forced onto the negative electrode by the external power supply. During use, the electrons are pushed onto the negative electrode by the chemical that is most easily oxidised.

TIP

Take particular care to use the terms *atom* and *ion* correctly.

TIP

Remember: The negative electrode has electrons forced onto it. In an electrolytic cell, the external power source is pushing the electrons around the external circuit. These electrons will transfer onto the positive ions that are attracted to that electrode; the electrons will be gained (OIL RIG).

20.6 Electrolysis

Electrolysis occurs in electrolytic cells. Electrical energy is provided by an external power source to bring about a non-spontaneous reaction. This exercise explores the electrolysis of molten binary ionic salts. A binary salt is one that is made of only two elements.

1   Electrolysis is the process of breaking down a substance.

    a   At which electrode does oxidation occur in an electrolytic cell?

    b   What are the signs of the anode and cathode in an electrolytic cell?

    c   Why do the electrolytes need to be molten in order for electrolysis to occur?

    d   Describe how current is carried in both the external circuit and in the electrolyte of an electrolytic cell.

2   Identify the products formed during the electrolysis of the following molten substances. In each case, identify which is produced at the anode and which at the cathode, give the equation occurring at each electrode and the overall equation.

    a $CuCl_2$

    b ZnO

    c   manganese(IV) oxide

    d   indium(III) bromide

20.7 Redox reactions in organic chemistry

In organic chemistry, we generally consider oxidation and reduction reactions in terms of the loss or gain of hydrogen and oxygen, but ideas about oxidation states can also be useful. In this exercise, you will look at the reactions of some of the functional groups met in Chapter 11, so it would be worth revisiting that content to refamiliarise yourself with how to name and draw organic compounds. The first questions provide the opportunity to practise this.

1   State the following for the compounds listed:

    i   the name of the compound

    ii   the name of the functional group

    iii   the name of the homologous series

    iv   if it can be classified as primary, secondary or tertiary.

    a $CH_3CH_2CH_2OH$

    b $CH_3CH(OH)CH_3$

    c CH_3CHO

d $CH_3CH_2CH_2COCH_3$

e $CH_3CH_2CH_2COOH$

2   Deduce the average oxidation state of the carbon atoms in each of the compounds listed:

a $CH_3CH_2CH_2OH$

b $CH_3CH(OH)CH_3$

c CH_3CHO

d $CH_3CH_2CH_2COCH_3$

e $CH_3CH_2CH_2COOH$

f C_3H_6

g C_3H_8

TIP

As these are average oxidation states, do not worry if they are not whole numbers.

3   This question is about the oxidation of alcohols.

a   Which type of alcohol is resistant to oxidation?

b   Which type of alcohol can be oxidised to form an aldehyde?

c   Which type of alcohol can be oxidised to form a carboxylic acid?

d   Which type of alcohol can be oxidised to form a ketone?

e   Other than an alcohol, what other type of compound can be oxidised to form a carboxylic acid?

4   A mixture of propan-1-ol and a suitable oxidising agent can produce two different products, depending on the apparatus used, as shown in Figure **20.3a** and **b**.

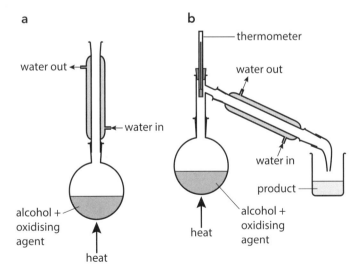

Figure 20.3: Oxidation of ethanol.

a   Give equations for the reactions that occur in these two experiments and suggest why the two different methods are required.

b   What name is given to the two practical techniques in Figure **20.3a** and **b**?

c   What would be produced if propan-2-ol were used in these experiments rather than ethanol? Give an equation for any reactions.

5   The oxidation of ethanol to ethanoic acid can be represented by the following equation:

$$CH_3CH_2OH + 2[O] \rightarrow CH_3COOH + H_2O$$

a   Deduce the oxidation half-equation for this reaction.

> **TIP**
>
> Oxidising agents in organic chemistry are often represented as [O] and reducing agents as [H].

> **TIP**
>
> In exam questions like question 4c, a condensed formula is fine, as long as it clearly shows the structure of the molecule, but drawing a structural formula would be even better.

> **TIP**
>
> Calculate the total oxidation number of all the carbon atoms in both molecules. The difference between these will be the number of electrons that are lost by ethanol. (Oxidation is loss of electrons.) Then balance the half-equation using H^+ and H_2O.

b   Acidified potassium dichromate(VI) is often used as an oxidising agent for this reaction. The half-equation for the reduction of potassium dichromate(VI) is as follows:

$$Cr_2O_7^{2-} + 14H^+ + 6e^- \rightarrow 2Cr^{3+} + 7H_2O$$

Give the overall redox equation for this reaction.

c   Acidified potassium manganate(VII) is often used as an oxidising agent for this reaction. The half-equation for the reduction of potassium manganate(VII) is as follows:

$$MnO_4^- + 8H^+ + 5e^- \rightarrow Mn^{2+} + 4H_2O$$

Give the overall redox equation for this reaction.

Exercise 20.8 Reduction reactions

In this exercise, you will practise writing equations for the reduction of aldehydes, ketones and carboxylic acids using hydrides. The reduction of alkenes and alkynes using hydrogen gas is met at the end of the exercise.

1   Aldehydes, ketones and carboxylic acids can be reduced to form alcohols. Complete and balance the following equations:

a $CH_3COOH + [H] \rightarrow CH_3CH_2OH$

b $CH_3COCH_3 + [H] \rightarrow$

c $HCHO + [H] \rightarrow$

2   Why is it difficult to reduce a carboxylic acid to an aldehyde?

> **TIP**
>
> [H] can be used in these reduction reactions to represent the reducing agent.

3   Two common reducing agents are lithium aluminium hydride, $LiAlH_4$, and sodium tetrahydridoborate, also known as sodium tetraborohydride, $NaBH_4$.

a   Calculate the oxidation state of hydrogen in these two compounds.

b   Both of these reducing agents can be considered to produce hydride ions, H^-. The mechanism for the reaction of a hydride ion with ethanal is shown in Figure **20.4**.

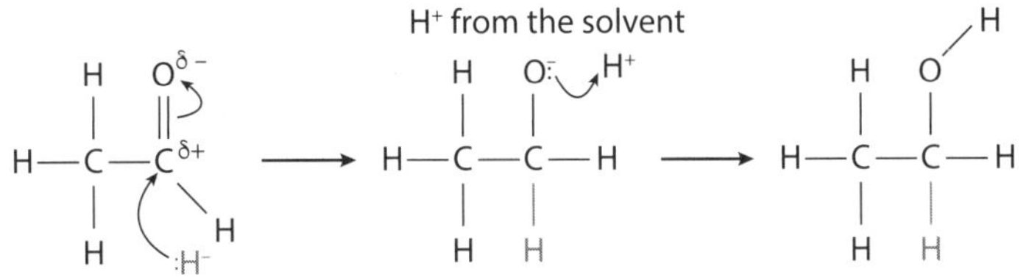

Figure 20.4: Mechanism for the reduction of ethanal.

The hydride ion acts as a *nucleophile*. What is the meaning of this term?

4   Alkenes and alkynes also undergo reduction reactions.

a   What reagent is commonly used for the reduction of an alkene or an alkyne?

b   Give an equation for the reduction of but-2-ene.

c   Give an equation for the reduction of but-2-yne.

5   The number of multiple bonds and rings in an organic compound is called its degree of unsaturation or index of hydrogen deficiency (IHD). Determine the degree of unsaturation of the following compounds:

a

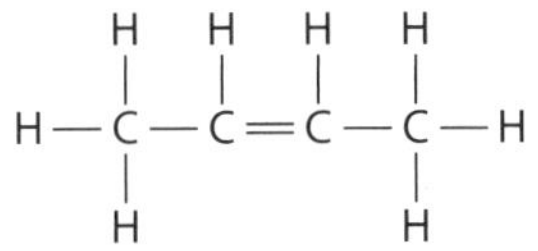

b

c

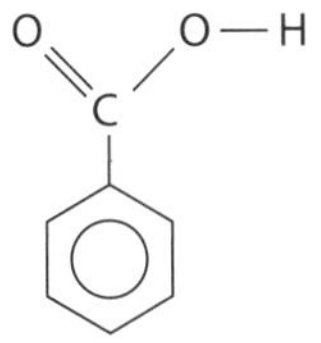

d

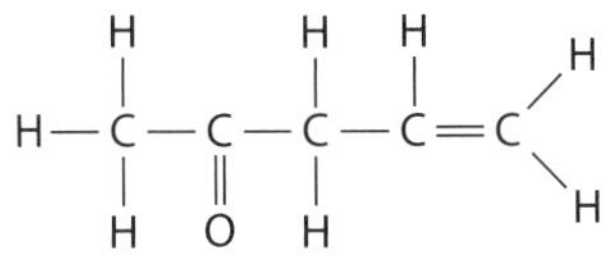

> **TIP**
>
> These compounds can be considered as metal hydrides, which are exceptions to the general rules used for the oxidation state of hydrogen.

> **TIP**
>
> Make sure your answers show the structure of the molecules by either drawing them or by using a condensed structural formula.

> **TIP**
>
> When determining degree of unsaturation,
>
> a double bond = 1,
> a triple bond = 2,
> a ring = 1.

Exercise 20.9 Standard electrode potentials

The voltage produced by a voltaic cell depends on the relative oxidising strength of the half-cells from which it is made. This is called its **standard electrode potential**. The strength of a substance as an oxidising agent can only be measured by comparing it to a **standard hydrogen electrode**. In this exercise, you will begin by practising calculating the **standard cell potential** when two half-cells are combined. You will then go on to look at the relationship between standard cell potentials and $\Delta G^{\ominus}$.

1   The standard electrode potential for $Zn^{2+}(aq) + 2e^- \rightleftharpoons Zn(s)$ is –0.76 V and the standard electrode potential for $Pb^{2+}(aq) + 2e^- \rightleftharpoons Pb(s)$ is –0.13 V.

   a   What does this tell you about the tendency of Zn^{2+} ions to gain electrons compared to that of Pb^{2+} ions?

   b   Using your answer to part **a**, determine the reactions that will occur in each half-cell when the two half-cells are combined.

   c   Deduce the overall redox equation.

   d   State whether the zinc or lead electrode is the negative electrode.

> **TIP**
>
> One way of working out which is the oxidation and which is the reduction half-equation is to use the values in the IB data book. Fluorine is a very reactive element; it very readily reacts to become F^- ions. The standard electrode potential for the F_2/F^- half-cell is very positive. This suggests that the more positive the electrode potential, the more likely that reaction will be the reduction half-equation.

2   Using the standard electrode potentials given in the IB data book, write the overall reaction and calculate the electrode potential for the following reactions:

   a $Zn(s) \,|\, Zn^{2+}(aq) \,\|\, Cu^{2+}(aq) \,|\, Cu(s)$

   b $Pt(s) \,|\, Fe^{2+}(aq), Fe^{3+}(aq) \,\|\, Cr_2O_7^{2-}(aq), H^+(aq), Cr^{3+}(aq) \,|\, Pt(s)$

   c $Sn(s) \,|\, Sn^{2+}(aq) \,\|\, Cl_2(g) \,|\, Cl^-(aq) \,|\, Pt(s)$

3   An experiment was set up to compare the following two cells under standard conditions:

   cell 1: $Zn(s) \,|\, Zn^{2+}(aq) \,\|\, H^+(aq), Cr_2O_7^{2-}(aq), Cr^{3+}(aq) \,|\, Pt(s)$

   cell 2: $Mg(s) \,|\, Mg^{2+}(aq) \,\|\, H^+(aq), Cr_2O_7^{2-}(aq), Cr^{3+}(aq) \,|\, Pt(s)$

   It was found that the voltage in cell 1 was +2.12 V, and in cell 2 the voltage was +3.73 V.

> **TIP**
>
> Standard electrode potentials used to be called standard reduction potentials, which was a useful name, as it reinforced the idea that a high reduction potential meant that something was highly likely to be reduced.

> **TIP**
>
> Unlike enthalpy calculations, electrode potentials are not molar quantities, and so, are not multiplied to match the balancing of an equation; they represent the potential for a reaction to occur. Simply reverse the sign of the oxidation standard electrode potential and then add the values of the two electrode potentials together.

a Give the overall equations for these two cells and use the values of the cell potentials to deduce the relative strength of zinc and magnesium as reducing agents.

b Deduce the cell potential if a new cell were set up using the magnesium half-cell and the zinc half-cell, and give the overall equation for this new cell.

c Identify whether the zinc or magnesium electrode would be the anode in this new cell.

4 Using the electrode potentials in the IB data book, predict whether each of the following reactions will be spontaneous, and explain your answer in each case. For those that are spontaneous, give the overall equation for the reaction.

a Fe and Sn^{2+}

b I^- and Mg

c H_2SO_3 and Ag^+

> **TIP**
>
> Remember to balance the number of electrons when combining the half-equations.

5 Using the electrode potentials in the IB data book, predict whether each of the following reactions will be spontaneous and explain your answer in each case. For those that are spontaneous, give the overall equation for the reaction.

a H^+ and Mn^{2+}

b I_2 and Fe^{2+}

c Fe^{2+} and Br_2

6 The standard cell potential can be used to predict if a reaction is likely to occur spontaneously or not. $\Delta G^{\ominus}$ can be used in a similar way.

a What values of the standard cell potential indicate that a reaction is likely to be spontaneous?

b What values of $\Delta G^{\ominus}$ indicate that a reaction is likely to be spontaneous?

7 Calculate $\Delta G^{\ominus}$ in kJ mol^{-1} for the following reactions, which were met previously in question **2**, given that $F = 96\,500$ C mol^{-1}.

a $Zn(s) \mid Zn^{2+}(aq) \parallel Cu^{2+}(aq) \mid Cu(s)$

b $Pt(s) \mid Fe^{2+}(aq), Fe^{3+}(aq) \parallel Cr_2O_7^{2-}(aq), H^+(aq), Cr^{3+}(aq) \mid Pt(s)$

c $Sn(s) \mid Sn^{2+}(aq) \parallel Cl_2(g) \mid Cl^-(aq) \mid Pt(s)$

> **TIP**
>
> Check your units when answering exam questions like question 7. The units of $\Delta G^{\ominus}$ calculated using $\Delta G^{\ominus} = -nFE^{\ominus}$ are J mol^{-1}.

> **TIP**
>
> In simple terms, reading from left to right, the left-hand half-equation can be thought of as driving the right-hand half-equation forward. The oxidation of zinc or magnesium (and therefore, their 'power' as reducing agents) is driving the reduction of $Cr_2O_7^{2-}$ to Cr^{3+}. The more positive the overall voltage produced, the more 'powerfully' the reaction is being driven.

> **TIP**
>
> Oxidation always occurs at the anode.

> **TIP**
>
> In question 5, there is a choice of half-equations. For example, in part **a** there is a choice between Mn^{2+}/Mn and MnO_4^-/Mn^{2+}. It is important to remember that one equation must be reduction and the other oxidation. H^+ ions can only be reduced (the maximum oxidation state of hydrogen is +1), and so, Mn^{2+} must be oxidised.

Exercise 20.10 Electrolysis of aqueous solutions

Exercise 20.5 looked at the electrolysis of molten ionic substances. In this exercise, you will look at the electrolysis of solutions and their application in electroplating and answer questions on how electrode potentials can be used to predict the products of electrolysis.

1 Identify the ions present in the following solutions and state which will be attracted to the anode and which to the cathode of an electrolytic cell:

a aqueous tin(II) chloride solution

b aqueous magnesium sulfate solution

c aqueous sodium nitrate solution

d aqueous calcium bromide solution.

2 A general principle is that, during the electrolysis of aqueous solutions, oxygen or halogens (apart from fluorine) are produced at the anode and hydrogen or a metal is produced at the cathode.

a State three factors that affect the identity of the products formed during the electrolysis of an aqueous solution.

b Using the standard electrode potentials in the IB data book, explain why the halogens are produced rather than oxygen.

c Using the standard electrode potentials in the data book, explain why copper is produced at the cathode of an electrolytic cell rather than hydrogen in the electrolysis of copper(II) sulfate solution.

3 a Identify the substance formed at the anode and cathode during the electrolysis of the aqueous solutions shown in Table **20.3**, using inert electrodes under standard conditions, and give the half-equations for the reaction at each electrode.

	Solution	Product at anode	Product at cathode
i	sodium chloride		
ii	magnesium bromide		
iii	copper(II) sulfate		
iv	acidified water		

Table 20.3: Products of electrolysis.

b Why is it necessary to acidify the sample of water in part **iv** before electrolysis is possible?

TIP

Oxidation occurs at the anode, so consider whether or not the ions can be oxidised. For example, can H^+ ions be oxidised? Positively charged ions are attracted to the negative electrode, so the negative electrode must be the…

TIP

When considering reduction reactions, the more positive (or less negative) the standard electrode potential, the more favourable is the reduction reaction. When considering oxidation, the equations and their electrode potentials should be reversed. Again, the more positive (or less negative), then the more favourable the oxidation reaction.

4   An electrolytic cell was set up using an aqueous solution of copper(II) nitrate of concentration 1 mol dm^{-3} using inert electrodes.

    a   Suggest a suitable substance from which inert electrodes can be made.

    b   Give half-equations for the reactions at both electrodes.

    c   How will the concentration of the copper(II) nitrate solution change over time?

    d   What will happen to the pH of the electrolyte as electrolysis proceeds?

    e   Describe what would be observed as electrolysis proceeds.

> **TIP**
>
> *Observed* means what you would see. Consider the colour of the solution and what the substances produced at the electrodes look like.

5   Electroplating is the process of coating an object with a thin layer of a metal using electrolysis.

    a   Should the object being coated be attached to the anode or cathode of an electrolytic cell?

    b   What should the other electrode be made from?

    c   What type of substance is usually used as the electrolyte?

6   Sketch a diagram to show how a simple metal object, such as a spoon, could be coated with silver. Include the following labels on your diagram:

- anode/cathode

- positive/negative electrode

- direction of movement of electrons

- the name of a suitable electrolyte

- equations at both electrodes.

EXAM-STYLE QUESTIONS

1   In which of the following reactions does sulfur have the biggest change in oxidation number?

    A $3H_2SO_4 + 2NaBr \rightarrow 2NaHSO_4 + Br_2 + SO_2 + 2H_2O$

    B $9H_2SO_4 + 8NaI \rightarrow 8NaHSO_4 + 4I_2 + 4H_2O + H_2S$

    C $H_2SO_4 + 2KMnO_4 \rightarrow K_2SO_4 + Mn_2O_7 + H_2O$

    D $H_2SO_4 + NaCl \rightarrow NaHSO_4 + HCl$

2   Determine the coefficient for the number of electrons in the following half-equation:

    ___ NO_3^- (aq) + ___ H^+(aq) + ___ $e^- \rightarrow$ ___ N_2(aq) + ___ H_2O(l)

    A   3

    B   5

    C   8

    D   10

3 Consider the following reaction:

$2MnO_4^-(aq) + 16H^+(aq) + 10Cl^-(aq) \rightarrow 2Mn^{2+}(aq) + 8H_2O(l) + 5Cl_2(g)$

In which option have the substances been correctly identified?

	Oxidising agent	Species oxidised
A	$MnO_4^-(aq)$	$Cl^-(aq)$
B	$MnO_4^-(aq)$	$Mn^{2+}(aq)$
C	$Cl^-(aq)$	$Cl_2(g)$
D	$Mn^{2+}(aq)$	$Cl^-(aq)$

4 Which of the following equations is a redox reaction?

A $MgO(s) + 2HCl(aq) \rightarrow MgCl_2(aq) + H_2O(l)$

B $HCl(aq) + NaOH(aq) \rightarrow NaCl(aq) + H_2O(l)$

C $2NaOH(aq) + Cl_2(g) \rightarrow NaOCl(aq) + NaCl(aq) + H_2O(l)$

D $MgCO_3(s) \rightarrow MgO(s) + CO_2(g)$

5 Which statement is correct?

A In a voltaic cell, the anode is positive and the cathode is negative.

B In an electrolytic cell, the anode is positive and the cathode is negative.

C In a voltaic cell, oxidation occurs at the positive electrode.

D In an electrolytic cell, positively charged ions are attracted to the anode.

6 This question is about the electrolysis of molten zinc chloride. Which statement is correct?

A Zinc metal is formed at the anode.

B Hydrogen gas is formed at the negative electrode.

C Oxygen gas is formed at the positive electrode.

D Chlorine gas is formed at the positive electrode.

7 For the voltaic cell shown in Figure 20.5, which statements are correct?

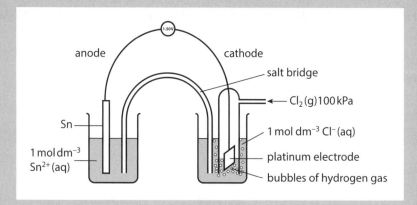

Figure 20.5: Sn/Sn²⁺ and Cl₂/Cl⁻ voltaic cell.

CONTINUED

    I   Electrons move in the external circuit from the tin electrode to the chlorine electrode.

    II Positive ions in the salt bridge move towards the tin electrode.

    III The concentration of tin ions in solution increases during the process.

    A I only

    B II only

    C I and III

    D II and III

8 Consider the following standard electrode potentials:

$SO_4^{2-}(aq) + 4H^+(aq) + 2e^- \rightleftharpoons H_2SO_3(aq) + H_2O(l)$ $E^\ominus_{cell} = +0.17$ V

$Ag^+(aq) + e^- \rightleftharpoons Ag(s)$ $E^\ominus_{cell} = +0.80$ V

What is the cell potential, in V, for the spontaneous reaction that occurs when these two half-cells are connected in a voltaic cell?

    A +0.97 V

    B −0.63 V

    C +0.43 V

    D +0.63 V

9 Which statement is correct for the following spontaneous reaction?

$2Fe^{3+}(aq) + Sn^{2+}(aq) \rightarrow 2Fe^{2+}(aq) + Sn^{4+}(aq)$

    A $E^\ominus_{cell} > 0$ and Fe^{3+} is a better reducing agent than Sn^{2+}

    B $E^\ominus_{cell} > 0$ and Fe^{3+} is a better oxidising agent than Sn^{4+}

    C $E^\ominus_{cell} > 0$ and Sn^{4+} is a better reducing agent than Fe^{3+}

    D $E^\ominus_{cell} > 0$ and Sn^{2+} is a better oxidising agent than Fe^{2+}

10 Given the following electrode potentials, which statement is correct?

$Al^{3+}(aq) + 3e^- \rightleftharpoons Al(s)$ $E^\ominus = -1.66$ V

$Zn^{2+}(aq) + 2e^- \rightleftharpoons Zn(s)$ $E^\ominus = -0.76$ V

$\frac{1}{2}I_2(s) + e^- \rightleftharpoons I^-(aq)$ $E^\ominus = +0.54$ V

$Fe^{3+}(aq) + e^- \rightleftharpoons Fe^{2+}(aq)$ $E^\ominus = +0.77$ V

    A For the reaction between iodine and aluminium, $E^\ominus_{cell} = 2.20$ V, and the reaction will happen spontaneously.

    B $\Delta G^\ominus > 0$ for the reaction between Fe^{3+} and Al.

    C If an Al^{3+}/Al half-cell is connected to a Zn^{2+}/Zn half-cell, then under standard conditions the zinc half-cell will be the anode.

    D If a current is passed through a 1 mol dm^{-3} mixture of both Zn^{2+} and Al^{3+} ions, then the aluminium ions are more likely to be reduced than the zinc ions.

11 Vanadium is a typical transition metal, in that it exhibits variable oxidation numbers.

a Give the oxidation number of vanadium in the species shown in Table **20.4**. [3]

Species	Oxidation number of vanadium
VCl_2	
VO_2^+	
NH_4VO_3	

Table 20.4: Oxidation numbers of vanadium.

b Aqueous V^{3+} ions react with zinc to form V^{2+}. Give the equation for this reaction. [1]

c V^{2+} ions react with nitric acid according to the following equation:

$V^{2+}(aq) + NO_3^-(aq) + 2H^+(aq) \rightarrow VO^{2+}(aq) + 2NO_2(g) + H_2O(l)$

Give the half-equations for this reaction, clearly stating which is reduction and which is oxidation. [2]

12 A 0.50 g sample of hydrated ammonium iron(II) sulfate with formula $(NH_4)_2SO_4 \cdot FeSO_4 \cdot xH_2O$ was dissolved in dilute sulfuric acid and made up to a total volume of 250 cm³. A 25.00 cm³ portion of this was then analysed by titration with 0.00100 mol dm³ $KMnO^4$ solution; 25.50 cm³ of the $KMnO_4$ solution were required. In the reaction, the iron(II) ions are oxidised to iron(III).

The half-equation for the reduction of the manganate(VII) ion is as follows:

$MnO_4^-(aq) + 8H^+(aq) + 5e^- \rightarrow Mn^{2+}(aq) + 4H_2O(l)$

a Deduce the balanced equation for the reaction between Fe^{2+} and MnO_4^- ions. [1]

b Calculate the number of moles of $KMnO_4$ used per titre. [1]

c Calculate the number of moles of Fe^{2+} ions that are oxidised during the reaction. [1]

d Calculate the number of moles of $(NH_4)_2SO_4 \cdot FeSO_4 \cdot xH_2O$ present in the original sample. [1]

e Deduce the relative formula mass of $(NH_4)_2SO_4 \cdot FeSO_4 \cdot xH_2O$, and hence, deduce the value of x. [3]

13 The results shown in Table **20.5** were obtained during a simple displacement experiment to deduce the reactivity of four metals, W, X, Y and Z.

	W(s)	X(s)	Y(s)	Z(s)
W nitrate(aq)		reaction	no reaction	reaction
X nitrate(aq)	no reaction		no reaction	no reaction
Y nitrate(aq)	reaction	reaction		reaction
Z nitrate(aq)	no reaction	reaction	no reaction	

Table 20.5: Results of displacement reactions.

CONTINUED

a Deduce the order of reactivity of the metals from most reactive to least reactive. [2]

b If metal W is copper, suggest an identity for metal Y. [1]

c If metal W is copper, describe what would be observed in the reaction of W nitrate with metal Z. [2]

14 In a voltaic cell, chemical energy is converted into electrical energy. Figure 20.6 shows a voltaic cell made using iron and copper half-cells.

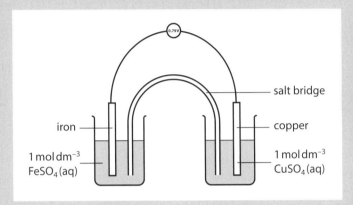

Figure 20.6: Iron/copper voltaic cell.

a Give the half-equations for the reactions at the anode and the cathode. [3]

b Give the overall reaction for the voltaic cell. [1]

c Describe any changes that would be seen in each beaker. [4]

15 Rechargeable batteries make use of reversible chemical reactions.

Some of the first readily available rechargeable batteries for use in household gadgets, like toys and clocks, were nickel–cadmium batteries. These use a metallic cadmium electrode and a nickel oxide hydroxide, NiO(OH), electrode separated by a potassium hydroxide electrolyte.

The equations for the reactions at the electrodes as the battery is discharged are as follows:

$Cd(s) + 2OH^-(aq) \rightarrow Cd(OH)_2(s) + 2e^-$ $\qquad E^\ominus = +0.82$ V

$NiO(OH)(s) + H_2O(l) + e^- \rightarrow Ni(OH)_2(s) + OH^-(aq)$ $\quad E^\ominus = +0.49$ V

a Deduce the overall reaction during discharging of the battery. [1]

b Calculate the standard cell potential. [1]

c Given that Faraday's constant is 96 500 C mol^{-1}, calculate $\Delta G^\ominus$. [1]

d Identify which reaction will occur at the anode when the battery is being recharged. [1]

16 This question is about the electrolysis of copper(II) bromide solution using platinum electrodes. Using the standard electrode potentials in the IB data book, explain why copper and bromine are produced rather than hydrogen and oxygen. [4]

Chapter 21

Electron sharing reactions

CHAPTER OUTLINE

In this chapter you will:

- understand what a radical is

- understand the radical substitution reactions of alkanes with halogens.

KEY TERMS

Make sure you understand the following key terms before you do the exercises.

radical: a species (atom or group of atoms) with an unpaired electron. Radicals are very reactive because of this unpaired electron

homolytic fission: a covalent bond breaks such that one electron goes back to each atom making up the original bond

substitution reaction: a reaction in which one atom or group is replaced by another atom or group

---

Exercise 21.1 Radicals

In this exercise, you will begin by practising identifying **radicals**, which are sometimes also known as *free radicals*. These are generally very reactive. You will then look at some examples of reactions that involve radicals.

1   Identify which of the following are radicals:

  a   P

  b   I

  c   S

  d   N

  e   Mg

2   Identify which of the following are radicals:

  a   NO

  b N_2O

  c N_2O_4

TIP

If there is an odd number of electrons, then it must be a radical. If there is an even number of electrons, then you will need to consider the electron configuration and whether its valence shell orbitals are paired or unpaired.

---

d SO_3

e PCl_4^+

f PCl_4^-

g ClO

h CH_3O

3   Radicals can be formed by the **homolytic fission** of a covalent bond.
    Give equations to show the homolytic fission for the following reactions:

a   breaking of the Br—Br bond in Br_2

b   breaking of the O—O bond in H_2O_2

c   breaking of the N—N bond in N_2O_4

4   Radicals are highly reactive and can react with each other, or with another
    molecule, to form a covalent bond. Write equations for the following reactions:

a   the reaction of a methyl radical, $CH_3\cdot$, with a hydroxyl radical, $OH\cdot$

b   the reaction of two ethyl radicals

c   the reaction of a chlorine radical with ethane

5   The **substitution reactions** of halogens with alkanes in the presence of ultraviolet
    light or heat are examples of radical reactions. Write the overall equations for the
    following reactions. Use molecular formulas in your answers.

a   reaction between bromine and ethane

b   reaction between chlorine and propane

c   reaction between bromine and methane

6   The reaction of chlorine with propane can produce a number of
    different products.

a   Draw the structural formulas for all of the possible di-substituted products.

b   Give the molecular formulas of the compound with the theoretical maximum
    number of substituted atoms.

Exercise 21.2 The radical substitution mechanism

The mechanism for the reaction of a halogen with an alkane is broken down into
three parts: initiation, propagation and termination. As the reaction involves highly
reactive radicals and proceeds through a number of steps, there will be a large number
of different particles that can collide at random. In this exercise, you will look at the
principle steps in the mechanism and at some of the other products that can be
formed by these random collisions.

> **TIP**
>
> Work out the total
> number of outer-shell
> electrons. If there is
> an even number of
> electrons, then these
> will be paired and the
> substance will not be
> a radical.

> **TIP**
>
> A dot is sometimes
> used to show that
> an atom or group
> of atoms is a radical.

1 Give the meanings of the terms *initiation*, *propagation* and *termination*.

2 In the initiation step, a halogen molecule is broken down into two halogen atoms.

    a Give an equation to show this, using bromine as your example.

    b What name is given to this type of bond breaking?

    c Name two ways of providing sufficient energy for this reaction.

    d What happens to the number of radicals present in a mixture of an alkane and a halogen during an initiation step?

    e Explain why it is the halogen–halogen bond that breaks during the initiation stage, rather than a C—H bond in the alkane.

3 The propagation step of the reaction mechanism involves two stages.

    a Give the equations for these two stages using the reaction of chlorine with ethane as your example.

    b The propagation steps can be described as a *chain reaction*. Explain this term.

    c Use the equations in your answer to part **a** to show how the number of radicals in the reaction mixture changes during the propagation steps.

4 Termination steps reduce the number of radicals present in a reaction mixture. Give three examples of termination steps for the reaction between ethane and bromine.

5 Give equations to show how a di-substituted product could be formed by the reaction of ethane with chlorine.

6 Explain how both 1-bromopropane and 2-bromopropane are formed as alternative products in the reaction of propane with bromine.

> **TIP**
>
> These two propagation stages must be given in the correct order. The first involves the reaction of a radical that was produced in the initiation step.

EXAM-STYLE QUESTIONS

1 Which of the following contains one or more unpaired electron?

    A Ti^{2+}

    B CO

    C Na^+

    D OH^-

2 The table shows the average bond enthalpies of a variety of bonds at 298 K.

Bond	Average bond enthalpy / kJ mol^{-1}
C—H	414
C—O	358
C—C	346
O—H	463
O—O	144

CONTINUED

Suggest the most likely radicals that would be formed if diethyl peroxide were to decompose homolytically. The structure of diethyl peroxide is shown in Figure **21.1**.

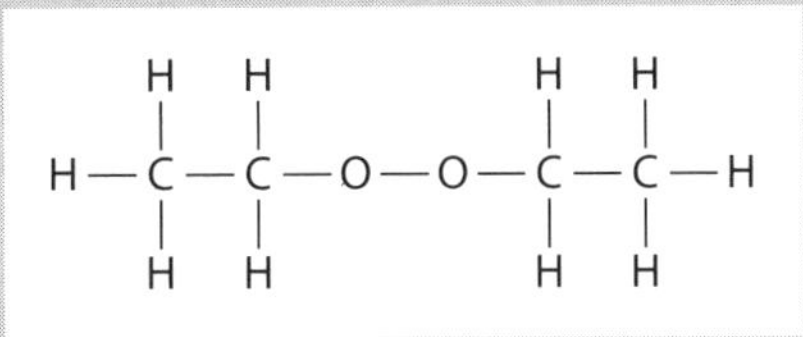

Figure 21.1: The structure of diethyl peroxide.

A $CH_3CH_2OOCH_2CH_3\bullet$ and $\bullet H$

B $CH_3CH_2OOCH_2\bullet$ and $\bullet CH_3$

C $CH_3CH_2\bullet$ and $\bullet OOCH_2CH_3$

D $2CH_3CH_2O\bullet$

3 Which of the following products could be formed in the reaction of methane with bromine?

I C_2H_6

II CH_3Br

III HBr

A I only

B II only

C II and III

D I, II and III

4 Which of the following terms cannot be correctly used when describing the reaction of propane with chlorine?

A radical substitution

B chain reaction

C electrophilic substitution

D homolytic fission

5 The following equations show the decomposition of ozone:

$O_3 + Cl\bullet \rightarrow ClO\bullet + O_2$

$ClO\bullet + O \rightarrow Cl\bullet + O_2$

Which of the following statements about these equations is correct?

A $Cl\bullet$ is a catalyst in this reaction and $ClO\bullet$ is an intermediary.

B $ClO\bullet$ is a catalyst in this reaction and $Cl\bullet$ is an intermediary.

C $Cl\bullet$ and $ClO\bullet$ are both catalysts in this reaction.

D $Cl\bullet$ and $ClO\bullet$ are both intermediaries in this reaction.

6 Bromine reacts with propane to form 1-bromopropane in the presence of UV light.

a Give the overall equation for the reaction. [1]

b Describe the role of UV light in the mechanism for this reaction. Use an equation to explain your answer. [2]

c Give equations to show the propagation steps for the formation of 1-bromopropane. [2]

CONTINUED

7 A proposed mechanism for the photolytic decomposition of ketones to form an alkane and carbon monoxide is shown in Figure **21.2**.

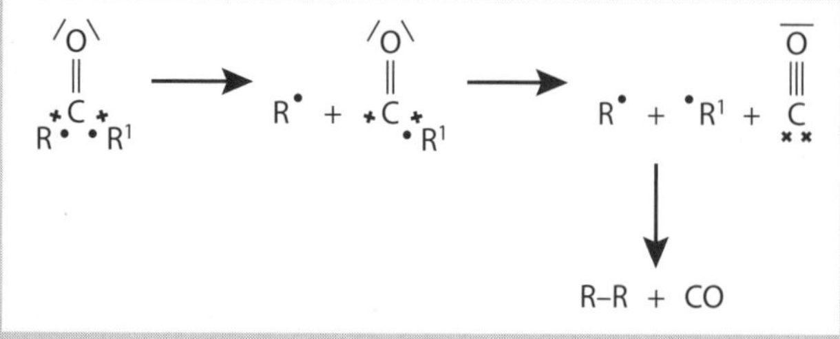

Figure 21.2: Photolytic decomposition of ketones.

Add curly arrows to the diagram to show the movement of the electrons. [3]

8 The polymerisation of alkenes can be initiated using a radical initiator represented as X•. The first step in the propagation can be represented by the equation in Figure **21.3**.

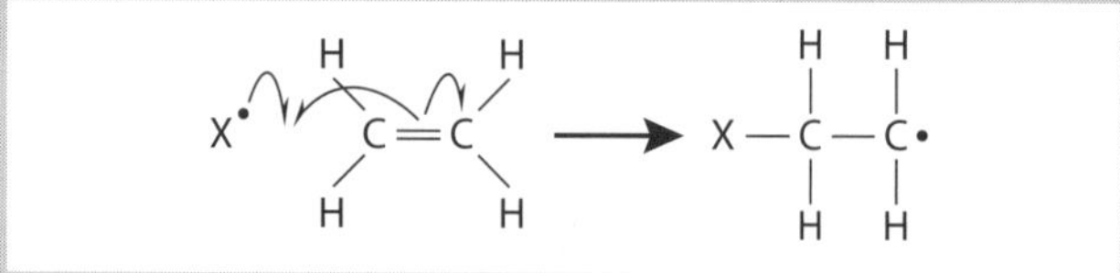

Figure 21.3: Radical polymerisation.

Suggest an equation for the addition of another ethene molecule to the product of this reaction. [2]

Chapter 22
Electron-pair sharing reactions

CHAPTER OUTLINE

In this chapter you will:

- understand the term *nucleophile*

- describe nucleophilic substitution reactions

- understand the term *heterolytic fission*

- understand the term *electrophile*

- understand why alkenes are more reactive than alkanes

- construct equations for the reaction of alkenes.

> understand the Lewis definition of acids and bases

> understand the mechanism for nucleophilic substitution reactions

> explain how the nature of the leaving group affects the rate of nucleophilic substitution reactions

> understand the mechanism for electrophilic addition reactions

> understand the reactions of unsymmetrical alkenes with hydrogen halides

> understand the mechanism for electrophilic substitution reactions.

KEY TERMS

Make sure you understand the following key terms before you do the exercises.

nucleophile: a molecule or a negatively charged ion, possessing a lone pair of electrons, which is attracted to a more positively charged region in a molecule (region with lower electron density) and donates a lone pair of electrons to form a covalent (coordination) bond. A nucleophile is a Lewis base

leaving group: an atom/ion/group of atoms that is lost from the substrate when a bond is broken in a reaction

heterolytic fission: a covalent bond breaks so that both electrons go to the same atom

> CONTINUED

addition reaction: in organic chemistry, a reaction in which a molecule is added to a compound containing a multiple bond without the loss of any other groups

electrophile: a reagent (a positively charged ion or the positive end of a dipole) that is attracted to regions of high electron density and accepts a pair of electrons to form a covalent bond. An electrophile is a Lewis acid

Lewis acid: an electron-pair acceptor

Lewis base: an electron-pair donor

carbocation: an organic molecular species with a positive charge on a carbon atom

Markovnikov's rule: 'rule' that can be used to predict the major product when HX adds to an unsymmetrical alkene. When H—X adds across the double bond of an alkene, the H atom becomes attached to the C atom that has the larger number of H atoms already attached

Exercise 22.1 Nucleophilic substitution reactions

Nucleophiles are attracted to regions of low electron density, such as the $\delta+$ end of the polar bond in a halogenoalkane. In this exercise, you will meet some examples of reactions involving nucleophiles.

1 Identify which of the following reagents can act as nucleophiles:

    a OH^-

    b H^+

    c NH_3

    d CN^-

    e H_2O

    f Na^+

2 Halogenoalkanes commonly undergo substitution reactions.

Complete the following equations for substitution reactions with halogenoalkanes and name the organic product formed in parts **a–c**.

    a $CH_3CH_2CH_2Cl + OH^- \rightarrow$

    b $CH_3Br + NH_3 \rightarrow$

    c $CH_3CH_2CH(I)CH_3 + H_2O \rightarrow$

    d $(CH_3)CBr + CN^- \rightarrow$

> TIP
>
> Draw the Lewis structure for each reagent and think about whether it can donate a pair of electrons to form a covalent bond.

3 Identify the **leaving group** in each of the equations in question 2.

4 What other name is sometimes used to describe the nucleophilic substitution reaction of a halogenoalkane with hydroxide ions or water?

5 During nucleophilic substitution reactions, the carbon-halogen bond undergoes **heterolytic fission** and a new covalent bond is formed between carbon and the nucleophile.

   a Draw a diagram to show the formation of a bond between a halogenoalkane and a nucleophile. Use curly arrows to represent the movement of the electrons. Use Nu: to represent the nucleophile.

   b What name is given to the type of covalent bond formed during the reaction?

Exercise 22.2 Addition reactions

Alkenes commonly undergo **addition reactions**. Only *one* of the bonds in the double bond breaks during these reactions. This is because one of the bonds in the double bond is weaker than the other. In this exercise, you will practise writing equations for this type of reaction.

1 Substances that react with alkenes are commonly **electrophiles**. Why are electrophiles attracted to the carbon-carbon double bond in an alkene?

2 Identify which of the following substances can act as electrophiles:

   a HBr

   b Na^+

   c H_2O

   d OH^-

   e NO_2^+

3 Name the alkene and the reagent that could be used to make the following compounds:

   a 1,2-dibromobutane

   b ethanol

   c 2-iodobutane

4 Draw an equation to show how an electrophile reacts with an alkene. Use curly arrows to represent the movement of the electrons and E^+ to represent the electrophile.

Exercise 22.3 Lewis acids and bases

Defining acids and bases in terms of accepting or donating an electron pair allows the use of ideas about acid–base behaviour in non-aqueous environments. In this exercise, you will practise identifying **Lewis acids** and **Lewis bases** and then look at some examples of acid–base reactions.

1 What type of bond is formed during a Lewis acid–base reaction?

2 OH^- is a Brønsted–Lowry base as it can accept a proton to form H_2O, as shown by the equation for its reaction with NH_4^+

$$OH^- + NH_4^+ \rightarrow NH_3 + H_2O$$

Explain why OH^- can also be described as a Lewis base.

3 H_2O can be described as a Brønsted–Lowry acid as it can donate a proton to form OH^- as shown in the equation for its reaction with ammonia:

$$H_2O + NH_3 \rightarrow NH_4^+ + OH^-$$

Explain why H_2O can be described as a Lewis acid.

4 Explain why the formation of complex ions is an example of a Lewis acid–base reaction.

5 Identify if the following substances can act as Lewis acids or Lewis bases:

  a NH_3

  b $AlCl_3$

  c Cu^{2+}

  d Cl^-

  e CO

  f BF_3

6 The following reactions are all Lewis acid–base reactions. For each one, identify which substance acts as the Lewis acid and which as the Lewis base.

  a $2NH_3 + Ag^+ \rightarrow [Ag(NH_3)_2]^+$

  b $CH_3Cl + OH^- \rightarrow CH_3OH + Cl^-$

  c $BF_3 + NH_3 \rightarrow BF_3NH_3$

  d $HF + NaNH_2 \rightarrow NaF + NH_3$

  e $Cd^{2+} + 4CN^- \rightarrow [Cd(CN)_4]^{2-}$

  f $CH_3NH_2 + BH_3 \rightarrow CH_3NH_2BH_3$

Exercise 22.4 Nucleophilic substitution mechanisms

Nucleophiles are Lewis bases because they donate a pair of electrons. In this exercise, you will look at the nucleophilic substitution reactions met in Exercise 22.1 again but in much more detail. This exercise looks at two different mechanisms for these reactions and the factors that affect how the reaction happens and its rate.

1 a Explain the mechanism for the reaction of the primary halogenoalkane 1-bromoethane with aqueous sodium hydroxide. Use curly arrows to show the movement of the electrons.

   b Draw an energy profile diagram for the reaction. Include a drawing of the transition state substance present at the peak of the profile.

   c The mechanism for this reaction is known as S_N2. What do S, N and 2 represent?

   d Give the rate equation for this reaction.

2 a Explain the mechanism for the reaction of the tertiary halogenoalkane 2-bromo-2-methylpropane with aqueous sodium hydroxide. Use curly arrows to show the movement of the electrons.

   b Draw an energy profile diagram for the reaction. Include a drawing of the **carbocation** formed during the reaction.

   c Why is the carbocation formed during the reaction described as an *intermediate* rather than as a *transition state*?

   d Describe the shape and bond angles of the carbocation.

   e The mechanism for this reaction is known as S_N1. What does the 1 represent?

   f Give the rate equation for the reaction.

3 In the hydrolysis of a single isomer of an optically active halogenoalkane, the optical purity of the product will depend on whether the reaction happens by the S_N1 or S_N2 mechanism.

   a Explain why the S_N2 mechanism produces an optically pure product.

   b Explain why the S_N1 mechanism produces a racemic mixture.

4 A single enantiomer of a secondary halogenoalkane was hydrolysed and the products analysed. It was found that the mixture contained 16% of one enantiomer and 84% of the other. Calculate the proportion of molecules that reacted via an S_N1 mechanism and the proportion that reacted via an S_N2 mechanism.

5 Describe the trend in the rate of hydrolysis of 1-iodoethane, 1-bromoethane and 1-chloroethane.

6   Explain the trend in the rate of hydrolysis of 1-iodoethane, 1-bromoethane and 1-chloroethane.

7   Identify whether breaking of the carbon–halogen bond or forming of the carbon–nucleophile bond is the rate-determining step in the S_N1 mechanism.

8   The S_N2 mechanism occurs by a single step, which involves the simultaneous formation of the carbon–nucleophile bond and breaking of the carbon–halogen bond. Given the trend in the rate of hydrolysis depends on the identity of the leaving group, suggest whether the bond forming or bond breaking process is more significant.

Exercise 22.5 Electrophilic addition reactions of alkenes

This exercise looks at the mechanism of electrophilic addition reactions met in Exercise 22.2. There are only very small differences in the mechanisms for the different reactions, so, in this exercise, the focus is on these and on **Markovnikov's rule**, which is used when an addition reaction has more than one possible product.

1   What name is given to the type of bond breaking during electrophilic addition reactions?

2   a   In the reaction between hydrogen bromide and ethene, which end of the hydrogen bromide molecule approaches the carbon–carbon double bond and why?

    b   Draw the mechanism for the reaction of ethene with hydrogen bromide. Use curly arrows to show the movement of the electrons.

    c   What name is given to the type of ion formed as an intermediate during this reaction?

3   Figure **22.1** shows the mechanism for the reaction of bromine with ethene.

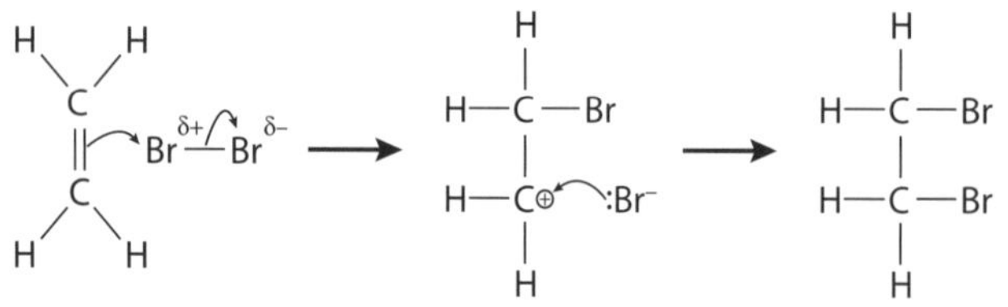

Figure 22.1: Mechanism for the reaction of bromine with ethene.

    a   The bromine molecule is correctly shown with a dipole, even though halogen molecules are non-polar. Explain what causes the dipole in the bromine molecule.

    b   Figure **22.1** shows the intermediate with a positive charge on the carbon atom. This intermediate can alternatively be drawn as a bromonium ion with the charge on the bromine atom. Draw a diagram of this alternative intermediate.

4   In the addition of water to an alkene, an acid catalyst is used. Draw the mechanism for the reaction of 2-methylbut-2-ene with water to show the role of the acid catalyst. Use curly arrows to show the movement of the electrons.

5   **a**   Draw the structures of the two possible products formed when propene reacts with hydrogen bromide.

    b   Use Markovnikov's rule to predict the major product in this reaction.

6   Identify if the following reactions are likely to form one or two products. Name the products. If two products are possible, identify which will be the major product.

    a   HCl + 2-methylpropene

    b   HBr + but-2-ene

    c H_2O + but-1-ene in the presence of an acid catalyst

    d Br_2 + propene

7   **a**   Draw the two possible intermediates formed when hydrogen bromide reacts with but-1-ene.

    b   Identify these intermediates as primary, secondary or tertiary.

    c   Which intermediate is more stable?

    d   Justify your answer to part **c**.

8   Explain Markovikov's rule in terms of the relative stability of the carbocation intermediates formed during electrophilic addition reactions.

Exercise 22.6 Electrophilic substitution reactions

Benzene has a π ring system of 6 delocalised electrons that extends around the ring of carbon atoms. This means that it has a high electron density, so it will undergo electrophilic reactions. In this exercise, you will explore these reactions and why, unlike the electron-rich alkenes, benzene tends to undergo substitution reactions rather than addition reactions.

1   Draw the mechanism for the electrophilic substitution of benzene using E^+ to represent an electrophile. Include curly arrows in your diagram.

2   Describe the structure of the intermediate formed during the electrophilic substitution reaction. Include the number of atoms and electrons in the delocalised structure in your description.

3   Give the full mechanism for the nitration of benzene using a concentrated sulfuric acid catalyst. Identify the reagent and give equations that show the formation of the electrophile and the regeneration of the catalyst.

EXAM-STYLE QUESTIONS

1 Which of the following reactions is a nucleophilic substitution reaction?

A $CH_3CH_2OH + 2[O] \rightarrow CH_3COOH + H_2O$

B $C_2H_4 + HBr \rightarrow CH_3CH_2Br$

C $C_6H_6 + HNO_3 \rightarrow C_6H_5NO_2 + H_2O$

D $CH_3CH_2CH_2Br + OH^- \rightarrow CH_3CH_2CH_2OH + Br^-$

2 Which of the following reagents can be used to convert a halogenoalkane into an alcohol?

A acidified potassium manganate(VII) solution

B concentrated sulfuric acid

C lithium aluminium hydride

D aqueous sodium hydroxide

3 Which of these reactions does not include heterolytic fission?

A free radical substitution

B electrophilic addition

C nucleophilic addition

D electrophilic substitution

4 Which of the following substances can act as an electrophile?

A HBr

B NH_3

C CN^-

D K^+

5 In which of the following reactions would 2-bromobutane be formed?

A butan-2-ol + Br_2

B but-1-ene + Br_2

C but-2-ene + HBr

D butanal + Br_2

6 Which of the following is correct?

	Type of reaction	Example
A	electrophilic substitution	$CH_3CH_2Br + H_2O \rightarrow CH_3CH_2OH + HBr$
B	nucleophilic addition	$CH_3CHCH_2 + H_2O \rightarrow CH_3CH_2CH_2OH$
C	electrophilic addition	$CH_3CH_2Br + NH_3 \rightarrow CH_3CH_2NH_2 + HBr$
D	nucleophilic substitution	$CH_3CH_2Br + CN^- \rightarrow CH_3CH_2CN + Br^-$

7 Which of the following substances would produce a secondary carbocation as an intermediate during its reaction with HBr?

A ethene

B propene

C 2-methylpropene

D 2-methylbut-1-ene

CONTINUED

8 Which statement is **not** correct?

   A Electrophiles are electron-pair acceptors and act as Lewis bases.

   B Nucleophiles are electron-pair acceptors and act as Lewis acids.

   C Electrophiles are electron-pair donors and act as Lewis acids.

   D Nucleophiles are electron-pair donors and act as Lewis bases.

9 Identify which of the following statements about the S_N2 mechanism is correct.

   A Hydrolysis of an optically pure single enantiomer will produce a racemic mixture of two optically active products.

   B The rate of hydrolysis of 1-chloropropane is faster than the hydrolysis of 1-bromopropane.

   C The reaction occurs in a single step.

   D The halogenoalkane acts as the nucleophile.

10 Identify which of the following statements are correct.

   I NH_3 can act as both a Brønsted–Lowry base and a Lewis base.

   II Cl^- ions can act as both a Brønsted–Lowry base and a Lewis base.

   III Cu^{2+} ions can act as both a Brønsted–Lowry acid and a Lewis acid.

   A I and II only

   B I and III only

   C II and III only

   D I, II and III

11 a Complete the gaps in Figure **22.2** to give the displayed formula of the organic product formed when ethene reacts with the reagents indicated.   [4]

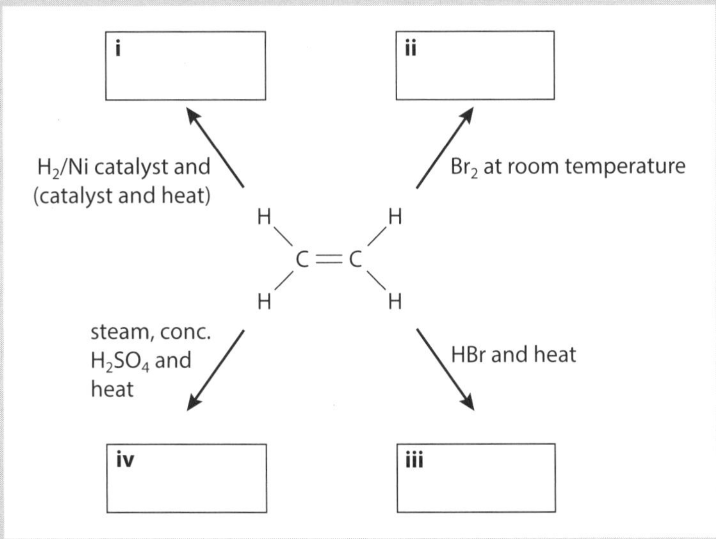

Figure 22.2: Reaction scheme for ethene.

   b The reactions of alkenes are typically electrophilic addition reactions. What is meant by the term *electrophilic addition*?   [2]

   c Explain why alkenes react with electrophiles.   [1]

12 Draw and name the products formed in the following reactions: [6]

a
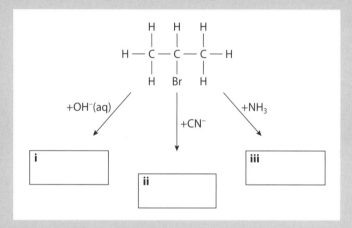

b

c

13 a Complete the gaps in Figure **22.3** to give the displayed formula of the organic products formed when 2-bromopropane reacts with the reagents indicated. [3]

Figure 22.3: Reaction scheme for 2-bromopropane.

b Give the formula of the other product formed in the reactions in Figure **22.3**. [1]

c The reactions in Figure **22.3** are nucleophilic substitution reactions. What is meant by the term *nucleophilic substitution*? [2]

d Explain why halogenoalkanes react with nucleophiles. [1]

e Explain why halogenoalkanes are more reactive than alkanes. [1]

14 Draw and name the products formed in the following reactions: [6]

a

b

c

CONTINUED

15 Alcohols can be prepared both from alkenes and from halogenoalkanes.

    a **i** Draw the displayed formula of an alkene that could be used to produce just butan-2-ol, rather than a mixture of butan-1-ol and butan-2-ol.   **[1]**

        ii Explain why the mechanism for this reaction produces a mixture of optical isomers.   **[2]**

    b Draw and name the mechanism for a reaction that could be used to produce a single enantiomer of butan-2-ol from a halogenoalkane.   **[3]**

    c The rate of formation of an alcohol from a halogenoalkane depends on a number of factors. Explain the effect of changing the identity of the halogen atom on the rate of reaction.   **[2]**

16 This question is about the reactions of compound X shown in Figure **22.4**.

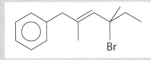

Figure 22.4: Compound X.

    a Draw the product that would be formed when compound X is reacted with aqueous sodium hydroxide, and give the name of the most probable mechanism for the reaction.   **[2]**

    b Give the equation for the reaction of X with a mixture of concentrated nitric and sulfuric acids, and give the name of the mechanism of the reaction.   **[3]**

    c Draw the product that would be formed when X is reacted with Br_2.   **[1]**

    d Draw the products that would be formed when X is reacted with HBr, identify which would be the major product, and give the name of the mechanism for the reaction.   **[4]**

> Glossary

acid deposition   a more general term than acid rain that refers to any process in which acidic substances (particles, gases and precipitation) leave the atmosphere to be deposited on the surface of the Earth – it can be divided into wet deposition (acid rain, fog and snow) and dry deposition (acidic gases and particles)

acid dissociation constant (K_a)   equilibrium constant for the dissociation of a weak acid. In general, for the dissociation of acid HA, $HA(aq) \rightleftharpoons H^+(aq) + A^-(aq)$, the expression for the acid dissociation constant is

$$K_a = \frac{[A^-(aq)][H^+(aq)]}{[HA(aq)]}$$

the higher the value of K_a, the stronger the acid

acid rain   rain with a pH of less than would be expected from dissolved atmospheric carbon dioxide (5.6). It is caused by dissolved oxides of nitrogen and sulfur

acid   a substance that reacts with a base/alkali to form a salt

activation energy (E_a)   the minimum energy that colliding particles must have before collision results in a chemical reaction

activity series   a list of metals, carbon and hydrogen in order of how easily they are oxidised to form positive ions

addition polymerisation   a large number of monomers are joined together into a polymer chain; no other groups are lost in the process. Alkenes (containing C=C) undergo addition polymerisation

addition reaction   in organic chemistry, a reaction in which a molecule is added to a compound containing a multiple bond without the loss of any other groups

adsorption   the tendency of atoms/molecules/ions to 'bond' to a surface either through a chemical or a physical interaction

aliphatic   organic compounds not containing a phenyl group

allotropes   different forms of the same element; e.g. diamond, graphite and fullerene are allotropes of carbon

alloy   homogeneous mixtures of two or more metals or of a metal with a non-metal

amphiprotic   a substance that can donate a proton (acting as a Brønsted–Lowry acid) and accept a proton (acting as a Brønsted–Lowry base), e.g. HCO_3^-

amphoteric   a substance that can act as an acid and a base

anion   a negative ion. It is formed when an atom gains (an) electron(s) so that the ion has more electrons (−) than protons (+)

aromatic   in organic chemistry, aromatic compounds are those that contain a phenyl group

Arrhenius factor (A) (pre-exponential factor)   a constant that takes into account the frequency of collisions with the correct orientation

atom economy   a measure of how efficient a particular reaction is in converting as much of the starting materials as possible into useful products

$$\text{atom economy} = \frac{\text{molar mass of desired product}}{\text{total molar mass of all reactants}} \times 100\%$$

The higher the atom economy, the greener the process, because more of the starting materials end up in the desired product

atom   the smallest part of an element that can still be recognised as that element; in the simplest picture of the atom, the electrons orbit around the central nucleus; the nucleus is made up of protons and neutrons (except for a hydrogen atom, which has no neutrons)

atomic number (Z)   the number of protons in the nucleus of an atom

Aufbau principle   the process of putting electrons into atoms to generate the electron configuration

average bond enthalpy   the average amount of energy required to break one mole of covalent bonds, in a gaseous molecule under standard conditions; 'average' refers to the fact that the bond enthalpy is different in different molecules and, therefore, the value quoted is the average amount of energy to break a particular bond in a range of molecules

Avogadro constant has the same numerical value as the Avogadro number but units of mol^{-1}, i.e. 6.02×10^{23} mol^{-1}. The symbol L or N_A is used for the Avogadro constant

Avogadro's law equal volumes of ideal gases measured at the same temperature and pressure contain the same number of molecules

base ionisation constant (K_b) equilibrium constant for the ionisation of a weak base, B, which ionises according to the equation:

$B(aq) + H_2O(l) \rightleftharpoons BH^+(aq) + OH^-(aq)$

$$K_b = \frac{[BH^+(aq)][OH^-(aq)]}{[B(aq)]}$$

the higher the value of K_b, the stronger the base

base a substance that reacts with an acid to form a salt

biodegradable can be broken down by microorganisms in the environment

boiling point the temperature at which a liquid boils under a specific set of conditions – usually we will be considering the boiling point at atmospheric pressure

boiling change of state from a liquid to a gas at the boiling point of the substance

bond enthalpy the enthalpy change when one mole of covalent bonds, in a gaseous molecule, is broken under standard conditions. Bond breaking requires energy (endothermic), ΔH is positive; bond making releases energy (exothermic), ΔH is negative

bond order the number of covalent bonds between two atoms. A single bond has a bond order of 1. A double bond has a bond order of 2, and a triple bond has a bond order of 3. When molecules/ions are best described as resonance hybrids, the bond orders will involve fractions

Born–Haber cycle an enthalpy level diagram breaking down the formation of an ionic compound into a series of simpler steps

Brønsted–Lowry acid a proton (H^+) donor

Brønsted–Lowry base a proton (H^+) acceptor

buffer solution a solution that resists changes in pH when small amounts of acid or alkali are added

calorimetry experimental determination of the heat given out/taken in during chemical reactions/ physical processes

carbocation an organic molecular species with a positive charge on a carbon atom

catalyst a substance that increases the rate of a chemical reaction without itself being used up in the reaction. A catalyst acts by allowing the reaction to proceed by an alternative pathway of lower activation energy

cation a positive ion. It is formed when an atom loses (an) electron(s) so that the ion has more protons (+) than electrons (−)

chemical equation this tells us the mole ratio in which reactants combine and the relationship to the number of moles of products formed

chemical properties how a substance behaves in chemical reactions

chromatography a technique used to separate the components of a mixture due to their different affinities for another substance and/or solubility in a solvent

cis–trans isomerism where two compounds have the same structural formula, but the groups are arranged differently in space around a double bond or a ring

climate change the change in the Earth's climate due to man-made factors, such as the increase in atmospheric carbon dioxide due to the increased burning of fossil fuels

collision theory a method that is used to explain the variation of rate of reaction. A reaction can occur only when two particles collide in the correct orientation and with $E \geq E_a$

combustion burning, an exothermic reaction that occurs when a substance reacts with oxygen. Usually these reactions produce a flame and continue once the initial heat source is removed

complete combustion the burning of a substance in a plentiful supply of oxygen

complex a species consisting of a central atom or ion surrounded by a number of ligands to which it is bonded by dative covalent bonds

compound a pure substance formed when two or more elements combine chemically in a fixed ratio

concentration quantity of solute dissolved in a unit volume of solution; the volume that is usually taken is 1 dm^3 (one litre); the quantity of solute may be expressed in g or mol, so the units of concentration are $g\ dm^{-3}$ or $mol\ dm^{-3}$

condensation polymerisation monomers, each containing two functional groups, join together to form a long chain, with the elimination of a small molecule, such as water or hydrogen chloride, each time two monomers join together

condensed electron configuration an abbreviated form of an electron configuration where the previous noble gas atom is written in square brackets followed by the remainder of the full electron configuration

condensed structural formula shows how the atoms are joined together in a molecule but does not show all of the bonds, e.g. $CH_3CH_2CH_2OH$

conjugate acid–base pair two species that differ by one proton (H^+); when an acid donates a proton, it forms the conjugate base (CH_3COO^- is the conjugate base of CH_3COOH); when a base gains a proton, it forms the conjugate acid (H_3O^+ is the conjugate acid of H_2O)

continuous spectrum a spectrum consisting of all frequencies/wavelengths of light

convergence limit the point in a line emission spectrum where the lines merge to form a continuum. The frequency of the convergence limit in the series of lines where the electron falls down to $n = 1$, may be used to determine the ionisation energy of hydrogen

convergence when the lines in an emission spectrum get closer together at higher energy/frequency

coordination bond a type of covalent bond in which both electrons come from the same atom. Also called a dative bond or coordinate covalent bond

covalent bond the electrostatic attraction between a shared pair of electrons and the nuclei of the atoms making up the bond

covalent network structure the structure of substances such as diamond and graphite that contain an extended network of covalently bonded atoms and not individual molecules. This is also called a giant covalent structure

degenerate a set of orbitals with the same energy

delocalisation the sharing of a pair of electrons between three or more atoms

deposition the change of state from a gas to a solid

dipole the separation of charge due to its uneven distribution

dipole–dipole forces intermolecular forces between molecules with a permanent dipole

dipole–induced dipole forces intermolecular forces between a polar molecule with a permanent dipole inducing a dipole in a neighbouring non-polar molecule

displacement reaction a reaction in which one element in a compound is replaced by another

distillation a separation technique used to separate the solvent from a solution or separate liquid components of a mixture that have different boiling points

ductile can be drawn out into wires

dynamic equilibrium macroscopic properties (all concentrations of reactants and products) are constant and the rate of the forward reaction is equal to the rate of the reverse reaction

electrochemical cell a device that interconverts chemical energy and electrical energy

electrolysis the breaking down of a substance (in molten state or solution) by the passage of electricity through it

electrolytic cell an electrochemical cell that converts electrical energy into chemical energy

electromagnetic spectrum the range of frequencies of radiation

electron configuration the arrangement of the electrons in an atom or ion

electron domain geometry the arrangement of the electron domains around a central atom

electron domain a lone pair, the electron pair that makes up a single bond or the electron pairs that together make up a multiple bond. Each single, double or triple bond counts as one electron domain when working out shapes of molecules

electronegativity a measure of the attraction of an atom in a molecule for the electron pair in the covalent bond of which it is a part. A more electronegative atom attracts electrons more strongly

electrophile a reagent (a positively charged ion or the positive end of a dipole) that is attracted to regions of high electron density and accepts a pair of electrons to form a covalent bond. An electrophile is a Lewis acid

element a chemical substance that cannot be broken down into a simpler substance by chemical means. Each atom has the same number of protons in the nucleus

emission spectrum electromagnetic radiation given out when an electron in an atom falls from a higher energy level to a lower one. Only certain frequencies of electromagnetic radiation are emitted – a line spectrum. Each atom has a different emission spectrum. For hydrogen, the emission spectrum in the visible region consists of a series of coloured lines that get closer together at higher frequency

empirical formula the simplest whole number ratio of the elements present in a compound

enantiomers the non-superimposable mirror images of a chiral molecule

endothermic reaction a chemical reaction in which heat is taken in from the surroundings – the reaction vessel gets colder; ΔH for an endothermic reaction is positive

energy level the energetic 'distance' of an electron from the nucleus of an atom

energy sub-levels the main energy levels, or shells, in an atom are divided into sub-levels. There are different types of sub-level, known as s, p, d and f sub-levels

enthalpy change (ΔH) the heat energy exchanged with the surroundings at constant pressure

entropy (S) a measure of the disorder of a system (how the matter is dispersed/distributed) or how the available energy is distributed among the particles. Standard entropy ($S^\ominus$) is the entropy of a substance at 100 kPa and 298 K; units are J K^{-1} mol^{-1}. $\Delta S^\ominus$ is the entropy change under standard conditions – a positive value indicates an increase in entropy, i.e., the system becomes more disordered/the energy becomes more spread out (less concentrated)

equilibrium law / equilibrium constant the ratio of the concentrations (raised to the powers of the coefficients in the stoichiometric equation) of products to reactants at equilibrium is equal to the equilibrium constant, K.

So, for the reaction: $H_2(g) + I_2(g) \rightleftharpoons 2HI(g)$

$$K = \frac{[HI(g)]^2}{[H_2(g)][I_2(g)]}$$

evaporation the change of state from a liquid to a gas that can occur at any temperature above the melting point

exothermic reaction a chemical reaction that results in the release of heat to the surroundings – the reaction vessel gets hotter; ΔH for an exothermic reaction is negative

expanded octet when a central atom in a molecule or ion can have more than eight electrons in its outer shell

experimental (or actual) yield the amount of desired product actually formed in a reaction

filtration a separation technique used to separate insoluble solids from a liquid or solution

first electron affinity the enthalpy change when one electron is added to each atom in one mole of gaseous atoms under standard conditions: $X(g) + e^- \rightarrow X^-(g)$. The first electron affinity is exothermic for virtually all elements

first electron affinity enthalpy change when one electron is added to each atom in one mole of gaseous atoms under standard conditions:

$$X(g) + e^- \rightarrow X^-(g)$$

The first electron affinity is exothermic for virtually all elements

first ionisation energy the minimum amount of energy required to remove an electron from a gaseous atom/ the energy required to remove one electron from each atom in one mole of gaseous atoms under standard conditions. The energy for the following process:

$$M(g) \rightarrow M^+(g) + e^-$$

formal charge the charge that an atom in a molecule/ ion would have if we assumed that the electrons in a covalent bond were equally shared between the atoms that are bonded – i.e., we assume that all atoms have the same electronegativity. Formal charge arises when there is a charge on an ion and when coordination bonds are formed. The two electrons in a coordination bond are shared equally between the donating atom (which, therefore, has a formal charge of +1) and the receiving atom (which then has a formal charge of −1)

freezing the change of state from a liquid to a solid

fuel cell a type of electrochemical cell that uses the reaction between a fuel (such as hydrogen or methanol) and an oxidising agent (e.g. oxygen) to produce electrical energy directly; it uses a continuous supply of reactants from an external source

fuel something that is burnt to produce energy

functional group an atom or group of atoms that gives an organic molecule its characteristic chemical properties. A functional group also influences the physical properties of a compound

general formula   the formula of a family of molecules that can be used to determine the molecular formula of any member of the series

Gibbs energy change (ΔG) or free energy change ΔG is related to the entropy change of the universe and can be defined using the equation $\Delta G = \Delta H - T\Delta S$. For a reaction to be spontaneous, ΔG for the reaction must be negative. $\Delta G^{\ominus}$ is the standard energy change

group   vertical column in the periodic table. These are numbered from 1 to 18, including the transition metal groups

half-equation   a balanced equation that shows only the oxidation half or the reduction half of a redox reaction

half-life   the time taken for the concentration of a reactant or number of radioactive nuclei in a sample to fall to half of its original value

heat   the energy that flows from something at a higher temperature to something at a lower temperature because of the temperature difference between them

Hess's law   the enthalpy change accompanying a chemical reaction is independent of the pathway between the initial and final states

heterogeneous mixture   a mixture of two or more substances, that does not have uniform composition and consists of separate phases. A heterogeneous mixture can be separated by mechanical means. An example is a mixture of two solids

heterolytic fission   a covalent bond breaks so that both electrons go to the same atom

homogeneous mixture   a mixture of two or more substances with the same (uniform) composition throughout the mixture – it consists of only one phase. Examples are solutions or a mixture of gases

homologous series   a series of compounds with the same functional group, in which each member differs from the next by $-CH_2-$

homolytic fission   a covalent bond breaks such that one electron goes back to each atom making up the original bond

Hund's rule   electrons fill orbitals of the same energy (degenerate orbitals) to give the maximum number of electrons with the same spin

hybridisation   the mixing of atomic orbitals when a compound forms to produce a new set of orbitals (the same number as originally), which are better arranged in space for covalent bonding

hydrocarbon   a compound containing carbon and hydrogen only

hydrogen bonding   an intermolecular force resulting from the interaction of a lone pair on a very electronegative atom (N/O/F) in one molecule with an H atom attached to N/O/F in another molecule. These forces may also occur between atoms in different parts of the same molecule

hydrolysis   a reaction in which a covalent bond in a molecule is broken by reaction with water; most commonly, hydrolysis reactions occur when a molecule is reacted with aqueous acid or aqueous alkali

ideal gas   a theoretical model that approximates the behaviour of real gases. It can be defined in terms of macroscopic properties (a gas that obeys the equation $PV = nRT$) or in terms of microscopic properties (the main assumptions that define an ideal gas on a microscopic scale are that the molecules are point masses – their volume is negligible compared with the volume of the container – and that there are no intermolecular forces except during a collision)

incomplete combustion   the burning of a substance in a limited supply of oxygen

infrared spectroscopy   an analytical technique used to identify the functional groups in an organic molecule due to their absorption of radiation in the infrared region of the electromagnetic spectrum

intermolecular forces   forces between different molecules. These include London forces, permanent dipole–permanent dipole interactions and hydrogen bonding

internal energy (sometimes called chemical energy)   the name given to the total amount of energy (kinetic and potential) in a sample of a substance

intramolecular forces   forces within a molecule – usually covalent bonding

ion product constant for water (K_w)   an equilibrium constant for the dissociation of water:

$K_w = [H^+(aq)][OH^-(aq)]$

K_w has a value of 1.0×10^{-14} at 25 °C. The ion product constant is also known as the ionic product constant

ion   a charged particle that is formed when an atom loses or gains electron(s); a positive ion is formed when an atom loses an electron(s) and a negative ion is formed when an atom gains an electron(s)

ionic bonding   the electrostatic attraction between oppositely charged ions

ionic equation   an equation that leaves out the formulas of substances which are not changed during a reaction

ionisation energy   see first ionisation energy

isotopes   different atoms of the same element with different mass numbers, i.e., different numbers of neutrons in the nucleus. Isotopes have the same chemical properties but different physical properties

lattice   usually used when describing crystals; a structure with a regular, repeating 3D arrangement

Le Chatelier's principle   if a system at equilibrium is subjected to some change, the position of equilibrium will shift in order to minimise the effect of the change

leaving group   an atom/ion/group of atoms that is lost from the substrate when a bond is broken in a reaction

Lewis (electron dot) formula   a diagram showing all the valence (outer-shell) electrons in a molecule (or ion). Also called a Lewis structure

Lewis acid   an electron-pair acceptor

Lewis base   an electron-pair donor

ligand   negative ion or neutral molecule that uses lone pairs of electrons to bond to a transition metal ion to form a complex ion. Coordination bonds are formed between the ligand and the transition metal ion

limiting reactant   the reactant that is used up first in a chemical reaction; when the amount in moles of each species is divided by their coefficient in the stoichiometric equation, the limiting reactant is the one with the lowest number; all other reactants are in excess

line spectrum   the emission spectrum of an atom consists of a series of lines that get closer together at higher frequency; only certain frequencies/wavelengths of light are present

London (dispersion) forces   intermolecular forces arising from temporary (instantaneous) dipole–induced dipole interactions

lustrous   shiny

macromolecule   a very large molecule

malleable   can be hammered into different shapes

Markovnikov's rule   'rule' that can be used to predict the major product when HX adds to an unsymmetrical alkene. When H—X adds across the double bond of an alkene, the H atom becomes attached to the C atom that has the larger number of H atoms already attached

mass number (A)   the total number of protons plus neutrons in the nucleus of an atom

mass spectrometry   an analytical technique used to determine the relative abundance and mass (strictly mass to charge ratio) of gaseous particles. It can be used to determine the isotopic composition of an element

mechanism   a series of elementary steps that make up a more complex reaction. Each step involves the collision of two particles

melting point   the temperature at which melting occurs

melting   the change of state from a solid to a liquid

metallic bonding   the electrostatic attraction between the positive ions and the delocalised electrons in a metallic lattice

metalloid   elements, such as Si, Ge and Sb, that have some of the properties of both metals and non-metals or properties that are intermediate between those of a metal and non-metal

miscible   able to mix to form a homogeneous mixture

mixture   two or more substances mixed together. The components of a mixture can be mixed together in any proportion (although there are limits for solutions). The components of a mixture are not chemically bonded together, and so, retain their individual properties. The components of a mixture can be separated from each other by physical processes

mobile phase   the phase that moves in chromatography, e.g. the solvent moving up the paper in paper chromatography

molar mass (M)   the mass that contains 1 mol of particles (atoms. molecules, ions) and is its A_r or M_r in grams. The units of molar mass are g mol^{-1}

mole ratio   the relationship between the number of moles of the various substances in a reaction

mole   the unit of the amount of substance. The amount of substance that contains the Avogadro number (6.02×10^{23}) of particles (atoms, ions, molecules, etc.)

molecular formula   the total number of atoms of each element present in a molecule of the compound; the molecular formula is a multiple of the empirical formula

molecularity   the number of reactant 'molecules' that take part in a particular elementary step in a reaction mechanism

molecule   an electrically neutral particle consisting of two or more atoms chemically bonded together

monomer   a molecule from which a polymer chain may be built up, e.g. ethene is the monomer for polyethene

neutralisation reaction   a chemical reaction in which an acid reacts with a base/alkali to form a salt plus water. Neutralisation reactions are exothermic

non-polar   a bond or molecule in which charge is distributed evenly

non-renewable energy sources   sources of energy that are finite – they will eventually run out, e.g. coal

nuclear symbol   a symbol showing the atomic number and mass number of an element, $^A_Z X$

nucleophile   a molecule or a negatively charged ion, possessing a lone pair of electrons, which is attracted to a more positively charged region in a molecule (region with lower electron density) and donates a lone pair of electrons to form a covalent (coordination) bond. A nucleophile is a Lewis base

optical isomerism   optical isomers rotate the plane of plane-polarised light in opposite directions (by the same amount as long as concentrations are equal). Optical isomers have the same molecular and structural formula, but groups are arranged differently in space and the individual optical isomers are non-superimposable mirror images of each other

orbital diagrams   diagrams that show the full electron configuration of atoms/ions using arrows (electrons) in boxes (orbitals)

orbital   a region of space in which there is a high probability of finding an electron; it represents a discrete energy level. There are s, p, d and f orbitals. One orbital can contain a maximum of two electrons

order of a reaction   the power of the concentration of a particular reactant in the experimentally determined rate equation e.g. in the rate equation:

rate = $k[A]^m[B]^n$, the order with respect to A is m and the order with respect to B is n

overall order of reaction   the sum of the powers of the concentration terms in the experimentally determined rate equation e.g. in the rate equation:

rate = $k[A]^m[B]^n$, the overall order is $m + n$

oxidation state (oxidation number)   the degree of oxidation of an atom in terms of counting electrons. It is a purely formal concept that regards all compounds as ionic and assigns charges to the components accordingly; it provides a guide to the distribution of electrons in covalent compounds

oxidation   loss of electrons or increase in oxidation state. Oxidation can also be defined in terms of the gain of oxygen or the loss of hydrogen, but these are less general definitions

oxidising agent (oxidant)   oxidises other species and, in the process, is itself reduced; an oxidising agent takes electrons away from another species

paper chromatography   a separation technique that separates different solutes according to how the solutes are partitioned between water on the fibres of the paper and the solvent

partition   the tendency of a solute to distribute itself between two immiscible solvents due to its solubility in each

Pauli exclusion principle   two electrons in the same orbital must have opposite spins

percentage yield   the percentage yield compares the actual experimental yield and the theoretical maximum yield:

$$\% \text{ yield} = \frac{\text{experimental yield}}{\text{theoretical yield}} \times 100$$

period   horizontal row in the periodic table. Hydrogen and helium are in Period 1

periodicity   the repetition of properties

pH range of an indicator   the pH range over which intermediate colours for an indicator can be seen because comparable amounts of the un-ionised and ionised forms are present

pH   a measure of the concentration of H^+ ions in an aqueous solution; it can be defined as the negative logarithm to base ten of the hydrogen ion concentration in aqueous solution

$$pH = -\log_{10}[H^+(aq)]$$

physical properties   properties such as melting point, solubility and electrical conductivity, relating to the physical state of a substance and the physical changes it can undergo

pi (π) bond   bond formed by the sideways overlap of parallel p orbitals; the electron density in the pi bond lies above and below the internuclear axis

plastic   the common term for synthetic polymers

pOH a measure of the concentration of hydroxide ions in an aqueous solution

polar a bond or molecule in which there is an uneven distribution of charge

polymerisation the process of joining together a large number of monomers to form a long chain molecule (polymer). There are two types of polymerisation: addition and condensation

polymers long-chain molecules, usually based on carbon, which are formed when smaller molecules (monomers) join together

potential energy profile diagram a diagram showing the change in the potential energy (y-axis) of a system as a reaction proceeds (x-axis is the reaction coordinate)

principal quantum number the number used to describe the main energy level or shell of an atom. The first shell has the principal quantum number one, the second two, and so on. The symbol n is sometimes used. The maximum number of electrons in a given shell can be calculated using the formula $2n^2$

proton (^{1}H) nuclear magnetic resonance spectroscopy an analytical technique used for structural determination. It is used to identify the hydrogen atoms (protons) in a molecule

radical a species (atom or group of atoms) with an unpaired electron. Radicals are very reactive because of this unpaired electron

rate constant (k) a constant of proportionality relating the concentrations in the experimentally determined rate expression to the rate of a chemical reaction; the rate constant is only a constant for a particular reaction at a particular temperature

rate equation (rate expression/rate law) an experimentally determined equation that relates the rate of a reaction to the concentrations of the substances in the reaction mixture, e.g. rate = $k[A]^m[B]^n$

rate of reaction the speed at which reactants are used up or products are formed or, more precisely, the change in concentration of reactants or products per unit time:

$$\text{average rate} = \frac{\text{change in concentration}}{\text{time}}$$

It could also be defined in terms of change in mass or volume etc over time

rate-determining step the slowest step in a reaction mechanism. It is the step with the highest activation energy

reaction intermediate a substance that is produced in one step of a reaction and then goes on to be used in a subsequent step

reaction quotient (Q) the ratio of the concentrations of the reactants and products (raised to the appropriate powers) at any point in time. An expression for Q is exactly the same as that for the equilibrium constant – except that the concentrations are not equilibrium concentrations.

So, for the reaction: $H_2(g) + I_2(g) \rightleftharpoons 2HI(g)$

$$Q = \frac{[HI(g)]^2}{[H_2(g)][I_2(g)]}$$

redox reaction a reaction involving both oxidation and reduction; if one species is oxidised, another species else must be reduced

reducing agent (reductant) reduces other species and, in the process, is itself oxidised; a reducing agent gives electrons to another species

reduction gain of electrons or decrease in oxidation state. Reduction can also be defined in terms of the loss of oxygen or the gain of hydrogen, but these are less general definitions

relative atomic mass (A_r) *the weighted average of the masses of the atoms of the isotopes*

relative formula mass if a compound contains ions, the relative formula mass is the average mass of the formula unit relative to the mass of $\frac{1}{12}$ of an atom of carbon-12

relative molecular mass (M_r) the average mass of a molecule of a compound relative to the mass of $\frac{1}{12}$ of an atom of carbon-12; M_r is the sum of the relative atomic masses for the individual atoms making up a molecule

renewable energy sources sources of energy that are naturally replenished - they will not run out, e.g. solar energy or wind power

resonance hybrid the actual structure of a molecule/ion for which resonance structures can be drawn can be described as a resonance hybrid made up of contributions (not necessarily equal) from all possible resonance structures

resonance structure   one of several Lewis formulas that can be drawn for some molecules/ions

reversible reaction   a reaction that can go either way, so the reactants become the products, but the products of the reaction can also react to re-form the reactants. The symbol $\rightleftharpoons$ shows that a reaction is reversible. A reversible reaction will eventually reach a state of equilibrium

R_f (retardation factor) value   in chromatography:

$$R_f = \frac{\text{distance solute moves}}{\text{distance solvent front moves}}$$

salt bridge   completes the circuit in a voltaic cell by providing an electrical connection between two half-cells, allowing ions to flow into or out of the half-cells to balance out the charges in the half-cells. The salt bridge contains a concentrated solution of an ionic salt, such as KCl

salt hydrolysis   the reaction of the conjugate base of a weak acid or the conjugate acid of a weak base with water

salt   a compound formed when the hydrogen ion (H^+) in an acid is replaced by a metal ion (or ammonium ion)

second electron affinity   the enthalpy change for the following process:

$$X^-(g) + e^- \rightarrow X^{2-}(g)$$

second ionisation energy   the minimum energy required to remove the outermost electron from each ion in a mole of gaseous ions with a 1+ charge to form a mole of gaseous ions each with a 2+ charge under standard conditions:

$$M^+(g) \rightarrow M^{2+}(g) + e^-$$

secondary cell   a cell (battery) that can be recharged using mains electricity and is often called a rechargeable battery. The chemical reactions in a rechargeable battery are reversible and can be reversed by connecting them to an electricity supply

sigma (σ) bond   bond formed by the axial (head-on) overlap of atomic orbitals; the electron density in a sigma bond lies mostly along the axis joining the two nuclei

skeletal formula   a representation of the structure of a molecule that shows only the bonds in the carbon skeleton and any groups joined to the carbon skeleton. The carbon atoms are not shown explicitly nor are hydrogen atoms joined to carbon

solubility   a measure of the maximum amount of a solute that can dissolve in a given volume of solvent

solute   a substance that is dissolved in another substance (the solvent) to form a solution

solution   that which is formed when a solute dissolves in a solvent

solvation   a process used to separate a mixture of two or more substances, due to differences in solubility

solvent   a substance that dissolves another substance (the solute); the solvent should be present in excess of the solute

specific heat capacity   the energy required to raise the temperature of 1 g of substance by 1 K (1 °C). It can also be defined as the energy to raise the temperature of 1 kg of substance by 1 K. Specific heat capacity has units of $J\ g^{-1}\ K^{-1}$ or $J\ g^{-1}\ °C^{-1}$. Units that are also encountered are $kJ\ kg^{-1}\ K^{-1}$ or $J\ kg^{-1}\ K^{-1}$

spectator ion   a substance that is not changed during a chemical reaction

standard ambient temperature and pressure (SATP)   298 K and 100 kPa

standard cell potential   the electromotive force (voltage) produced when two half-cells are connected under standard conditions (all concentrations 1 mol dm^{-3} and pressure 100 kPa). This drives the movement of electrons through the external circuit from the negative electrode to the positive electrode

standard electrode potential   the electromotive force (voltage) of a half-cell connected to a standard hydrogen electrode, measured under standard conditions; all solutions must be of concentration 1 mol dm^{-3} and pressure 100 kPa. A standard electrode potential is always quoted for the reduction reaction

standard enthalpy change of atomisation ($\Delta H_{at}^\ominus$)   the enthalpy change when one mole of gaseous atoms is formed from an element in its standard state under standard conditions

standard enthalpy change of combustion ($\Delta H_c^\ominus$)   the enthalpy change (heat given out) when one mole of a substance is completely burnt in oxygen under standard conditions

standard enthalpy change of formation ($\Delta H_f^\ominus$)   the enthalpy change when one mole of a substance is formed from its elements in their standard states under standard conditions. $\Delta H_f^\ominus$ for any element in its standard state is zero

standard enthalpy change of neutralisation (ΔH_n) the enthalpy change when one mole of H_2O molecules is formed when an acid (H^+) reacts with an alkali (OH^-) under standard conditions, i.e

$$H^+(aq) + OH^-(aq) \rightarrow H_2O(l)$$

the enthalpy change of neutralisation is always exothermic

standard hydrogen electrode the standard half-cell relative to which standard electrode potentials are measured. Hydrogen gas at 100 kPa (1 bar) pressure is bubbled around a platinum electrode of very high surface area in a solution of H^+ ions of concentration 1 mol dm^{-3}

The reaction occurring in this half-cell is
$$2H^+(aq) + 2e^- \rightleftharpoons H_2(g)$$
and this is assigned a standard electrode potential ($E^{\ominus}_{cell}$) of 0.00 V

standard lattice enthalpy ($\Delta H^{\ominus}_{latt}$) the enthalpy change when one mole of ionic compound is broken apart into its constituent gaseous ions under standard conditions, e.g., for NaCl:

$$NaCl(s) \rightarrow Na^+(g) + Cl^-(g) \qquad \Delta H^{\ominus}_{latt} = +771 \text{ kJ mol}^{-1}$$

lattice enthalpy can be defined in either direction, i.e. as the making or breaking of the lattice, but in the IB syllabus it is usually defined in terms of breaking apart the lattice

standard solution a solution of known concentration

standard temperature and pressure (STP) 273 K, 100 kPa pressure

state symbols used to indicate the physical state of an element or compound; these may be either written as subscripts after the chemical formula or in normal type: (aq) = aqueous (dissolved in water); (g) = gas; (l) = liquid; (s) = solid

states of matter solid, liquid and gas

stationary phase in chromatography, the phase that does not move; this may be the water coating the fibres in paper chromatography or the solid adsorbent in thin-layer chromatography

stereochemical formula a diagram of a molecule that shows the spatial arrangement of the atoms/groups. Solid wedges show a bond coming out of the plane of the paper/screen and dashed wedges shows bonds going into the plane

stereoisomers molecules with the same molecular formula and structural formula, but the atoms are arranged differently in space; *cis–trans* isomers and optical isomers are stereoisomers

strong acid an acid, such as HCl, H_2SO_4, HNO_3, that dissociates completely in aqueous solution

$$HCl(aq) \rightarrow H^+(aq) + Cl^-(aq)$$

strong base a base that ionises completely in aqueous solution; strong bases are the Group 1 hydroxides (LiOH, NaOH, etc.) and $Ba(OH)_2$

structural formula a representation of a molecule that shows the arrangement of the atoms

structural isomers two or more compounds that have the same molecular formula but different structural formulas, i.e., the atoms are joined together in a different way

sublimation the change of state from a solid to a gas

substitution reaction a reaction in which one atom or group is replaced by another atom or group

system/surroundings system refers to the chemicals themselves, whereas the surroundings refers to the solvent, the air and the apparatus – all that surrounds the chemicals

temperature a measure of the average kinetic energy of particles

theoretical yield the maximum possible amount of the desired product formed in a reaction

thin-layer chromatography (TLC) a separation technique similar to paper chromatography that separates different solutes according to how strongly they are adsorbed onto the stationary phase

titration a technique that involves adding measured volumes of a solution (from a burette) to another solution to determine the amounts that react exactly with each other

transition metals/elements the elements in the central part (d block) of the periodic table. There are various ways of defining a transition metal. IUPAC definition: 'an element whose atoms have an incomplete (partially filled) d subshell or forms positive ions with an incomplete (partially filled) d subshell'

transition state (activated complex) a maximum on the potential energy profile/the highest energy species on the reaction pathway between reactants/intermediates and intermediates/products

valence electrons   outer-shell electrons

valence-shell electron-pair repulsion (VSEPR) theory   the theory by which the shapes of molecules and ions can be deduced

van der Waals forces   the collective name given to the forces between molecules and includes London (dispersion) forces, dipole–dipole interactions and dipole–induced dipole interactions but not hydrogen bonding and ion–dipole interactions

volatility   a measure of how easily a substance evaporates

voltaic cell   an electrochemical cell that converts chemical energy into electrical energy

weak acid   an acid, such as a carboxylic acid (ethanoic acid, propanoic acid, etc.) or carbonic acid (H_2CO_3), that dissociates only partially in aqueous solution

$$CH_3COOH(aq) \rightleftharpoons H^+(aq) + CH_3COO^-(aq)$$

weak base   a base that ionises only partially in aqueous solution, e.g., ammonia and amines

$$NH_3(aq) + H_2O(l) \rightleftharpoons NH_4^+(aq) + OH^-(aq)$$

yield   the amount of the desired product obtained from a chemical reaction

› Acknowledgements

The authors and publishers acknowledge the following sources of copyright material and are grateful for the permissions granted. While every effort has been made, it has not always been possible to identify the sources of all the material used, or to trace all copyright holders. If any omissions are brought to our notice, we will be happy to include the appropriate acknowledgements on reprinting.

Thanks to the following for permission to reproduce images:

Cover; Stuart Cox/Getty Images *Inside* Figure 11.1 Kim Christensen/Alamy Stock Photo